TWO LOVES
I HAVE

To my father,
who loved the Sonnets

TWO LOVES I HAVE

A new reading of
Shakespeare's Sonnets

J.D. Winter

sussex
ACADEMIC
PRESS
Brighton • Chicago • Toronto

Copyright © J. D. Winter, 2016.

The right of J. D. Winter to be identified as Author of this work has been asserted in
accordance with the Copyright, Designs and Patents Act 1988.

2 4 6 8 10 9 7 5 3 1

First published 2016, in Great Britain by
SUSSEX ACADEMIC PRESS
PO Box 139
Eastbourne BN24 9BP

SUSSEX ACADEMIC PRESS
Independent Publishers Group
814 N. Franklin Street, Chicago, IL 60610

and in Canada by
SUSSEX ACADEMIC PRESS (CANADA)

British Library Cataloguing in Publication Data
A CIP catalogue record for this book is available from the British Library.

Library of Congress Cataloging-in-Publication Data
Names: Winter, Joe, 1943– author.
Title: Two loves I have : a new reading of Shakespeare's Sonnets /
J. D. Winter.
Description: Brighton ; Chicago : Sussex Academic Press, 2016. | Includes
bibliographical references.
Identifiers: LCCN 2015048165 (print) | LCCN 2015051356 (ebook) |
ISBN 9781845197964 (pbk : alk. paper) | ISBN 9781782843108
(ebook) | ISBN 9781782843115 | ISBN 9781782843122
Subjects: LCSH: Shakespeare, William, 1564–1616. Sonnets. | Sonnets,
English—History and criticism.
Classification: LCC PR2848 .W57 2016 (print) | LCC PR2848 (ebook) | DDC
821/.3—dc23
LC record available at http://lccn.loc.gov/2015048165

Typeset & designed by Sussex Academic Press, Brighton & Eastbourne.
Printed by TJ International, Padstow, Cornwall.

Contents

Introduction

The sonnet-sequence printed by Thomas Thorpe in London in 1609 is not easy to make full sense of. Of the 154 poems the first 126 are to or about a young man; and while the first 17 of these are a unit, and otherwise a few pairs go together, the general effect is of loose groupings according to theme with a number of more or less random placings. A gradual if somewhat circular progression in the poet's thoughts as to the relationship can be discerned. But the relationship itself is unclear. It is not the kind of love it is based on that blurs the issue, though some thought may go in that direction. It is not the question of the young man's identity that may slightly obscure things for the reader, though a great deal of research has gone on attempts to answer it. Indeed the fascination of literary historians with this point has tended to divert scholarship from the business of looking at the poems as poems. It is more the relationship of the youth to the sonnets themselves that seems to leave something to be answered.

In the main body of the collection Shakespeare vows many times over that the purpose of his writing is to immortalise the beauty and excellence of his dear friend; and yet one has very little idea from them all of what the inspirer of the poems was actually like: of his *presence* in them. It is as if Shakespeare's love is at one and the same time a mental construct with the person himself absent, and the object of his affections who fills his world. (His at times undifferentiated use of the word "love" encourages a slight lack of focus in this respect.) Of course to a degree it is what love is like, an attachment to the idea as well as to the person; but the declared intent of the writer, to capture in words something forever true of the individual, seems short on individuality. In part this is due to the convention of the love-poetry of the time, a direct inheritance of the mediaeval courtly tradition, positively cherished in the Elizabethan sonnet-sequence. Beauty is described in a reworked cliché of the ideal. The distance between speaker and loved one is all but impassable, the paragon on a higher plane. Yet as one comes to the second section of the present sequence one realises a deeper intent on the part of the writer. Up to 126 he is concerned with perfection; beyond that, the reverse. If there is a hesitation in the reader's empathy, in the first series, on account of the youth's seeming in some sense unreal, we may be sure it is part of the larger scheme of the sequence as a whole. This said, the point of the individual poems is never in doubt; and their beauty often takes the breath away.

After sonnet 126 there are 28 to or about a woman. Quickly one is aware of a more realised character (though the subject would not have agreed with the depiction). There is less of a sense of order to these poems, apart from the last two that act as a conclusion or *envoi*; and the several other differences between this section and that to the man create a further point of interest for the reader. As he is etherealised so she is thuddingly coars-ened: the distortion is equal and opposite. This in spite of the fact of her stereotype being altogether forgotten in a number of the poems (never so with the man). Distorted or not, she is the more tangible and real figure. Both characters are often addressed in the second person, and perhaps (some of) those poems and others too were presented to them or sent as letters. Some in either section refer to a love affair between the two of them that cost the writer dear. There have been several attempts to identify her also; and it should always be remembered that both she and the young man may have been invented by the poet to make a sonnet-drama, for reasons of his own. I am pretty sure they existed, but it cannot be proved; nor, for the purposes of reading and appreciating the poems, does it matter. They are real to the Sonnets.

My approach is to read the poems as poems: to see where their strengths lie, and on occasion their comparative weaknesses. To interpret some of the layers of meaning, especially in the rhyming couplet at poem's end. To comment on their formal beauty, and their rhetorical composure, at the same time as their sharply personal aspects; and on individual lines, phrases and words. To discern something of the poems' intent. It is a tricky task, open at every point to challenge; for in the arts of literary criticism and appreciation everything is subjective. I hope that over the course of my notes the difference between the 'two loves' of my title (from sonnet 144) will become apparent. By this I mean the two kinds of love that the poems to the man and the woman respectively illustrate. Finally, my aim is to make the Sonnets more accessible to the general reader, to furnish all readers with food for thought; and to pay tribute to perhaps the most astonishing set of personal poems ever written.

The man behind the tempest of dramatic characters that descended on the Elizabethan and Jacobean theatre, and still and always will charge the stage, anywhere and everywhere, with a magnificent fury and freshness, cannot easily be associated with a placid inner life. More likely is a vortex, a spinning charged world where he fought for and clung to his deepest reality. This is a world the Sonnets show. To illustrate and develop certain points I have drawn on an eclectic knowledge of poetry that has come to me over the years. I regard the act of reading poetry as a spontaneous one before all else; and so hope to be forgiven what may be seen as a slightly unconventional modus operandi. I hope, too, that the reader will bear with me as I bring the microscope up close to the text on occasion, to run the risk of overstaying a welcome in the dance of words. For some fifty years the Sonnets have been on my mind; it is time to take a look at what is there.

A response to poetry that is accurate but not over-organised seems to fit with its own nature: and without further ado, that is the intent of the pages that follow. Background will emerge in some cases; theories may be ventured and left hanging; and it may be that by not travelling in a straight line, I shall end up not so far away from where I started. Yet, as with a fourteen-line poem, at the same time it may be a long way indeed.

THE SONNETS

From fairest creatures we desire increase,
That thereby beauty's rose might never die,
But as the riper should by time decease, 3
His tender heir might bear his memory.
But thou, contracted to thine own bright eyes,
Feed'st thy light's flame with self-substantial fuel, 6
Making a famine where abundance lies,
Thyself thy foe, to thy sweet self too cruel.
Thou that art now the world's fresh ornament, 9
And only herald to the gaudy spring,
Within thine own bud buriest thy content
And, tender churl, mak'st waste in niggarding. 12
    Pity the world, or else this glutton be,
    To eat the world's due, by the grave and thee.

Sonnets 1 to 17 are addressed to a young man, ostensibly to encourage him to a certain course of action. To write seventeen sonnets on the advisability of begetting an heir is a curiosity in itself. Some think the youth may have been William Herbert, a young aristocrat known to be averse to marrying. (The initials W.H. appear somewhat mysteriously in the printer's dedication.) His identification is however a highly vexed question and one which I shall not explore, as it has the barest effect, if any, on a response to the sonnets as poetry. My view is that the poet took up the theme (for whatever reason) and found his way forward with it, both as a writer of sonnets, exploring the potential of his chosen form, and as an explorer at large in a difficult realm: the language of first-person love. His plays deal with this on stage; but a different world is entered by the writer writing as himself. The group of seventeen, constructed about a prosaic message as it is, acts as a gateway to it.

    This is not to say the feeling behind the words, his advice to the young man to 'get a son' (sonnet 7), is insincere. There can be several reasons for a course of action, some more conscious than others. A reader of poetry makes an individual judgement on such a matter; but in any case sincerity (that no imaginative writer takes an absolute position on) is not what one is looking for, but rather an authentic voice. It is this voice, creator of a storm of statements that speak from the page as if the writer's persona were one of the dramatist's own great characters, that I shall try to some small degree to follow.

Sonnet 1 delights in the assurance and grace of its opening; and, differently, in the sudden note of exasperation that one is tempted to hear in lines 5–6. Salvador Dali's golden Narcissus is before us; and an older person, exhorting him to think beyond himself. Lines 5–6 gather weight with a splendid underlying emphasis. 9* is balanced between surrender and sarcasm; the reader can take it either way. I am persuaded by the line's pure clarity and poise that a more or less total surrender is already on the cards. The ambiguity in the writer's position is itself thrillingly real; and one suspends judgement as to the exact nature of his personal involvement with the subject. 'By' in line 14 is a little vague: the suggestion is that the youth is as greedy as the grave, conspiring with it to leave nothing of himself behind.

Finally we may mention Shakespeare's sonnet-form, the three alternately rhyming quatrains and the final couplet, that others had used to some extent but that he made his own. The dynamic of its use – the craftsmanship of the poet who shapes the instrument he plays on – is touched on in the following pages. By and large it is as great a wonder as anything that at any particular moment is presented in an individual poem.

---

* An unreferenced number over 14 in the text is the sonnet number; otherwise it is the current sonnet's line.

When forty winters shall besiege thy brow
And dig deep trenches in thy beauty's field,
Thy youth's proud livery, so gaz'd on now,   3
Will be a tattered weed of small worth held.
Then being asked where all thy beauty lies,
Where all the treasure of thy lusty days,   6
To say within thine own deep-sunken eyes
Were an all-eating shame and thriftless praise.
How much more praise deserved thy beauty's use,   9
If thou couldst answer, 'This fair child of mine
Shall sum my count and make my old excuse,'
Proving his beauty by succession thine.   12
    This were to be new made when thou art old,
    And see thy blood warm when thou feel'st it cold.

A sonnet is traditionally reserved for the theme of love, though a constellation of ideas may emerge and revolve to present it. It is probably the easiest theme to treat of conventionally, to prettify; the least apt to yield up the inner beauty of the individual voice. The topic has always seemed to require a surrender to the conventional idea of the lover; all too often there is something of a dull composite personality behind a love-poem's words. One of his later sonnets expresses Shakespeare's impatience at the dull and ridiculous language of ardour that poets so often employ. But throughout his own sequence we meet the living person, often with a slight sense of shock. Here he is before us contrasting the ravaged state of later middle age (as forty was then), and by implication surely something like his own, with 'youth's proud livery' (3). The contrast works: almost with a shudder one sees or feels him there.

    The 'deep-sunken eyes' (7) of age have haunted me a half-century, taking up residence behind the scenes in my own head as a warning; eyes of an 'all-eating shame' (8) that when it is too late, will know their owner did not manage to fulfil expectations. Shakespeare can do this: bewilderingly a word, an expression can take on an added intent. It may be personal to the reader (as here), amusing, far-searching in its range, or deadly; any or all of these. It is a choice of word, or subordinate idea, with a built-in radar for further action, undeliberate as to specifics, but equipped for the quest that all poetry (as distinct from mere verse) can undertake at one level or another. Ambiguity is not what makes the pulse beat in poetry; nevertheless it lies at the core.

Already the supposed raison d'être of the piece, the same in all the first seventeen, to breed or in some way be cursed, is unconvincing. But Shakespeare evidently enjoyed finding arguments for it. He may very well have read the translation of Erasmus's *Epistle to persuade a young gentleman to marriage*, that appeared in Thomas Wilson's *The Arte of Rhetorique* (1553) as an example of the Oration Deliberative. It was a popular book at the time, and one can imagine it playing a part as the poet cast about for a new variation on his theme. Erasmus speaks of a fruitful tillage of the ground, for example, that may have given rise to a line in sonnet 3. The inventiveness of the writer, as he presents and re-presents reasons to 'get a son', seems almost to be a cause for merriment. And yet each of the early sonnets is intent, at some level, with a steady seriousness.

Look in thy glass and tell the face thou viewest,
Now is the time that face should form another,
Whose fresh repair if now thou not renewest,   3
Thou dost beguile the world, unbless some mother.
For where is she so fair whose uneared womb
Disdains the tillage of thy husbandry?   6
Or who is he so fond will be the tomb
Of his self-love, to stop posterity?
Thou art thy mother's glass, and she in thee   9
Calls back the lovely April of her prime;
So thou through windows of thine age shalt see,
Despite of wrinkles, this thy golden time.   12
    But if thou live remembered not to be,
      Die single, and thine image dies with thee.

The message itself is mechanical. Why is Shakespeare penning these poem-injunctions, with their blatantly contrived arguments, these variations on an idea with a repetitiveness already a little wearisome at heart? If the young man is his mother's glass (mirror), why is it assumed his own child will closely resemble its father? One cannot imagine the recipient of the poem will do more than smile at the repeated plea. But he may smile more broadly at the laddish dig in the ribs at 5–6. And his heart may well be caught by the unaffected reference to his mother at his age. To us now the sexist language of 5–6 makes 9–10 an unexpected delight; but one imagines that for the young man, the sudden allusion will momentarily put the rest out of his mind. Of course it may merely be a part of the argument – but why bring the mother on stage rather than the father? Does the poet see a feminine element in the youth (see 20)? The direct familial touch, charming as it is, seems almost out of place; certainly it would appear so in the latter part of the series, 18–126, where the familiarity between the two men is more intense, of a different nature entirely. Perhaps a kind of avuncular suggestion is a part of the poet's persona at this stage. At any rate the speaker seems to reveal a minor detail of a personal hinterland, so to speak; even if it amounts to no more than a guess at how someone used to look. One has no idea of what if anything it may tell us of the author; simply that it gives us a sense of an untroubled exterior life on the speaker's part, where people are referred to with no sense of strain or upset, or of moving in a larger-than-life world.

It is a vexed question, what one may call the validity of the autobiographical element of the Sonnets. There are other more definite suggestions of the poet's bare factual life than this to come, and yet they could all have been made up. I am inclined to go on the impression the lines leave on me after time. As far as recollections go, this is as appealing as any. Yet one should never forget that Shakespeare is an absolute master of the conceit, the adoption of a far-fetched comparison to make an effect; and the same conjuring skills lie always to hand.

The image of the last line deftly touches on the glass metaphor to conclude with a certain telling depth. The couplet that ends his adopted sonnet-shape was to become, in poem after poem, one of the poet's hallmark effects. One can already observe, in his use of the form as a whole to present an argument, how he has taken its measure as a rhetorical device. We cannot assume the order of the pieces is Shakespeare's own, but a good case can be made for the sequence as we have it as pretty well the right one; and without doubt the first seventeen go nowhere but at the beginning. The poet is learning in them to speak in a sonnet-way, that for him includes an unfathomable extra touch at poem's end. One is given a cue here as to the power of some of the sonnets to come.

Unthrifty loveliness, why dost thou spend
Upon thyself thy beauty's legacy?
Nature's bequest gives nothing, but doth lend,   3
And being frank she lends to those are free.
Then, beauteous niggard, why dost thou abuse
The bounteous largess given thee to give?   6
Profitless usurer, why dost thou use
So great a sum of sums, yet canst not live?
For having traffic with thyself alone,   9
Thou of thyself thy sweet self dost deceive;
Then how, when Nature calls thee to be gone,
What ácceptable audit canst thou leave?   12
   Thy unused beauty must be tombed with thee,
   Which usèd lives th'executor to be.

One of the plainest pieces in its comparative lack of phrases and passages that illuminate by their sheer poetry, this nevertheless engages as a perfect minor example of rhetorical persuasiveness. Its addressee, one imagines, will at least have enjoyed the artistry on offer, while possibly squirming at the directness of the accusation of sexual self-absorption. Again, he may laugh at that: there is much in the sequence to do with laddish double meanings. And yet the Muse is present. The opening two words, a sigh of remonstrance and surrender; the gust of feeling that dies away, to be replaced by a kind of rapier-point sophistry (how often a Sonnet proceeds along such lines); the succession of questions interlaced with supposedly telling points, that yields to a final couplet with almost uncanny clinching effect – all this makes a fine poem. The perfect overall control of line and form, alliteration and repetition and rolling phrase, and above all perhaps the financial metaphor extended throughout, lends its strength. 'Executor' (14) finely equates the capacity of a supposed child to carry out the requirements of the will with the execution, or creation, of the father's beauty. If the piece is unconvincing in its apparent motive, a deeper one is not far to seek. The sonneteer is learning his trade and the surface argument serves him well.

This is not to say his admiration for the youth is contrived, nor even his concern for his "survival" in a child, though the latter carries considerably less conviction. But what seems to me to announce itself from the depths is the sense of a mind grappling with its material, that is ultimately the material of love. I would note here the personal pronoun – thou, thyself, thee, thy – that comes to serve almost as an unseen stepping-stone along the intuitive path of the reading mind. This is to do with far more than the writer's admiration for the young man. It is to lead into an exploration of identity, of writer and recipient both.

Those hours that with gentle work did frame
The lovely gaze where every eye doth dwell,
Will play the tyrants to the very same, 3
And that unfair which fairly doth excel.
For never-resting time leads summer on
To hideous winter and confounds him there, 6
Sap checked with frost and lusty leaves quite gone,
Beauty o'ersnowed and bareness everywhere.
Then were not summer's distillation left, 9
A liquid prisoner pent in walls of glass,
Beauty's effect with beauty were bereft,
Nor it nor no remembrance what it was. 12
    But flowers distilled, though they with winter meet,
    Leese but their show; their substance still lives sweet.

Time makes an entrance, a character in its own right. It is to play as mighty a part as any of the poet's dramatic characters. A "bloody tyrant" in sonnet 16 and something like a devastating world-god as the sequence finds its true voice, it steals onstage in the softest of guises. The footfall of the first two lines has a charm all its own. And while the character reveals its hand as the poem proceeds, the picturesque expressions still leave something of a lulling effect. This is to change later.

    The sestet is a rather beautiful dalliance with the practice of perfumery. This was quite a business in Shakespeare's time; the essence of the tenth line was common enough in prosaic terms. But here is an exemplar of the poetic effect, an alchemy due in part in this case to a tension between animate and inanimate, 'prisoner pent' and mere matter. It can go on meaning different things: I have to confess, with a part of my mind I see a tie-up with the very much more modern practice or business of storing the male reproductive essence for later use. While this is not ugly in itself it is scarcely inspiring to the imagination; and yet it does not impinge on the line's stellar beauty. Here is an extract from an article in *Popular Science*, June 1899: "No botanist can read the line 'A liquid prisoner pent in walls of glass' and not recognise the exact portrayal of the living vegetable cell. The living protoplasm is a liquid prisoner sure enough, hemmed in by walls transparent. . . . The first scientific glimpse of the 'prisoner pent in walls of glass' came about 1670, through the lenses of Nehemiah Grew, a Puritan physicist and botanist." Lucretius and Goethe are cited as other poets who have discerned a scientific outline before the scientists have seen it for themselves. The writer of the article is no doubt one of many who at different times have seen, and will see, a connection with states of being that when the line was written can scarcely have been envisaged. The words of poetry are cast in stone but there is a world to be made with it.

In line 14 'leese' is 'lose. 'Still' is nice: the echo, with the double meaning, laying a finishing touch out of sight, as it were. So the whole piece moves imperceptibly into place; and one is left to let it do what it will.

Then let not winter's ragged hand deface
In thee thy summer ere thou be distilled:
Make sweet some vial; treasure thou some place   3
With beauty's treasure ere it be self-killed.
That use is not forbidden usury
Which happies those that pay the willing loan;   6
That's for thyself to breed another thee,
Or ten times happier be it ten for one.
Ten times thyself were happier than thou art,   9
If ten of thine ten times refigured thee;
Then what could death do if thou shouldst depart,
Leaving thee living in posterity?   12
    Be not self-willed, for thou art much too fair
    To be death's conquest and make worms thine heir.

Again one can see the recipient smiling at yet another version
of the argument, with an extra nod of appreciation at the word-
play. Usury was legal but considered beyond the pale, witness
The Merchant of Venice; the maximum rate of 10% is exploded
here up to the power of three, to make a point that is manifestly
not the point. The neat 'self-willed' in line 13 sets up the recip-
ient for a coup de grâce; and the final line as if with a triumphant
laugh sweeps aside his defences. The word not only incisively
echoes 'self-killed' but carries a triple meaning of its own:
mulish, bequeathing all to yourself alone, and an implied sense
stemming from an Elizabethan use of 'will' as the sexual organ
(male or female). The conclusion has the macabre fling of a
union with death itself with worms as the result. But who is the
recipient?

    And is there a recipient? The question of autobiographical
fact in the Sonnets has no clear end: but one tends to assume a
real addressee and him (if perhaps not later her) reading at least

a fair number of them. I have mentioned William Herbert; a more usual candidate is Henry Wriothesley, third Earl of Southampton, to whom the long poems *Venus and Adonis* and *Lucrece* are addressed. There the tone is subservient, in the way of one seeking patronage in a public dedication, quite unlike the sly familiar tone so quickly to be overheard in the sequence. Common sense allows us to suppose Shakespeare did not make "thou" and "thyself" out of thin air, and similarly, in my view, that when he offers us gratuitous information (as later, twice, that he – the poet – is lame), that it is so. But there are degrees of what looks like fact, some softer than others ('thou art thy mother's glass', 3.9, does not *say* the writer knew or saw her); and common sense equally tells us to render unto Caesar the things that are a literary historian's, and elsewhere the things that belong to the ever-living in a poem. The two areas overlap and I shall not be able to stay away from the former entirely; and indeed it raises fascinating questions on its own account. But with little to say on the latter area as far as the jeu d'esprit above is concerned, this seems as good a place as any to clarify an intention to steer clear of the historian's patch, by and large, the more to take part in another quest. My aim is to experience as fully as I may the poetry of the Sonnets, and to offer others some thoughts that may or may not be of assistance on their own way to doing so: for which privilege I give thanks to whatever gods may be.

Lo, in the orient when the gracious light
Lifts up his burning head, each under eye
Doth homage to his new-appearing sight,   3
Serving with looks his sacred majesty;
And having climbed the steep-up heavenly hill,
Resembling strong youth in his middle age,   6
Yet mortal looks adore his beauty still,
Attending on his golden pilgrimage.
But when from highmost pitch, with weary car,   9
Like feeble age he reeleth from the day,
The eyes, 'fore duteous, now converted are
From his low tract, and look another way.   12
    So thou, thyself outgoing in thy noon,
    Unlooked on diest unless thou get a son.

An exercise in the high style, this has its own engaging quality, on an undemanding level. The quatrains proceed in perfect step and the couplet brings what almost feels like a dressage event to a precise close. The homophone in the final word allows the majestic presence its name at last, yet still at one remove, as if a certain distance and mystery are to be preserved. Neatness is one thing – line 8 is neat – poetry another. 'Lifts up his burning head' (2) compels my inner attention, a swift magical sequence of deliberate light steps, after which we are returned to cliché. It is not in Shakespeare's interest here to talk of glories of the sunset; and his predilection is always to use it with dark overtones of the approaching night, as opposed to the rays of early morning (as in sonnet 33). In some ways he too was a man of cliché. And yet this sonnet has its own beauty.

There is a lot to be said for the perfect control of a chosen form. All the great writers have it, indeed all the great artists of whatever medium. A means of establishing an agreement with the reader's (listener's, observer's) own mind, so that it can allow itself to be carried along, the form of a written work of art is not always clearly definable in the modern age. This does not mean it is not there; only that there is a greater difficulty in gaining an objective slant to an act of critical appreciation. It is easier to write about Shakespeare's sonnets than the novels of James Joyce.

And to my mind more rewarding: for what a piece such as the above can remind of is the basis of art, a simplicity of outlook that chimes with an aspect of existence no more or less than the inheritance of everyman. On one level the apotheosis of banality, on another sonnet 7 entertains in its music and quietly informs as to a certain universal experience. Shakespeare the director lets Time's persona try on an outfit. He will be more ambitious for it later. His next piece not only entertains in its sounding pattern; the poem itself is a small musical world.

Music to hear, why hear'st thou music sadly?
Sweets with sweets war not, joy delights in joy.
Why lov'st thou that which thou receiv'st not gladly,　　3
Or else receiv'st with pleasure thine annoy?
If the true concord of well-tunèd sounds,
By unions married, do offend thine ear,　　6
They do but sweetly chide thee, who confounds
In singleness the parts that thou shouldst bear.
Mark how one string, sweet husband to another,　　9
Strikes each in each by mutual ordering;
Resembling sire and child and happy mother,
Who all in one, one pleasing note do sing;　　12
　　Whose speechless song, being many, seeming one,
　　Sings this to thee: 'Thou single wilt prove none.'

In personal terms this is very different from the last sonnet. There could scarcely be a greater contrast between the opening addresses: one is declaimed, the other anything but. "Sadly" at the time had more of seriousness and less of gloom in it than now; the youth is in a sombre frame of mind. 'I am never merry when I hear sweet music,' says Jessica to Lorenzo in *The Merchant of Venice*, and is informed in part-answer, 'The reason is, your spirits are attentive: / . . . The man that hath no music in himself, / Nor is not moved with concord of sweet sounds, / Is fit for treasons, stratagems and spoils; / . . . Let no such man be trusted. Mark the music.' The echo in line 5 is telling, and gives rise to the idea (still a little far-fetched) that Shakespeare took something of the youth's character for the minor heroine. In 84 we are told he is 'fond on praise'. No further idiosyncrasy on his part emerges in all the 126 sonnets addressed to him; merely generalisation as to character, as in 'kind and true' (105), or alternatively 'lascivious grace' (40) or 'straying youth' (41); and reference to a certain glow or sheen the speaker clearly finds attractive. But here in line 1 is someone we can know. Often Shakespeare seems in part to be talking to himself when addressing the youth: not here. One can almost hear the first line starting a conversation. The hint of true personality the poet employs is enough for him to visit his theme afresh.

And a beautiful job he makes of it. The whole piece is a musical composition. In the new impulse added (typically) to the line of thought as the sestet begins, I have always heard plucked notes. 'Mark how one string, sweet husband to another . . .' In *Macbeth* one can seem to hear dogs barking as the king snarls at the First Murderer, 'Ay, in the catalogue ye go for men; / As hounds, greyhounds, mongrels, spaniels, curs, / Shoughs, water-rugs, and demi-wolves are clept / All by the name of dogs . . .' I do not know of any other poet who can do this.

If the plea to sire a child had been restricted to this sonnet it would have made (comparative) sense. Why should one not want to see a young person in the bosom of a family? The oddness of the repeated plea, together with the variety of argument found to support it, tells of something else at work. My guess is a private joke between the poet and the young man, maybe arising from a concern on the parents' part; this then turned (Shakespeare being Shakespeare) to a preoccupation with the deepest themes of poetry, love, immortality, death, beauty, the seed there from the start, in the friendship's closeness. At the same time the poet was tuning his instrument. Here a single note is struck through many. The extended metaphor may be said to work to perfection.

Is it for fear to wet a widow's eye
That thou consum'st thyself in single life?
Ah, if thou issueless shalt hap to die,   3
The world will wail thee like a makeless wife;
The world will be thy widow and still weep
That thou no form of thee hast left behind,   6
When every private widow well may keep,
By children's eyes, her husband's shape in mind.
Look what an unthrift in the world doth spend   9
Shifts but his place, for still the world enjoys it;
But beauty's waste hath in the world an end,
And kept unused, the user so destroys it.   12
    No love toward others in that bosom sits,
    That on himself such murd'rous shame commits.

So far as the mock debate goes, the proposition of "singleness" under a rain of blows, a further suggestion comes into play, not a little surprising and almost hilariously artificial. Whatever stops a young person of good health marrying, it is unlikely to be the unbearable thought of his weeping widow (unless he is off to the wars). Yet the poet achieves a remarkable turn upon the conceit, by which "the world" takes centre place (mentioned five times). 'Thou dost beguile the world' (sonnet 3) warns in passing; here the idea of the macrocosm is paramount. Beauty is its ornament, the individual its debtor for life; the backdrop to the shadow-boxing in the foreground all at once is an eternal one. The couplet summarily returns us to a stage on which individuals are dominant. The accusation of narcissism is back with a vengeance: 'no love toward others' (13) has a personal barb attached, to be delivered more gently, and yet more vehemently, in the next poem. The force of 'destroys' and 'murd'rous shame' takes us aback; it goes with a slight acceleration of pace and feeling over the piece as a whole. The final line suggests auto-eroticism, a wasting of potency. Yet the lingering impression still may be a plangent tone behind the scenes, a regret at an opportunity for the richness of new life denied, a deprived 'makeless [mateless] wife' (4) given over to her grief.

'By children's eyes' (8) is an interesting phrase. By context it is bound to mean 'by the eying of [her] children', but it may also mean what it more directly says. Are not the eyes a vital centre? They become so later in the sequence, opposed to the mind, in another, more essential debate.

For shame deny that thou bear'st love to any,
Who for thyself art so unprovident.
Grant if thou wilt, thou art belov'd of many,   3
But that thou none lov'st is most evident;
For thou art so possessed with murd'rous hate,
That 'gainst thyself thou stick'st not to conspire,   6
Seeking that beauteous roof to ruinate,
Which to repair should be thy chief desire.
O change thy thought, that I may change my mind!   9
Shall hate be fairer lodged than gentle love?
Be as thy presence is, gracious and kind,
Or to thyself at least kind-hearted prove.   12
    Make thee another self for love of me,
    That beauty still may live in thine or thee.

It is narcissism with a twist, hate of all the world (in depriving the future of the beauty he might bequeath it) indicating self-hate of a kind. Again the 'murd'rous' epithet (5), striking home like a dagger. After which line 9 has the ring of pure conviction. Yet the poet may still be playing at poetry: the involvement the line carries, ten short words of a simple, open appeal, may be a simulated charge, a magic of word-making, that represents little or nothing in the actual situation, whatever that may have been. I find the best way to look at it is to say, there is no actual situation. Whatever there was, the poet certainly does not wish to do more than allude to (though there are moments of great directness). But in the natural way of reading, as one suspends thoughts of doubt or disbelief, and takes line 9 entirely as it asks to be taken, it creates a moment of deep attachment I for one can believe in, for at least as long as the poem lasts. Whether or not it is (as I think) a line to echo down the ages, it has echoed down the narrow corridor of one person's life.

Its lovely follow-up in line 10, question by exhortation, completes the change of mood. The dagger is laid aside, an embrace extended; in 'for love of me' (13) for the first time an irrational cause comes into play. The suggestion of the argument's continuance ("prove you love one person at least", see line 1) is structural, the deeper level of reasoning merely of the heart. Love begins to take its place as the prime motive.

As fast as thou shalt wane, so fast thou grow'st
In one of thine, from that which thou departest;
And that fresh blood which youngly thou bestow'st   3
Thou mayst call thine, when thou from youth convertest.
Herein lies wisdom, beauty, and increase;
Without this, folly, age, and cold decay;   6
If all were minded so, the times should cease,
And threescore year would make the world away.
Let those whom Nature hath not made for store,   9
Harsh, featureless and rude, barrenly perish:
Look whom she best endowed, she gave the more;
Which bounteous gift thou shouldst in bounty cherish.   12
    She carved thee for her seal, and meant thereby
    Thou shouldst print more, not let that copy die.

The opening quatrain is uncharacteristically awkward in its
rhyme, that draws too much attention to itself: one has the
impression of a rushed job. Yet once into the writing the poet
finds his ease. One wonders at the circumstances of the writing
of this first group of sonnets with their insistent and unusual
request. A scenario that comes to mind, at least for a number of
them, is a challenge from the young man to his friend: a test at
once of skill and affection: one may even picture him sitting
there amused, and both touched and gratified, as the word-
magician beats the clock – who knows? In 1816 John Keats and
Leigh Hunt raced each other to write a sonnet *On the Grasshopper
and the Cricket*. Keats produced a charming piece starting 'The
poetry of earth is never dead' (also winning on time). Here we
seem to have an example of the poem developing its own convic-
tion from an uninspired start, the triplets of nouns and
adjectives taking on the rhetorical mantle, so to speak, and
allowing the sonnet-form to exercise its persuasive flow in the

Shakespearian fashion. The closing metaphor, taking up 'so fast thou grow'st' of line 1, allows Nature herself a certain character (as in sonnets 4, 67, 126 and elsewhere).

One is a little surprised at the man who was to stand up for so many of the lowly poor among the minor characters of his plays, taking a line in 9–12 that the most vociferous proponents of eugenics in the early 20th century might have echoed. (Not only Hitler; there were plenty nearer home.) It is of course anachronistically suspect to jump the centuries thus; attitudes are bred of the time; but illicit musings, or at least doubtful connections, are part of the pleasure of reading. In any case as we know it is one of a series of false attacks, a kind of tilting at windmills, to go with Cervantes almost back to the time the sonnets were written. Knowing what is to come, one looks forward with relief to the moment when the speaker discards the mantle of Don Quixote, and the sequence takes on its true (if not quite definable) intent. And yet these have their music too.

'Departest' (2): 'are [art] parted from'.

When I do count the clock that tells the time,
And see the brave day sunk in hideous night,
When I behold the violet past prime,   3
And sable curls all silvered o'er with white;
When lofty trees I see barren of leaves,
Which erst from heat did canopy the herd,   6
And summer's green all girded up in sheaves,
Borne on the bier with white and bristly beard;
Then of thy beauty do I question make   9
That thou among the wastes of time must go,
Since sweets and beauties do themselves forsake,
And die as fast as they see others grow.   12
    And nothing 'gainst time's scythe can make defence
    Save breed to brave him, when he takes thee hence.

A nocturne of a delicate melancholy in the octave, if subordinate in the sentence, has a voice of its own. The motif of human ageing, touched on in the fourth line, is wonderfully transferred to Nature in the eighth. Keats – perhaps Shakespeare's chief follower among poets – wrote of the second quatrain, 'He has left nothing to say about nothing or any thing.' The alliteration in the first eight lines adds a picturesque touch to a deepening apprehension. Again the poet tries out a fitting for a principal character, Time, that will itself be subordinate only to Love.

I find lines 9 and 10 almost unbearably beautiful. The slow, meditative pace, leisurely established, carries over into a dawning realisation that seems to arrive at the speed of light. The rest of the poem pads out the whole, the couplet nicely picking up the alliterative device as a coda; all conviction has died away. But something has been said that goes far beyond what I term the mock debate, whose purpose, to allow an expression of the dearest attachment, is becoming more and more apparent; and one senses to the author as well.

'Ridiculous the waste sad time / Stretching before and after', wrote T.S.Eliot, to conclude *Burnt Norton*, the first of his *Four Quartets*. His 'sad' has the Shakespearian overtone, perhaps, more colourless than emotional. His 'time' is altogether different. To compare the two lines (10 with the first of Eliot's quoted above) is to glimpse what Shakespeare offers, here, there and everywhere in his work. As if tracing the shades and ranges of an invisible map of the world, he catches – even as a modern physicist might – at a force that is all around us. All authors of the imagination, perhaps all artists are concerned with it, some (as Eliot) more from a distance. It is the simplest and least comprehensible aspect of existence, governing us as surely as gravity: the there-and-not-there-ness of personal closeness.

O that you were yourself, but love you are
No longer yours than you yourself here live;
Against this coming end you should prepare,   3
And your sweet semblance to some other give.
So should that beauty which you hold in lease
Find no determination; then you were   6
Yourself again after yourself's decease,
When your sweet issue your sweet form should bear.
Who lets so fair a house fall to decay,   9
Which husbandry in honour might uphold
Against the stormy gusts of winter's day
And barren rage of death's eternal cold?   12
    O none but unthrifts! Dear my love, you know
    You had a father; let your son say so.

To be "not yourself" (line 1) suggested what it does now. The poem may have arisen from the youth's feeling off-colour. The chop-logic that ensues creates little of interest in the octave; while the third quatrain is both entertaining and forceful, and the couplet remarkably direct in its appeal. Yet the presentation of the opening argument is a graceful one, charming the ear, and especially in my case, for some reason, with a slight sound-echo of 'beauty' (5) in 'determination' ('ending', 6). The pronoun play of lines 1–2, noted above in sonnet 4, in its very insistence is a signal to something behind the scenes. How do you write of love? The poet Robert Graves comments, 'Lovers in the act dispense / With the meum-tuum sense' to which I reply, very well, but 'Scribblers of what lovers do / Make poetry of I and You'. In his sonnets towards the end of the sequence, to the Dark Lady as she is known, Shakespeare is not averse to speaking of the "act" but the pronoun play goes on (for example 149.1–4). I think in the present sonnet in particular it can be said to hint at an uncertainty with identity. The writer may or may not have intended it as such, but the poem offers the reading to a modern mind, scarcely buried as it is in the first phrase.

The good householder is re-introduced from sonnet 10; and again there is a wonderful progression from one line to another. In sonnet 12 human age was caught up in Nature's grasp; here it is the reverse, the twelfth line a resounding and picturesque climax, the work of the quatrains now over. The couplet intensifies the vocative 'love' of the opening and makes a simple, quite irrational plea. Or rather a plea with the merest form of rationality, for the sake of the overall structure, clearly there to support quite another roof.

Not from the stars do I my judgement pluck,
And yet methinks I have astronomy;
But not to tell of good or evil luck, 3
Of plagues, of dearths, or seasons' quality;
Nor can I fortune to brief minutes tell,
Pointing to each his thunder, rain and wind; 6
Or say with princes if it shall go well,
By oft predict that I in heaven find.
But from thine eyes my knowledge I derive, 9
And, constant stars, in them I read such art
As truth and beauty shall together thrive,
If from thyself to store thou wouldst convert; 12
    Or else of thee this I prognosticate,
    Thy end is truth's and beauty's doom and date.

A humorous smile in the octave, which the reader is able to take on trust, in the sense of being at home with the speaker's tone of voice, his feelings, changes to . . . what? So often the Shakespearian riddle in the Sonnets, the level of sincerity is up in the air, as free as a kite, there and not there. A beautifully-written sestet merely delivers another set-piece argument. In his sonnet-sequence *Astrophel and Stella* (published 1591, probably before at least most of Shakespeare's were composed), Philip Sidney has his hero discover his fate from 'those two stars in Stella's face'. Some see a parodic strain in the Shakespearian collection, and certainly he wearied of his fellow-poets' use of cliché (sonnet 130); but my view is a little different. The sonneteering tradition of his time had lifted wholesale the courtly apparatus of a knight's address to his lady, that had simply infested the mediaeval literary mind-set. No doubt for a number of different reasons he chose to enter the tradition; and taking advantage of the underlying artificiality, he used it to address a man. This does two things. It highlights the said artificiality, thus beginning to clear the way for a more realistic love-poetry. And more to the point, it allows him to venture into Olympus, the realm of the gods. By which I mean he is able to write about the human eternity. The film *Forrest Gump* has its hero in leg-braces as a boy, that dramatically fall off as he runs away from bullies. I hope I have not wrecked the reader's enjoyment of the poems by the comparison (or of the film for that matter). At any rate, the braces are not to last for long.

A couple of incidental points interest me. The poet's calm remark in the second line (of a piece with the unobtrusive polymath of the plays); and his ability to make an ugly word almost beautiful in the thirteenth. Perhaps I am overstepping the bounds of subjectivity, self-indulgence and general irrelevance here, but reading poetry is a personal matter and this is a personal reaction. I have always thought – or hoped – Edward Thomas saw the name Adlestrop on a station platform and wondered if he could put the gawkiest of words into a poem and make it fair. I can't imagine Shakespeare being self-conscious with a word in the same way; but in any case it happens. A poet's alchemy is not confined to Olympus.

When I consider everything that grows
Holds in perfection but a little moment,
That this huge stage presenteth nought but shows 　　　3
Whereon the stars in secret influence comment;
When I perceive that men as plants increase
Cheerèd and checked even by the self-same sky, 　　　6
Vaunt in their youthful sap, at height decrease,
And wear their brave state out of memory;
Then the conceit of this inconstant stay 　　　9
Sets you most rich in youth before my sight,
Where wasteful time debateth with decay
To change your day of youth to sullied night. 　　　12
　　And all in war with time for love of you,
　　As he takes from you, I engraft you new.

This stands with the next two sonnets as the end stage in the initial argument on the means of keeping beauty alive in the world – its procreation – and as a bridge to Shakespeare's second and true argument, that he is finally able to admit to in sonnet 18. The first four lines of 16 clarify 'engraft' (14 above); otherwise the metaphor has a tantalising hint of a new approach, that the reader may guess at, but nothing is sure. It falls into place as one reads on.

A point of linkage out of the way, one may go back to the beginning and wonder at the balance struck in the first two lines. A heavy lightness, perfectly poised, as though a world were held in the hand: for an instant a future Prospero contemplates the fairy-tale of existence. The poet is talking not so much of time as of change; and the poem gradually comes down to hard tacks. After a sweeping dismissal of astrological forecasting in the last piece line 4 has a certain fascination. There is, or may be, influence but it is secret, not known. The stars and planets, an audience of sorts to our goings-on, weigh in; or there is a sense in which they have their own say. With our improved current understanding of the heavens (and indeed of 'everything that grows', 1) we enter a position both of now and the past. It is another case of a modern mind taking words a little differently; and of a phrase or line that will always have a hint of new readings, which return to the same one. An increase in knowledge does not deflect the intent behind a remark of poetry.

Line 8, that flickers with a recognition of existence as heroic and futile in one, leads to an apprehension of all that is precious that surely goes beyond the apparent point of reference, 'your day of youth' (12). As we read we do not doubt the addressee's own existence or that it is dear (and dearer than that word) to the poet. The splendid penultimate line cannot be gainsaid. Yet it can be extended. The 'you' at its end is the youth; but is not the precarious substance of life's magic also on hand, addressed as it were behind its representative, whom we are sensible of as at some indefinable point, that varies from reader to reader? There is a tension here and a mystery. Why is it we know so little of what the young man was actually like? In the sonnets addressed to him we are led to and from the person, to and from the brief perfection of all (line 2), and either at times is the near and at times the far. This is the interplay behind the scenes, to be caught at but not to be traced, a music beneath the music. It may be said to be the characteristic of these poems, the burden of their song.

But wherefore do not you a mightier way
Make war upon this bloody tyrant, Time,
And fortify yourself in your decay   3
With means more blessèd than my barren rhyme?
Now stand you on the top of happy hours,
And many maiden gardens, yet unset,   6
With virtuous wish would bear your living flowers,
Much liker than your painted counterfeit.
So should the lines of life that life repair,   9
Which this, time's pencil or my pupil pen,
Neither in inward worth nor outward fair
Can make you live yourself in eyes of men.   12
    To give away yourself keeps yourself still,
    And you must live, drawn by your own sweet skill.

Again the first two lines, like a powerful gust, seem to whisk the boat into mid-stream, after which the oar-blades of the mind take over. The strong sweeping strokes of the lines, adapting themselves to the fine conditions offered by a couple of metaphorical stretches, bring the vessel safely home, with a finishing-line emerging by deft use of an image from the second of these. If from line 5 it is all display, still a note of savage intensity stays with us from the start. And the reader has an inner eye woken, so to speak, by the elucidation of the final phrase of 15. There offered, here at once withdrawn as comparatively worthless, is a further way of keeping fresh the sapling of youth's beauty: its re-creation in the poet's own words.

    The wish for his poetry to be able to offer such a service seems to peep through. But he cannot yet make the full claim, reverting to the banal. Yet even with the hint of such a means the end in view is for an instant transformed. It is in the mind that the marvel of the young man shall stand. We are turned a little more to the generalisation, even as the signal is removed. By love's celebration love shall last.

I wonder if the odd contemporary reader, however, might not have recoiled slightly, as many a modern may do, at the wearily mechanical image of beauty in the second quatrain, introduced as it is by "barren" in line 4. The third quatrain is well-known for its compressed syntax, though the general meaning is clear enough. (One might discern a touch of writer's – or rower's – cramp.) 'Time's pencil' (10) may refer to the present poem, in parallel with 'my pupil pen'; or to a portrait of the youth (see line 8 and note to 47). The pencil is a paintbrush; the last line suggests the youth is to be his own artist. It is a relief the arguments for the process are almost at an end.

Who will believe my verse in time to come
If it were filled with your most high deserts?
Though yet heaven knows it is but as a tomb   3
Which hides your life, and shows not half your parts.
If I could write the beauty of your eyes,
And in fresh numbers number all your graces,   6
The age to come would say, 'This poet lies;
Such heavenly touches ne'er touched earthly faces.'
So should my papers, yellowed with their age,   9
Be scorned, like old men of less truth than tongue,
And your true rights be termed a poet's rage
And stretchèd metre of an antique song.   12
    But were some child of yours alive that time,
    You should live twice, in it and in my rhyme.

This is the last in the series that may have been inspired by Erasmus' Epistle (see note to sonnet 2). I can imagine the two of them crowing over the Epistle together. (Perhaps the young man's parents gave it him to read.) The order of the first seventeen may or may not be Shakespeare's as opposed to the publisher Thomas Thorpe's, and so for the rest of the collection; but in many respects it works and (with a suitable mental reservation) will have to do. The alternative is ignoring the order as we have it altogether, which makes a deal less sense. While the poet decries the merits of his verse it forms almost the entire subject-matter of the piece, more so than in any other; and as if to return to the living strength of 'I engraft you new' (15), in the end it is allowed equal standing with the formulaic solution to the apparent problem. Which of course is no problem at all.

    Whether or not the Epistle triggered the Sonnets, the true inspirer, the "onlie begetter", to lift Thorpe's dedicatory words from their context, was a poet's involvement with friendship, beauty, youth and love. I find this sonnet very touching for his sense of his words' inadequacy. Shakespeare's sublime confidence in the enduring power of his verse, a staple of what is to come, has this behind it. In sonnet 65 he asks who, where, or what there can be to challenge the onward march of Time (a cliché he would abhor), and answers, 'O none, unless this miracle have might, / That in black ink my love may still run bright.' It is always a miracle, one that he hoped for, that we see exist. What is extraordinary in art is simply its appearance on the face of the globe. We are about to explore a mountain range.

The third quatrain above has within it a glimpse of the writer at his work. Oh that we could see those 'old men'! I take the 'antique song' (12) to be the sonnet-form (or sonnet-sequence). Appearing first in Italy in the 13th century it has lasted well. W. H. Auden's *In Time of War*, written in the late 1930s, has a marvellous new "take" on the form, while preserving its base in pristine fashion. The Bengali poet Jibanananda Das does the same, differently, in *Rupasi Bangla* (*Bengal the Beautiful*), also written in the 'thirties, and published after his death in 1957. Both these are sequences of some length, and there are and will be others. Whether or not it lasts as long again it is a form, singly or in sequence, ideally fit for its purpose. In its fourteen lines, with a regular rhyme-scheme of some kind, and allowance for development in the octave and a fresh impetus in the sestet, it is perfectly framed to come to a conclusion that in essence is that of one sentence. If its purpose can be given a name, it may be no more than the revealing of a point the heart insists is to be made.

Shall I compare thee to a summer's day?
Thou art more lovely and more temperate.
Rough winds do shake the darling buds of May,   3
And summer's lease hath all too short a date.
Sometime too hot the eye of heaven shines,
And often is his gold complexion dimmed;   6
And every fair from fair sometime declines,
By chance or Nature's changing force untrimmed.
But thy eternal summer shall not fade,   9
Nor lose possession of that fair thou ow'st,
Nor shall death brag thou wand'rest in his shade,
When in eternal lines to time thou grow'st.   12
    So long as men can breathe or eyes can see,
    So long lives this, and this gives life to thee.

Shakespeare finds a new way into his theme. The 'eternal lines' of line 12 are clear a second later, as 'this' is honoured with a pure delight. On the face of it the poet may be seen to prize his poem; but is it not rather the impulse of poetry that he has at last allowed into the open, and given its full due? There is the grace of the young man, of Nature, and of the instrument. They are separate and one: and from them the poet has contrived an expression of a certain intent in life, to preserve the beautiful.

His passionate admiration for the youth is to the fore. Structurally this is so; and everything about the poem persuades us of it too. It is free and fresh, a breeze can almost be felt; we are outside, the day's change is all around us, the season's, life's; at one and the same time we see 'the darling buds of May' (3) . . . and that all is to be 'untrimmed' (8), marred, stripped of its ornament. Only 'the fair thou ow'st' ('own'st', 10) is to be protected. At one level it is a declaration of love for a person. At another it is an act of homage to a craft. The force of the latter, in the measured statement of the couplet at the end, is no less in its way than that of the spontaneous outburst of the opening line. But the integrity of the piece is never compromised.

It is a love-poem. Nothing could be more expressive of the poet's commitment than the closing words. The ritual exhortation of the first group of poems has disappeared as if it had never been; there is a sense of exuberant play, and something steadier, stronger. Something is burning behind the scenes. Whatever else is going on there, to make the full statement, the means employed does not for a moment interrupt the end. In a sense this poem, the first of a long series in which the poet has freed himself of an initial encumbrance, is the key to the rest of the section 1 to 126. We will continue to know or sense next to nothing of what the youth is actually like. Other worlds hover within that of the poet's regard for a person. But the personal aspect still is the be-all and end-all. And never is it more joyfully engaged in than here.

One or two details catch the eye: the simplicity of lines 5–6; and an image for which there are no words. 'Death, be not proud,' wrote John Donne a few years later, in a breathtaking sonnet of his own. Line 11 here has a lighter personification, and yet one that is more at home in the mind (at least mine). So much could be said on its vocabulary, pace, poise, and who knows what, and nothing would be said at all.

Devouring Time, blunt thou the lion's paws,
And make the earth devour her own sweet brood;
Pluck the keen teeth from the fierce tiger's jaws,   3
And burn the long-lived phoenix in her blood.
Make glad and sorry seasons as thou fleet'st
And do whate'er thou wilt, swift-footed Time,   6
To the wide world and all her fading sweets;
But I forbid thee one most heinous crime.
O carve not with thy hours my love's fair brow,   9
Nor draw no lines there with thine antique pen;
Him in thy course untainted do allow
For beauty's pattern to succeeding men.   12
    Yet do thy worst, old Time; despite thy wrong,
    My love shall in my verse ever live young.

The shackles are off. The tremendous opening quatrain is pitted, finally, against a simple statement of belief in the last line. Despite the physical reference in lines 9–10 I have always for some reason felt the 'love' of line 14 to be more the mental construct. Certainly I think it is entirely valid to see it in that way, as well as the other. There is never a clear dividing-line.

Shakespeare's new allegiance to the power of (his) verse has already become its own cliché, to some small extent. We know that he knows that nothing can stop the ageing process; but he has found a way of expressing his love for a person by means of a proposition (with which as readers we can concur): a trust in the power of poetry. The difference between this position and that of the first seventeen sonnets is liberating; the poet's hand is decisively the stronger. Here as on an eternal battlefield more and more ground is ceded to Time, only for it to be stopped in its tracks. The 'war upon this bloody tyrant' (16.2) is fully declared. It seems that along with finding a way to let the poetic imagination roam at height, the author has a perfect confidence in his chosen sonnet-form; it is second nature to him now.

The urgency is more real, the tone more expansive, than earlier on. But the poet is always capable of operating on different levels. We have the paradox of a line at once of majesty and tenderness, 'O carve not with thy hours my love's fair brow' (9), signifying little, merely an echo of a theme we know we are not to take literally. Two things make it acceptable and a delight. We are won over by its spare poetic power. And the privileged position of the speaker, who by accepting Time's depredations in the ordinary and magical worlds both, wins the right to reprimand it for a final dread intention, is dramatically compelling.

The couplets of both 18 and 19 begin to show us what Shakespeare can do with a sonnet's ending. Neat, pointed, compelling in its way before, it is now open and free to say more. While at times a thing of play as much as a true journey of thought, it always uses the consecutive rhyme to decisive effect; and whatever the hidden burden of the piece may be, is felt more as we come to the (final) full stop. There is always a telling economy in the couplet's inner construction. But on a handful of occasions the point to be made is of a piercing power, as we shall see.

A woman's face, with Nature's own hand painted,
Hast thou, the master-mistress of my passion;
A woman's gentle heart, but not acquainted   3
With shifting change, as is false women's fashion;
An eye more bright than theirs, less false in rolling,
Gilding the object whereupon it gazeth;   6
A man in hue all hues in his controlling,
Which steals men's eyes and women's souls amazeth.
And for a woman wert thou first created,   9
Till Nature, as she wrought thee, fell a-doting,
And by addition me of thee defeated,
By adding one thing to my purpose nothing.   12
    But since she pricked thee out for women's pleasure,
    Mine be thy love, and thy love's use their treasure.

This is extraordinary. One cannot assume the sonnets tell us anything about their writer's life, of course; at the same time one may make a reasonable assumption of relevance. I am aware that the story they seem to tell me as I read may be wrong. But it would be wrong to ignore the possibility of some light being shed. Tentatively therefore I offer the suggestion that the author found it necessary to make the sexual position clear, regarding the passionate friendship. There was none.

Perhaps the clarification was for his benefit, perhaps the youth's, or perhaps both. There is a moment in some boys' adolescence when something about them suggests a quite beautiful girl. A year or two later it is gone. Shakespeare is startlingly honest here. He is fascinated by the feminine element in the youth, admits it, knows (or realises) he harbours no genital interest, and says so. He is happy for his friend to sleep with women, confident he has his love. (My sense is that he may be making the position clear more for the youth's benefit than his own.)

Is it the sudden access in the freedom of expression (since sonnet 18) that has brought this on? Whatever the background it is a remarkable venture by the poet into the nature of attraction in what would appear to be a specific situation. It may also be one in which he has shown great courage.

The reader may be taken aback by the misogynistic sentiment on display (lines 4–5). It was unfortunately common at the time among writers, and the European tradition stretches back to Homer. The fickleness of women is a staple item of the mental graffiti of the male world. Shakespeare's portrayal of the Dark Lady later on has a certain set-piece dismissiveness to it, intensified for reasons of his own; though we also sense her as a powerful presence, a person who happens to be a woman, and with whom the poet is in love. And we cannot forget Portia, Cleopatra and other blazingly independent female characters from the plays. The misogyny we note in the Sonnets is more of a writer's conventional prop, less of an attack; though one could wish it were not there.

Shakespeare does however appear to feel strongly about women's use of cosmetics, as hinted at in line 1 and shown openly often in the sequence. (It is a minor but searing theme in *Hamlet*.) It is relevant to the theme of beauty, but also seems to come over as something of a personality quirk in itself, engaging in its way and tiresome also, as quirks can be.

The poem is filled with what we now term feminine rhyme. A suggestion of wavering, or change, may be discerned in the repeated cadence. Or it may be merely a pretty artifice. One is never sure of a creative writer's intention. Nor need one be.

So is it not with me as with that Muse,
Stirred by a painted beauty to his verse,
Who heaven itself for ornament doth use,   3
And every fair with his fair doth rehearse,
Making a couplement of proud compare
With sun and moon, with earth and sea's rich gems,   6
With April's first-born flowers, and all things rare
That heaven's air in this huge rondure hems.
O let me true in love but truly write,   9
And then believe me, my love is as fair
As any mother's child, though not so bright
As those gold candles fixed in heaven's air.   12
    Let them say more that like of hearsay well;
    I will not praise that purpose not to sell.

On the face of it this piece might have been written to the
woman, a more conventional rendering of the idea behind 130.
But with her in mind the poet is always more headstrong,
somehow, than the composed and lucid witness of these lines.
Their placing as given can be seen to make sense. A true, unvar-
nished beauty in verse is the only way to capture that of the
young man, painted by nature's hand and none other. It does
cross the mind that Thomas Thorpe may have been uncertain as
to the placing and used such a line of reasoning to insert it where
he did. The overall sequencing, while making a good deal of
sense as earlier suggested, does not quite seem authoritative.

Be that as it may, it is a piece of the utmost naturalness and
charm. Line 9 is beautiful in its plainness. It is every love-poet's
cri de coeur. But I am almost as fascinated by the preceding riches,
a cornucopia where everything is at once on top of each other
and finely apart. Line 8 is not averse to what might be called the
painted prettiness of alliteration, but such technical virtuosities

fall within the remit of the art of poetry. They do not use words to lie. Wonderful itself in its way, the line perfectly sets the stage for the transition from octave to sestet, to the words from the heart.

Sonnet 130 is far better-known for its outburst against the comparisons in love-poetry that were still so much the rage. It is altogether more vivid than this poem. There is no equivalent in this for 'I love to hear her speak . . . ' (130.9). Addressing the man Shakespeare is less concerned with the personal reality. Yet this is not to doubt the truth of the main point, in personal terms, being made here; it is simply that other terms, abstracts, universals, also fill his mind. Returning to the footling comparisons so much in fashion, I very much like the deadly 'gold' of the stars in line 12. The sardonic note of false description is felt even as we applaud the line for its loveliness. He punctures the poetaster and half-traps the reader too. The point is there to be taken. The businesslike ending makes its own plain statement, nicely in contrast with all the rest.

Overall it is the difference between decorativeness and beauty that he is writing about. Between carrying a bouquet and carrying conviction. Between entertaining oneself and honouring another. Between truth and lie.

My glass shall not persuade me I am old,
So long as youth and thou are of one date;
But when in thee time's furrows I behold,   3
Then look I death my days should expiate.
For all that beauty that doth cover thee
Is but the seemly raiment of my heart,   6
Which in thy breast doth live, as thine in me.
How can I then be elder than thou art?
O therefore love, be of thyself so wary   9
As I not for myself, but for thee will,
Bearing thy heart, which I shall keep so chary
As tender nurse her babe from faring ill.   12
    Presume not on thy heart when mine is slain;
    Thou gav'st me thine, not to give back again.

Beneath the somewhat ungainly trope of the true heart's plac-
ing, a warning is issued: do not roam in your affections (line 9).
Your heart (that is mine) shall be broken too. Shakespeare
manages the corporeal conceit with a sleight-of-hand that muf-
fles its absurd side. 'The seemly raiment of my heart' (6) is an
engaging term for the body and will tend to win the reader
over to the metaphorical exchange, which after all stands for a
real one. The same idea comes up in sonnet 133 with a more
complex interplay; a threesome of hearts almost jumps through
hoops; yet still the underlying truth of love's belonging is
revealed and the artifice falls away. In 133 incidentally, to the
lady, we see a sharper edge. 'Prison my heart in thy steel
bosom's ward' begins the sestet, while here a softer imperative
takes the current forward in line 9. What is known as the *volta*,
or turn, in the sonnet generally occurs there, a touch of dra-
matic resolution in the thought-process. Line 9 very often sets
off a new train of thought, or brings a new air of confidence to

the argument. The speaker's personality, in the latter part of every poem by this means well established, is then able to make a final point (often a complex one) in the couplet, and in doing so to gracefully withdraw. The reader is left to absorb the state of play.

The story-line is of course all from one person's point of view. The other character, whether the man or the woman, takes on a kind of reflected life, a shadow vivacity. Without doubt the woman is given the major role as a personality. Yet it is beyond question that he cared for the man more than for her. I am reminded of Beethoven's almost desperate love for his nephew. Perhaps a raging creative force, world-towering in its passions, sometimes may seek a safe haven, a soul to lock onto, almost a shrine of innocence. Shakespeare seems always to regard the young man in some deep sense as pure, if led astray. It is a different kind of caring.

Here an apprehension of old age in the speaker, even as it is brushed away, lingers a little from the start. The writer looks in the glass again in 62, this time head-on. Decay, including the thought of death, lays a hand on proceedings now and then, to steadily make itself known. The first series is haunted by Time's 'sickle hour' (126). Still it is used sparingly. At one level it may serve to set up a sense of distance, that will always have a part to play, in the description of closeness.

Is this the poet's quest? Whatever it may be said to be, I would draw attention to the marked use in this poem of a device that is to become integral in it. What I have loosely termed pronoun play – a *pas de deux* of I and thou, thine and mine – takes us a little further on to something inexplicable at the heart of love.

As an unperfect actor on the stage
Who with his fear is put beside his part,
Or some fierce thing replete with too much rage,　　　3
Whose strength's abundance weakens his own heart;
So I for fear of trust forget to say
The perfect ceremony of love's rite,　　　6
And in mine own love's strength seem to decay,
O'ercharg'd with burden of mine own love's might.
O let my books then be the eloquence　　　9
And dumb presagers of my speaking breast,
Who plead for love and look for recompense
More than that tongue that more hath more expressed.　　　12
　　　O learn to read what silent love hath writ;
　　　To hear with eyes belongs to love's fine wit.

Taken at face value this is a moving expression of a lover's sense
of inadequacy in the presence of the other. I am sure this is the
main way to take it. The octave seems to revolve about 'for fear
of trust' (5), a simple admission hanging undefined (trust in a
sympathetic audience? in himself to find the right words?), the
phrase itself finely launched by the foregoing 'fear' (2) and its
sound in 'fierce' (3). His 'books' (9) are the sheets of paper he
writes on (a meaning of the time). A rival poet may well be indi-
cated in line 12 (and lie in the background in 21). Later there
are a number of sonnets about at least one other such claimant
for the young man's attention. The final line has a certain assur-
ance, after the precarious poise gained up to that point, a long
lead-up informed by a tremor of fear. 'To hear with eyes' (14) is
a memorable phrase; and the concluding 'fine wit' ('discerning
sense') is of course what the writer would always wish for from
the other when speaking to him. The whole is an example of a
poem (the "book" to hand) playing a part itself in the argument

it presents. In the last line, for a second the speaker's embodiment, it seems to discover a slight confidence.

We can also put the sestet first, in a way. One's writing has one's heart. The poet hopes at length for greater recognition than some of the noisier voices of the time. The final line is addressed to all Shakespeare's readers. The octave on this approach can seem to express the frustration of a writer who does not find his work accepted by the present time as he would wish, because (as he knows) he has not been able to present it properly to the intermediaries of the literary world, 'o'ercharg'd with burden of [his] own love's might' (8). Shakespeare's long minor poems, *Venus and Adonis* and *Lucrece*, did well. (They may or may not pre-date this sonnet.) Their patron, the Earl of Southampton, may have been the young man of the sequence. But the poet may yet have had serious difficulty with his main work, the plays. There is a hiatus where there should be a natural linkage between the name of the playwright and the private person of Stratford (or any other private person, supposing the authorship question to have some grounds). Admittedly this is something of a forced reading: I introduce it partly because it can seem to express, to a delicate perfection, the situation of writers of all times unable to represent themselves properly.

It is far-fetched, speculative; a criticism of the second relevance. Can it be said not to lie within the poem's intent? The poem here is at a certain distance from the poet (whose own intent cannot be known, but can always allow for a later perspective).

But it is a digression from the particular. The statement of the speaker, in the situation of the poem, is paramount. He cannot speak his love but write it. In which context, one hopes the first reader had the wit to hear it.

Mine eye hath played the painter and hath stelled
Thy beauty's form in table of my heart;
My body is the frame wherein 'tis held,   3
And pérspective it is best painter's art.
For through the painter must you see his skill
To find where your true image pictured lies,   6
Which in my bosom's shop is hanging still,
That hath his windows glazèd with thine eyes.
Now see what good turns eyes for eyes have done: 9
Mine eyes have drawn thy shape, and thine for me
Are windows to my breast, wherethrough the sun
Delights to peep, to gaze therein on thee.   12
    Yet eyes this cunning want to grace their art;
    They draw but what they see, know not the heart.

A traditional conceit of intimacy, the harbouring in the heart of
the pure image of the adored, is used to represent love's close-
ness and its limit. ('Stelled' (1) is 'portrayed'.) The poet draws
on the idea of perspective with a fine precision. The portrait
artist does his work, the subject views the result on display in
the artist's shop – the metaphor is splendidly impersonal. Such
is love's strength, there would seem to be a physical reality that
allows for a perfect knowledge, each of the other; until the
conclusion with its note of doubt and warning.

It is a remarkable study on the art of perspective in brief, how
to look at things. 'For through the painter must you see his skill'
(5). The octave is about subjectivity on the artist's side, until
line 8 reminds us it is equally on the viewer's. This is all of
course within the metaphorical frame (which has to hold still
for the viewer/reader's further exploration, so to speak). The
third quatrain expands on the duality of the artist/viewer stance
that at times can seem as one. There is a moment of epiphany –

'Mine eyes have drawn thy shape, and thine for me / Are windows to my breast . . . ' – and the couplet takes us back to the sober fact of two sets of eyes, the separated view. The poem shimmers with the reality of the metaphor itself.

But as it falls away at the end, its work done, the point of it all, a personal apprehension, is left hanging, unframed except in the bare lines of the verse itself. Suspicion has entered the gates. A love story is to come that is at times of a savage darkness, with the deepest spots of blackness to be found in the writer himself. But even as the storm begins, and indeed till its end, the sun delights to peep through. It is a story that seems to have written itself, somewhat fitfully, one of many shades, and not to be hurried.

Let those who are in favour with their stars
Of public honour and proud titles boast,
Whilst I, whom fortune of such triumph bars,   3
Unlooked for joy in that I honour most.
Great princes' favourites their fair leaves spread
But as the marigold at the sun's eye,   6
And in themselves their pride lies burièd,
For at a frown they in their glory die.
The painful warrior famousèd for fight,   9
After a thousand victories once foiled,
Is from the book of honour razèd quite,
And all the rest forgot for which he toiled.   12
    Then happy I that love and am beloved
    Where I may not remove nor be removed.

A simple affection seems to run through this and bind it
together. It may be a good moment to mention the light reas-
suring emphasis that rhyme imparts, as it tacks its material into
place. There are no complexities here; the speaker is almost
child-like (as are we all) in his trust in love. Only the last three
words imply a concern for the future, and this only in the light
of a question raised in 22 and 24. No more than a sudden puff
of cloud on a far-off horizon; but it is there.

'Unlooked for' (line 4) I take to mean 'to an unexpected
extent'. The marigold was something of a poet's flower,
appearing in other sonnet-sequences of the time, such as Henry
Constable's. 'The marigold the leaves abroad doth spread, /
Because the sun's, and her power is the same', says he. T. Hill
in the *Profitable Art of Gardening* (1597) writes that it is 'named
ye husbandmans Dyall, for that the same so aptlye declareth the
hours of mornyng and evening, by the opening and shutting of
it'. (I am indebted to Katharine M. Wilson's *Shakespeare's*

Sugared Sonnets for the former and to Stephen Booth's *Shakespeare's Sonnets* for the latter item.) Line 12 can give one pause: an indefinable world of one man's achievements and ideals, suddenly as nothing

'Honour' is the keyword. In its public aspect it is transitory, a toy of opinion. In love's privacy is the genuine article (the poem indicates). Just as Shakespeare develops the theme of, say, true and false authority in a number of his plays, so behind his sonnet-sequence a theme of honour is ever-present. (The word itself is not often used.)

The writer is denied public recognition as it would seem. Later he is to complain bitterly, on occasion, of being at odds with the world. Sometimes he is deep in 'love's philosophy', to take a phrase from his near-contemporary John Donne; sometimes the courtly convention is there merely as a flimsy framework, to lend nominal support to a statement really about himself. More often it is something of both. The poetic ego of the writer is certainly one of the most arresting features of the Sonnets.

Lord of my love, to whom in vassalage
Thy merit hath my duty strongly knit,
To thee I send this written ambassage,   3
To witness duty, not to show my wit.
Duty so great, which wit so poor as mine
May make seem bare, in wanting words to show it,   6
But that I hope some good conceit of thine
In thy soul's thought, all naked, will bestow it;
Till whatsoever star that guides my moving   9
Points on me graciously with fair aspect,
And puts apparel on my tattered loving,
To show me worthy of thy sweet respect.   12
    Then may I dare to boast how I do love thee;
    Till then, not show my head where thou mayst prove me.

A lover's tentative request for some expression of affection, or as it may be of appreciation of his verse, is couched in the most modest and self-effacing of terms. At first the tone is self-parodic, even joky (line 4); one senses a roar of laughter on both sides, even as the lines begin to turn to the crux of the matter. A 'good conceit of thine / In thy soul's thought' (7–8) is needed for the poet's wit to flourish, 'to boast how I do love thee' (13). As it is his powers of expression are too feeble to do his thoughts of love justice. Perhaps he is asking the other to write a line or two for him, his true feeling, 'all naked' (8). This in turn will put 'apparel on my tattered loving' (11), encourage him to reply with his best poetry. In 23.8 his silence is due to his being 'o'er-charg'd with burden of my own love's might'; now, summoning up the courage to send another poem, he finds a reason closer to home. The third quatrain is delightfully veiled. The star at one remove is surely the young man himself. He may have wondered why the series of ardent declarations has appeared to dry up.

Shakespeare replies tenderly, careful not to accuse the other of neglect, revealing a hope in the very absence of a presumption of its fulfilment. At least this is how I take it. It is a quite charming love-letter.

As in many of the sonnets there is an underlying wit to the piece, a touch of easy word-play throughout, an amusement taken in developing the terms of the argument; and at the same time a sense almost of purity of feeling, a deep seriousness. Katharine M. Wilson finds the wit uppermost, taking the whole sequence to be a collection of parodies of sonnets by others, a comment on the poetic approach and style of the time. I see the lighter side as within the tone the two may have established with each other in conversation; and also as a means of reducing the youngster's possible embarrassment, or sense of pressure. Others do not see a youngster necessarily there at all, but a series of dramatic creations in sonnet-form for any of a number of reasons. It is the sudden appeal of line after line, phrase after phrase in the collection that ultimately convinces me of a basis in the writer's life. In the plays such moments are everywhere; but the use with them of the first person in the poems more or less seems to settle the matter for me. One does not of course have to settle for a particular alternative, but can let all possibilities co-exist (noted, half-noted or unnoticed) and enjoy each poem as it lasts. As it lasts, however, I find that such a line as 'And puts apparel on my tattered loving' (11) pierces the heart; and whether or not I have to, at some level that outlasts the poem's ending, I take the essence of the story to be true.

The reciprocity that lies in love is further explored in this poem. Every love story deals with it in some way; but perhaps nowhere is its secret more visited, more nearly laid hold of, than in this strange wayward collection.

Weary with toil, I haste me to my bed,
The dear repose for limbs with travel tired;
But then begins a journey in my head   3
To work my mind, when body's work's expired.
For then my thoughts, from far where I abide,
Intend a zealous pilgrimage to thee,   6
And keep my drooping eyelids open wide,
Looking on darkness which the blind do see.
Save that my soul's imaginary sight   9
Presents thy shadow to my sightless view,
Which like a jewel hung in ghastly night
Makes black night beauteous, and her old face new.   12
    Lo, thus by day my limbs, by night my mind
    For thee, and for myself, no quiet find.

The toil is that of travel (movingly enlarged upon in 50); but
many a writer, after hours at the desk, will have stumbled bed-
ward mumbling the first line, and many of other trades too.
Art is transferable by nature. Here it is the very simplicity of
the experience of the whole that lends it its authenticity.
'Intend' in line 6 means as much to set out on as to have in
mind (a meaning of the time, from the Latin *iter intendere*). Line
8 has a telling effect. After thinking about it for a time I am at
a loss; after not thinking about it I understand. The words
seem to penetrate the being and bring the darkness with them.
It is partly the alliteration (the use of the letter d in 7–8), and
partly the line's position (ending the octave); partly the bibli-
cal tone ('looking on', 'do see' and the sense of revelation), and
partly a lingering on the act (of eyelids staying open). All this
I saw when I thought; when I stopped thinking I saw, and felt,
the darkness. One can do much to explain an effect and miss
what it is.

A clip-clop of hooves (again see 50) can almost be heard in the dull-heavy beat, emphasised in the final line's slowing-down. The separate uses of 'for' add to the pause of its two commas, the line turning in on itself slightly as a different meaning obtains; though the mechanics are all over before we take them all in. In the light of an unease expressed elsewhere, the line may carry a hint of tormenting doubt as to his friend's loyalty. Yet even to comment on such a hint, and what it may portend, may allow its looming presence to be dissipated in the highways and byways of definition. As always, to bring up the microscope to clarify can add to the obscurity.

It is a risk commentary must take in its stride. There is always the original text to return to, uncluttered by the notes below it. To remark on the poem's broad theme, not being able to sleep must chime at some level with everyone of an age to read it. Insomnia is mentioned elsewhere in the Sonnets (see 61); and it is of huge import in *Macbeth*. Shakespeare knew whereof he spoke.

How can I then return in happy plight
That am debarred the benefit of rest,
When day's oppression is not eased by night,   3
But day by night and night by day oppressed,
And each, though enemies to either's reign,
Do in consent shake hands to torture me,   6
The one by toil, the other to complain
How far I toil, still farther off from thee?
I tell the day, to please him, thou art bright,   9
And dost him grace when clouds do blot the heaven;
So flatter I the swart-complexioned night,
When sparkling stars twire not, thou gild'st the even.   12
    But day doth daily draw my sorrows longer,
    And night doth nightly make grief's length seem stronger.

This follows on from the last, the writer appearing to explain his melancholic presence, or his absence, to the loved one. He lacks 'the benefit of rest' (2). It is a waking nightmare. The day's toil (line 7) may be more than that of travel, or different from it entirely; the night's is back to travelling in the mind. But whatever distance is covered in his interminable nocturnal journeying, the object of his affections lies further away. The third quatrain is the merest prettification, of exactly the sort the poet mocks in the verse of others. It would seem to be there for a conventional purpose, the love-theme now no more than a cover for a need that has overpowered him, to write of his blind depression.

    I am aware that to take the speaker at his word as to the depth of his suffering may be at odds with the light sonnet-tune the words are couched in. Rhyme can trip along somewhat; the speaker can switch all too soon from pathos to pertness (line 6 to line 12). Sometimes a sonnet can re-harness the apparent limitations of the tidiness it is tied to, the quick shuffle of line and rhyme, for a statement of dramatic power to rival anything in blank verse (as in 66). Yet often the writer/speaker will strike something of a pose. When that is sensed the declared emotive intent is moderated to a degree in an intuitive act of understanding on the part of the reader. Here I confess I sense something of a swarming darkness, and by and large go along with what is said. But others will settle on a different level of acceptance. And yet at the same time, I imagine, we will all suspend judgement.

Lines 9–12 provide a diversion from the dreariness of suffering, a light relief ('twire' is 'peek'); the contrast with the clouds, or blackness, of the internal weather is gracefully done. But it is show. He is in the abyss: too preoccupied with his own state to do more than pay a superficial compliment to the other. This does not mean his love is less; merely that he can pay it little attention. Day and night conspire to torment him (with a memorable image in line 6); and in 13–14 they have him on the rack. He is resigned to the darkness, engulfed in its waves, from which there is no respite. 'Length' in 14 may be a misprint for 'strength'; several editors assume it; and as well as getting away from the slightly odd 'length seem stronger' and adding emphasis, it may bring in a hint of his own hand stretching the rack (so to speak). But it is a conjecture.

What is not conjecture is that the friendship can adopt a different tone in different poems. One can see the poet as artist with a double palette, one of love, one of everything else. The speaker needs to bring in something of the night. The approach is chosen to suit the occasion; or it seems to choose itself. The eye travels down; a conclusion is reached; the speaker bows out; a word-painting emerges. Each hangs completed in its sonnet-frame.

When in disgrace with fortune and men's eyes,
I all alone beweep my outcast state,
And trouble deaf heaven with my bootless cries,   3
And look upon myself and curse my fate,
Wishing me like to one more rich in hope,
Featured like him, like him with friends possessed,   6
Desiring this man's art, and that man's scope,
With what I most enjoy contented least;
Yet in these thoughts myself almost despising,   9
Haply I think on thee, and then my state,
Like to the lark at break of day arising
From sullen earth, sings hymns at heaven's gate.   12
    For thy sweet love remembered such wealth brings,
    That then I scorn to change my state with kings.

A transformation in mood as 'I think on thee' (10), to be sure; but as remarkable, a transformation in inner state (to take the poem's keyword). He has opened up: still in the grip of the demon, he can talk about it; suddenly a number of causes for complaint are in the air. One can see him gesticulating, ticking the points off. My guess is that he has not felt able to see his friend for some time, not being in 'happy plight' (28.1), but at last has ventured a visit and can return to its memory as a blessed relief. But he is still locked in a deep gloom.

I have always been able to revel in the octave for its energy, its clarity, its honesty. It is one of those moments of poetry that it seems an offence to sully with the critic's eye. A couple of peripheral points: 'rich in hope' I take to indicate an optimistic outlook in general, rather than a narrow expectation of wealth. And there is the remarkable open plagiarism by T.S.Eliot of line 7.

Ash-Wednesday (1930) begins, 'Because I do not hope to turn again / Because I do not hope / Because I do not hope to turn / Desiring this man's gift and that man's scope / I no longer strive to strive towards such things . . . ' A mild kleptomania is a feature of Eliot's poems (this is the only direct example I know of from the Sonnets), and often the lines and phrases are given new breath in their new setting. But I have always felt that the faint touch of a second-hand mustiness can reflect on the aura of the later craftsman, however successful the re-working. There is something to be said for and against.

Line 9 takes the merciless self-examination to an almost intolerable pitch: and then at a chance thought the heart lifts. The recollection of his friend changes everything. The air is lightened; 'day's oppression' (28.3) is of another world. Beneath the tirade of an angry man is an unselfconscious child. Now he is rich.

When to the sessions of sweet silent thought
I summon up remembrance of things past,
I sigh the lack of many a thing I sought,   3
And with old woes new wail my dear time's waste.
Then can I drown an eye, unused to flow,
For precious friends hid in death's dateless night,   6
And weep afresh love's long since cancelled woe,
And moan th' expense of many a vanished sight.
Then can I grieve at grievances foregone,   9
And heavily from woe to woe tell o'er
The sad account of fore-bemoanèd moan,
Which I new pay as if not paid before;   12
    But if the while I think on thee, dear friend,
    All losses are restored and sorrows end.

Still sad, much calmer, almost with a rueful smile the poet observes himself in tears. From the plays one learns much of the thought but little or nothing of the emotional character of the man who wrote them. The overcharged soul we find in the Sonnets remedies the lack, at least to a degree: an invisible commentary; or a kind of thread, interwoven at root about the great flowering of the dramatic cast. The sequence leans more to the tragic; the riotous author, who loved to set off the wit of the "low life" against the gravity of the ruling class, has absented himself. (Perhaps he is present as a punster, as we shall see.)

The whispering sibilance in the first two lines is a thing of beauty in itself, as the buried echoes in 'remembrance' and 'past' tail off the salient s. Line 6 is immortal, 7 an apt and true remark as to what can go on at such 'sessions', 8 suspiciously like a touch of padding. 'Expense' (8) presumably means loss, of that which has expended itself; at any rate, carrying with it a natural emphasis from the octave's completion, the line has enough in it to take us along. If the sight is of loved ones 'hid' or 'cancelled' there is more to be said for it; but yet, in the exalted company it keeps, perhaps a raised eyebrow against.

The repetitiveness as a theme of the third quatrain is very neatly done. Yet it has been bettered. By implication at least a phrase of the 19th-century poet Gerard Manley Hopkins says it all and more. 'My cries heave, herds-long . . . ' rises from the depths of one of his sonnets of despair. A touch of wry amusement at the pitiable figure he cuts, that we may or may not sense in Shakespeare, is very much there (uniquely it may be for Hopkins); and what a picture it is. I see a great column of bovines, hear a variously-pitched lowing of complaints, one setting off another, one answering another. The comparison with a lone man's moans is irresistible. Hopkins' sonnet concludes, 'all / Life death does end and each day dies with sleep'. Shakespeare's conclusion is a more heartening one, in line with that of the previous piece. The comparison with Hopkins (who wrote several sonnets on a terrible inward darkness he was prone to) is instructive; and it is not only to do with the depth of despair or its finality. Where Hopkins is passionate Shakespeare is descriptive. It is for his characters that he reserves the full outcry.

The language of the couplet is refreshingly straightforward, after the convolutedness of 9–12 (warranted as it is). The privilege of love overcomes all loss. The relief is tangible.

Thy bosom is endearèd with all hearts
Which I by lacking have supposèd dead;
And there reigns love and all love's loving parts,⠀⠀⠀⠀3
And all those friends which I thought burièd.
How many a holy and obsequious tear
Hath dear religious love stol'n from mine eye,⠀⠀⠀⠀6
As interest of the dead, which now appear
But things removed that hidden in thee lie.
Thou art the grave where buried love doth live,⠀⠀⠀⠀9
Hung with the trophies of my lovers gone,
Who all their parts of me to thee did give;
That due of many now is thine alone.⠀⠀⠀⠀12
⠀⠀Their images I loved I view in thee,
⠀⠀And thou, all they, hast all the all of me.

I find this difficult. It seems to reduce the 'precious friends hid in death's dateless night' of the last piece (line 6) to friends he knows no more, dead to him alone, somehow gathered in his one true friend. Either they have all flocked to him and left the speaker, or because he is everything to the speaker, their claims on him ('their parts of me', 11) are all met by the speaker's due reverence towards the loved one alone. In other words they are actually or metaphorically attached to the friend; the speaker re-discovers their existence in him. 'Lovers' (10) probably means 'loving friends' (as in 126.4). Though the writer seems to redefine what he means by death in the previous sonnet I find I reject such intent. 30 is precious to me in meaning what it seems to mean on its own. If Shakespeare leeched its essence to conjure up a new concoction, he has every right to do it, and I have every right to ignore it. In 31, I am convinced, he is carried away by the tone, the sound, much as an operatic piece may set the voice above the words.

Indeed the whole of the above poem can unfold on the air like a song, a grave and solemn lament. As such it has a morbid beauty. It is a kind of great poetry woven from flim-flam. The mood behind it all is no more than a self-indulgent sadness; certainly nothing so noble as sorrow; yet the words have a magical effect. 'How many a holy and obsequious tear / Hath dear religious love stol'n from mine eye' (5–6) is the work of an artist in love with his art, and practising it for all he is worth, with little or no outside reference. It is the passion of a solipsist. Only the final line rescues the situation. The pronoun magic does its work; and I can accept that something has been said of love that needs the saying. But too much has to be conceded to the lead-up, and I remain uncomfortable with that.

As regards what has happened to the friends in 31, what is to be taken as literal and what metaphorical in their apparent existence as within the young man, a certain irritation I confess stops me paying due attention to the question. It is a more than usually meaningless conceit; and yet more than usually successful in the poetic dividend. To an extent Shakespeare is following a conventional line of sonnet-thought, at least part-way; and it may be that by conjuring from its very insincerity a note that can appear to ring true, he derives some enjoyment or satisfaction. But I cannot help wondering again whether he sanctioned the selection and ordering of the poems. It was an act of authorial sabotage if he did. To turn true tears into something lachrymose is, just a touch, to degrade the whole relationship, or at least the business of its being written about. But who is to say? It is an unusual situation. One can marvel at it, and shrug at it, in the same moment. In what are after all the most personal of poems, Shakespeare has an agenda of his own.

If thou survive my well-contented day,
When that churl death my bones with dust shall cover,
And shalt by fortune once more re-survey   3
These poor rude lines of thy deceasèd lover,
Compare them with the bett'ring of the time,
And though they be outstripped by every pen   6
Reserve them for my love, not for their rhyme,
Exceeded by the height of happier men.
O then vouchsafe me but this loving thought: 9
'Had my friend's Muse grown with this growing age,
A dearer birth than this his love had brought
To march in ranks of better equipage.   12
   But since he died, and poets better prove,
   Theirs for their style I'll read, his for his love.'

The opening line strikes a new tone. 'Well-contented' may have meant "paid in full" with the idea of a life that has had its due, not necessarily a happy one. The natural meaning now includes a touch of appreciative recognition, an inner contentedness with whatever life has handed out. With that sense in mind the phrase has almost been a lode-star to me: and yet it may not have been what Shakespeare meant. But it is what the poem can now mean that matters, provided that what lies within the possible intent of the author is not actually opposed. It is an instinctive, subjective judgement of the reading eye; and while on occasion a later, more informed view will cause a revaluation, more often than not one's first understanding will bear the test of time. The rhythmic ease, the sense of acceptance in the words around this one, a core of the heart's warmth that the second half of the poem reveals, all contribute to the judgement one makes here as one reads on. To consider the matter has us in touch, in an almost unfathomable way, with the reach of a poet's mind.

Several poems allude to the offerings of a rival poet or poets. If the youth was the Earl of Southampton, or someone in a similar position, there may have been others after his patronage. Odd to the modern age, the situation of a young man addressed in verse by other men, in terms of an ardent but largely Platonic love, while it must have been rare – almost all the sonnet-sequences of the time were by men addressed to women – was not so strange. Women were seen as wifely creatures by men: a discussion of the soul such a man might offer, with its medley of wit and earnestness, might well be directed to another man. And this in spite of the creation of Portia *et al.*, in Shakespeare's case. It is a curious feature of the collection, and will come to be seen as more so; but at the time, as one imagines, it was more readily taken on board.

A more striking feature, that catches the eye in many places, and can leave a lasting impression on the mind, is a self-dismissiveness on the writer's part. As the theme of immortalising his friend in verse begins to drop away, we see him more, perhaps, as he often can see himself. 'The thing itself . . . a poor, bare, fork'd animal' that King Lear is (probably) later, in the storm of the heavens and in what is left of his sanity, to see in Edgar, is somewhere there in the Shakespeare of the Sonnets. The outward sincerity is one thing; as here, it can be seen as part of the show. But over the collection as a whole there is a gathering sense of something else. Gradually, and despite any number of indications to the contrary, we are left with a deep, abiding impression of the poet's humility.

Full many a glorious morning I have seen
Flatter the mountain tops with sovereign eye,
Kissing with golden face the meadows green,   3
Gilding pale streams with heavenly alchemy;
Anon permit the basest clouds to ride
With ugly rack on his celestial face,   6
And from the forlorn world his visage hide,
Stealing unseen to west with this disgrace.
Even so my sun one early morn did shine   9
With all triumphant splendour on my brow;
But out alack, he was but one hour mine,
The region cloud hath masked him from me now.   12
    Yet him for this my love no whit disdaineth;
    Suns of the world may stain when heaven's sun staineth.

A wonderful freshness fills the first four lines; at the same time
one is aware of a practised hand "laying it on". (It could almost
be Hamlet on board ship, altering Claudius's letter.) The poet's
virtuosity constantly leaves the reader slightly edgy in this way.
But it is not an unpleasant effect, nor one at odds with a plau-
sible view of the poem's intent. Lines 5–8 picturesquely sketch
in the second part of the sun's journey, ending the octave with
the lightly suggestive (at this point) 'disgrace'. The sestet carries
a remarkable double effect, an optical illusion in words.

The first presentation of 'my sun' (9) is as the young man,
with whom Shakespeare could be for no more than an hour.
'Even so my sun . . . ' gives the metaphorical reading clearly
enough; and though 'he' and 'him' could be 'it', the emphasis in
11 especially backs up the closeness of 'my' (9). In which case
the couplet is a gentle – too gentle? – conclusion: I don't blame
him at all, as he or anyone can be niggardly if the sun in the sky
can be so discourteous as to snatch away its heavenly benison.

One takes in the narrative in an uncomplicated fashion till the last line, when the force of the last three words, that are bound to recall the young man, has an uncanny retrospective effect. 'My sun' can be the literal "sun of the world" that shone in splendour on my brow and then clouded over; but why should I blame it when 'heaven's sun staineth'? The youth hereby is guilty of some lapse in conduct, picking up also from 'disgrace', and from the repetitive thud of the last line that comes down like an accusation. Allowing 'but one hour' to his visitor has not disappeared as his transgression (from the first reading); but now it is that and more.

I think the reader is encouraged by the factors mentioned, not necessarily to re-read painstakingly, but to hold the possibility of a second and different reading in mind. And somehow the force of what one has read, heard in one's mind, is deepened. It is a lovely example of one of the ways that ambiguity in poetry can work. If (as is still possible) one takes 'my sun' first as the object in the sky (and 'he' and him' as 'it'), the couplet is at once pointed and powerful. But again, the language will have wrought an effect to the contrary, now in 9–12 rather than 14. Probably one carries both possibilities (maybe without realising it) from the start of the sestet, inclining more one way; and at the end one is left with a statement both satisfying in itself and of an undiscovered power. 'Suns of the world' and 'heaven's sun' balance it out: either can mean either. The mind is settled by the poise obtained; and also lightly charged.

The sonnet is the first of a number that respond in some way to the friend's unkindness or misdeeds. As we have seen, it has its own 'heavenly alchemy'.

Why didst thou promise such a beauteous day
And make me travel forth without my cloak,
To let base clouds o'ertake me in my way,   3
Hiding thy bravery in their rotten smoke?
'Tis not enough that through the cloud thou break
To dry the rain on my storm-beaten face,   6
For no man well of such a salve can speak
That heals the wound and cures not the disgrace.
Nor can thy shame give physic to my grief;   9
Though thou repent, yet I have still the loss.
Th' offender's sorrow lends but weak relief
To him that bears the strong offence's cross.   12
    Ah, but those tears are pearl which thy love sheeds,
    And they are rich and ransom all ill deeds.

The ambivalence holds. The poet addresses the sun, but the terms used gradually present another picture, a scene of drama that further resolves itself: a crisis is met and passed. The metaphor itself is never dispelled, the tears at the end paralleling the rain of line 6. The same word concludes the octave as in 33; one wonders if the sonnets were not written more or less together, after the same occasion. The 'disgrace' now is more tangible, this poem coming to terms with the reality of the betrayal (whatever it was). Under cover of the metaphor the drama of a lovers' quarrel is played out. In the last sonnet, as in the next, it seems the same grievance is at work, here both felt and forgotten, in the tears on either side.

    The poetic web sustains a certain magic. The mystery of a metaphor, that means both itself and what is behind it, is handled with a gossamer deftness. All but withdrawn in successive stages in the sestet, its survival is nominal yet vital. I am reminded of the Middle English poem *Pearl* in which the poet mourns the loss of – what would appear to be – his infant daughter. But he never says so. The gem-stone she starts as becomes a young woman in a vision whom he recognises. 'Ho watz ne nerre þen aunte or nece.' ('She was closer to me than aunt or niece.') But he keeps the lid on the well of dreams. *Pearl* is a long poem, the metaphor sustained over 101 verses and 1212 lines. But the same principle, that can reveal truth in a lack of explicitness, in the story-land of poetry, has a say here. I find a compelling simplicity in this little poem, deriving from a mastery of the art of implication.

The statement gathers strength to a remarkable degree. As if in a perfect crystal, the injured sense of the wronged party is captured in lines 11–12, almost offhandedly it would seem. Such is the writer's bewildering gift. (All editors assume a correction to 'cross', from an apparent printer's error of 'loss', repeated unconvincingly from line 10.) The substance of line 12 would have struck a chord with the narrator of *Pearl*, who carries his own sense of injury (in the child's loss) from the start almost to the very finish. Shakespeare would not have read the work as it appears to have been lost at the time. (It was discovered in a private library in the 19th century, nearly five hundred years after its composition, and has a claim to be the most beautiful poem in the English language.) It does not carry (nor would it be fitting to the theme) a touch of a reciprocity as at the ocean's depths, that this poem in its small way does; and that I begin to realise the work of Shakespeare as a whole does too. Slowly, in the Sonnets, something of that quality may emerge a little, as we continue.

'Sheeds' (line 13) was 'sheds'.

No more be grieved at that which thou hast done:
Roses have thorns, and silver fountains mud,
Clouds and eclipses stain both moon and sun,   3
And loathsome canker lives in sweetest bud.
All men make faults, and even I in this,
Authórising thy trespass with compare,   6
Myself corrupting, salving thy amiss,
Excusing thy sins more than thy sins are.
For to thy sensual fault I bring in sense;   9
Thy adverse party is thy advocate;
And 'gainst myself a lawful plea commence.
Such civil war is in my love and hate,   12
    That I an áccessory needs must be
    To that sweet thief which sourly robs from me.

One wonders at the change in tone after the first quatrain. Perhaps it was written at a different time from the rest. The sonnet clearly carries on from the last, the writer upset by the other's tears and offering comfort. Line 1 in its directness scarcely needs the anodyne loveliness of 2–4; yet the very clichés enliven the dramatic situation: we can almost visualise the one speaking the words the other hears chiefly as soothing sounds. This is all within the poetic *mise en scène* of course; what actually went on, that may have given rise to the poems, we have no idea. Perhaps – as I am inclined to think – the inside accurately reflects the outside; perhaps the reflection is distorted to a greater or lesser degree; perhaps there was no outside at all, and the poet is creating a drama out of nothing. But the outside doesn't really matter.

After line 4 the speaker seems more and more to be talking to himself, till at the end when the other is in the third person. The poet often switches from the descriptive to the discursive,

the grace of the one ceding to a quick-fire logic (or sophistry) in
the other, the two harnessed in tandem to the sonnet-form's
elegance. We are not told what the 'sensual fault' is – it may be
no more than a luxuriating in the company of others and
denying the hard-journeying writer his own dear time. The
speaker proceeds to prosecute himself, ticking off points as if in
a courtroom; until (again) he is in the position of his friend, this
time as wrongdoer, partner in crime. Upon which he reverses
position in a single word. The force of 'sourly' carries on to the
last three words; and the accusation stands against the other as
the accompanying framework falls away.

The poem is riddled with internal contradiction, from 'roses
have thorns' to the instances of outright paradox that direct
proceedings more and more to the end. We are left, I believe,
with an understanding on the one hand of a lovers' drama and
on the other of something at the heart of love itself. The drama
includes contradictory impulses – not to accuse and to accuse
the other, to accuse and not to accuse oneself. All of which leads
to a recognition at some level of the self and not-self at one.
Meaning is elusive here and I can only fumble at it.

But I have a picture in mind of a charged atom. Particles that
vigorously combat one another and fly apart are drawn together.
In poetic terms a verse-form that has always been used in some
way to speak of love finds itself, under Shakespeare's hand,
representing what it explores, as a part of the exploration. There
is much that is sour over the sequence as a whole. But all that
divides is drawn together, in the unity of the sonnet.

Let me confess that we two must be twain,
Although our undivided loves are one;
So shall these blots that do with me remain,   3
Without thy help, by me be borne alone.
In our two loves there is but one respect,
Though in our lives a separable spite,   6
Which though it alter not love's sole effect,
Yet doth it steal sweet hours from love's delight.
I may not evermore acknowledge thee,   9
Lest my bewailèd guilt should do thee shame;
Nor thou with public kindness honour me,
Unless thou take that honour from thy name.   12
    But do not so; I love thee in such sort,
    As thou being mine, mine is thy good report.

Lines 1–2 ingeniously bend the circumstances as the speaker fits them into a new argument, refusing to blame his friend at all for the distance that has arisen between them. He accepts the situation and adopts a stance of outright generosity – that may or may not have a twist at the end. The 'blots' (3) and 'bewailèd guilt' (10), his faults as from the last sonnet, seem now to draw more on a sense of his own personal dishonour (that we have seen admitted in 25, declared in 29, and are to see more strongly again in for example 111). Lines 9–12 are borne along by such an association; and the concluding phrase also makes use of it.

With the basic tenet of the poem stated, the second quatrain is marvellously compact, line 8 bringing in the point at issue with an acute yet softened emphasis. ('Separable' in line 6 is active, "bringing about separation"; 'spite' is misfortune.) The tone becomes somewhat louder ('I may not evermore acknowledge thee . . . ', 9) as the speaker takes stock and looks about him, as it were. And we come to the couplet, for which I don't think there are words to describe the tone. It is a constantly moving amalgam of meaning, on the one hand the perfect expression of a generous spirit, on the other a double-edged, even sly put-down. I simply cannot decide if Shakespeare intended the second suggestion, and it is of such a personal nature that it does seem to matter; and yet, once spotted, it can be said to lie within the poem's intent. The jury is out.

The poet urges his friend not to see him. 'Our undivided loves', 'but one respect', 'love's sole effect' all meet in his simple declaration, 'I love thee in such sort . . . ' And then the last line. It is a beautiful surrender to the idea he has created over the piece of his friend's virtue. He has said the fault is all his and he will not infect the other's reputation by visiting him. Their closeness, transformative for him, is meeting enough. The unexpected and noble finesse in 'mine is thy good report', with its implied avowal of trust, speaks for a heart charged with love. And then one reads the line differently.

If you and I are one, if I am yours and you are mine, my 'good report' (reputation or standing) is also yours. Despite the 'blots' that he has assumed, or of public opinion, Shakespeare knows at the deepest level he is not to blame, his conscience is clear. The boot is on the other foot. 'I love thee in such sort' as to be able to offer a chance of your reform, 'thou being mine'. On the first reading, beneath the artifice of the framework of the poem, lies an artless declaration. A self-effacing love simply is there. On a reverse reading of the same words, a different love speaks out. He would lead his friend to better ways. Can two such contradictory effects co-exist?

Perhaps with Shakespeare they can.

As a decrepit father takes delight
To see his active child do deeds of youth,
So I, made lame by Fortune's dearest spite,   3
Take all my comfort of thy worth and truth.
For whether beauty, birth, or wealth, or wit,
Or any of these all, or all, or more,   6
Entitled in thy parts do crownèd sit,
I make my love engrafted to this store.
So then I am not lame, poor, nor despised,   9
Whilst that this shadow doth such substance give,
That I in thy abundance am sufficed,
And by a part of all thy glory live.   12
　　Look what is best, that best I wish in thee;
　　This wish I have – then ten times happy me.

To take the ending first, this one makes for a ten times unhappy comparison with the last. Very often the closing couplet is a kind of marvel of workmanship on its own, with a secret drawer that can open and shut, and a key to it that cannot quite be held by the understanding, but operates on a reading of the poem. This is Shakespeare's art and I have seen it nowhere else: it is a treasure of the Sonnets. And here – I can only suppose he intended to come back to it. There is a shade of deeper meaning in the idea of a happiness that is at once unselfish and selfish – but the trouble is, it's not happiness but a childish glee that leaps from the page, infantilising both the father and the active child of the beginning, and consigning the sober tone of the rest to outer darkness.

Nevertheless, on their own lines 1–12 make a rather charming statement, growing in depth and power. An ending is needed (it would make a fine competition to supply one). But one may look at the poem we have, even if it lacks the true resolution of the couplet, that adds to a Shakespearian sonnet as a whole the sense of a privileged journey. 'Lame' in lines 3 and 9 can be taken as metaphorical, "ineffectual"; just as in 89 ('Speak of my lameness, and I straight will halt') it can refer to verse that is metrically clumsy. It can also be taken as literal fact. This seems to me a little more likely; and one can imagine the writer-actor denied the parts he may have dreamt of playing by a certain disability. Line 3 is appealing on that reading; but there is no court to decide the appeal.

Also on the autobiographical note one sees a very strong argument against those who posit the Earl of Oxford as the author, or any other aristocrat, simply in the several apparent references in the sequence to a lack of wealth, high birth, public standing in general. On the other hand there are interesting arguments against the Stratford Shakespeare and some for Oxford. One would like to see the whole debate conducted in calmer waters.

Lines 9–10 start the sestet with a moving flight of fancy, that plays on the Platonic idea of reality, a part of the intellectual life of the time. Briefly, the doctrine holds what we perceive as matter to be merely the shadow or reflection of ideal forms. The true (invisible) substance creates shadow. Shakespeare reverses the terms, turning the concept to his own use (as again, this time with more orthodox intent, in 53). To conclude, I return to the inadequacy of the couplet. One wonders how it might modulate the emphasis in line 12. I offer: 'Nor can day's weary age dim the eye longer, / That sees the star of morn shine ever stronger.' But this is worse: at least the original keeps up a sense of the Platonic ideal; and has its own live energy.

(Open for entries . . .)

How can my Muse want subject to invent
While thou dost breathe, that pour'st into my verse
Thine own sweet argument, too excellent   3
For every vulgar paper to rehearse?
O give thyself the thanks, if aught in me
Worthy perusal stand against thy sight;   6
For who's so dumb that cannot write to thee,
When thou thyself dost give invention light?
Be thou the tenth Muse, ten times more in worth   9
Than those old nine which rhymers invocate;
And he that calls on thee, let him bring forth
Eternal numbers to outlive long date.   12
   If my slight Muse do please these curious days,
   The pain be mine, but thine shall be the praise.

This is not unlike the exercise of a consummate stylist with little
at the moment to say. He takes a ready-made theme to hand –
the all and sum of his friend's sway over him – and proceeds, in
rich 'numbers' (12) or verses, to make it sound almost tinny.
Clearly he wanted to write a poem; but ironically enough, the
muse whose worth he trumpets forth is indeed slight in this
instance. It is his own talent, coming from god knows where,
that fills this piece. Line 13 is the key: 'my slight Muse' refers
to his poetic gift rather than to any source, and that is what the
poem truly celebrates, the line conveying a touch of anxiety as
to its reception at large. The piece is, in other words, a self-
indulgence; and an acceptable one so far as I am concerned,
given the grace of the 'numbers' and the rhetorical splendour of
the whole. But the relationship of the two men, that from the
poet's point of view sets the sequence 1–126 alight, is here (as
in a few others) scarcely existent. It is the courtly convention
that speaks and not the love.

'The pain be mine, but thine shall be the praise' (14). The writer allows the painstaking nature of his craftsmanship to stand as a reminder of what he has endured *vis-à-vis* his friend, the phrase underscoring his discontent in general; and we are back in 36 for a moment, with a nod to the idea of reputations. The personal relationship the sequence is founded on is tangible at the close. It may be said to breather a clearer air. But the artifice that leads up to that point is transparent; and not in the way a conceit is, but in a way that belies what should come as naturally as Keats' 'leaves to a tree'. The sonnet is brought into the fold, added to the collection; but as in 31, at a cost of thematic authenticity.

Part of wanting to write a sonnet is to engage with its rhetorical sweep. With a closing couplet to wind things up as only he was able, with the ease and grace of his 'numbers' to hand, one is tempted to see the poet, at least in part, as practising his trade and setting his wares on display, to 'please these curious [choosy] days' (13). And in part, no doubt, his friend was his inspiration and he wished to say so. Beneath a fine surface, then, there is something ill-fitting. And yet it is a thing of beauty.

O how thy worth with manners may I sing,
When thou art all the better part of me?
What can mine own praise to mine own self bring,   3
And what is't but mine own when I praise thee?
Even for this let us divided live,
And our dear love lose name of single one,   6
That by this separation I may give
That due to thee which thou deserv'st alone.
O absence, what a torment wouldst thou prove,   9
Were it not thy sour leisure gave sweet leave
To entertain the time with thoughts of love,
Which time and thoughts so sweetly doth deceive;   12
    And that thou teachest how to make one twain,
    By praising him here who doth hence remain.

Still marking time to an extent, the poet finds a different way to make a virtue of necessity. The time he would like with his loved one is denied him. We have no explicit reason for this (yet); though there have been hints and more of a betrayal of trust on the other's part. Again Shakespeare will go to any length, it seems, to avoid speaking harshly of him. The poem turns on a double meaning that takes too long to puzzle out (unless one's mind is as quick as the poet's). Once one has it it is delightful. And yet even then the satisfaction lies in a successful feat of mental engineering, as much as in a reiteration of the speaker's position, poignant though it be.

In 11–12 'love' appears the subject of 'doth deceive'; and the conjuring away of drear time and dark thoughts that its own thoughts bring, is trumped by another card absence has to play. It teaches the writer to endure his being distanced – and also that he can be with the other, the distance now nothing. 'To make one twain' (13) is to let them in their single love 'divided live' (5); and also (subtly subverting the adopted position) to let one share his identity with another, 'to double one person', as Booth has it. On the latter view he is with the other, absence self-cancelling; the two views obscure each other and yet (in the way of poetry) co-exist. At the start he cannot offer praise as it would be praising himself; but even as he welcomes the distance it is no more. A space has been found for praise with manners; offering the same with a clear conscience, he finds he is in some way back with his friend. This is indeed no torment.

'Here' (14) is key: whether it means where the speaker is and the other is not, or "in this poem" (and it seems something of both), it underlines the writer's solitary state, which is where (finally) we wind up. The other 'who doth hence remain' is in truth apart from him, after all the foregoing courtesies. However elaborate the artifice – and it is close to being a perpetual-motion machine – one is in no doubt of the poet's own position. It comes up again and again in the poems to the young man. In its way it could almost be a definition of selflessness.

Take all my loves, my love, yea, take them all;
What hast thou then more than thou hadst before?
No love, my love, that thou mayst true love call;   3
All mine was thine, before thou hadst this more.
Then if for my love thou my love receivest,
I cannot blame thee for my love thou usest;   6
But yet be blamed, if thou thyself deceivest
By wilful taste of what thyself refusest.
I do forgive thy robbery, gentle thief,   9
Although thou steal thee all my poverty;
And yet love knows it is a greater grief
To bear love's wrong than hate's known injury.   12
    Lascivious grace, in whom all ill well shows,
    Kill me with spites – yet we must not be foes.

This is best read in conjunction with the next, where the 'robbery' is more out in the open. There is a note of slightly frenzied despair in the speaker's signing away all that is dear to him to the other. The agitated chop-logic of lines 2–6, where he says his friend had that already, and has the right to do with it whatever he likes, increases the sense of a bubbling tension; and the more intent address in 7–8 has the clue to a deeper cause for concern. Yes, I hand over all my friends to you, 'all hearts / Which I by lacking have supposèd dead' (31.1–2, on one reading); but if you make free with them – or one of them – in a way your true self would abhor (8), your blame is merited. There is a warning: the young man may be betraying not so much the speaker as himself.

But he has hurt the speaker. The third quatrain (as so often) is charged with a deeper tone and finer poetry. As in 34 lines 11–12 carry a universal truth of love, altogether unforced, to complete and balance the exposition. ('Known' is 'expected'.)

Before we turn to the conclusion, it may be useful to look more closely at the structure the poet made his own.

A word is needed for the first twelve lines of a Shakespearian sonnet, let it be the dodeka (Greek for twelve, long o), that takes us to the edge of one kind of knowing; after which the material takes on a deeper texture. The Shakespearian couplet is *sui generis*. Its sense of finality is always dependent on a certain interplay of design; and can include a touch of chance in the reader's approach to an ambiguous wording. One may say the die is cast. Lines 11–12 here complete the presentation, as it may be said, of a naked vulnerable soul. Reason comes on stage in a more authoritative guise; and the force of the dodeka is absorbed in a final expansion of the theme. A second *volta* (turn) leads the reader into a new field of the understanding, where the mind and heart are at one.

In this case less remarkable progress is made in the couplet than on some other occasions. The directness of address at the start, that gathers in focus mid-sonnet, is further charged with the outright accusation in 'lascivious', and the recall of the imperative from the beginning: yet all is tempered by paradox and contained within admiration. We are reminded of the speaker's steady love; or rather the speaker reminds himself. The concluding effect of paradox in 'Kill me with spites [vexations] – yet we must not be foes' is a little obvious; there is not so much an inner breath of realisation, as a finishing twirl. But the open appeal of the whole is moving.

Those pretty wrongs that liberty commits,
When I am sometime absent from thy heart,
Thy beauty and thy years full well befits,   3
For still temptation follows where thou art.
Gentle thou art, and therefore to be won;
Beauteous thou art, therefore to be assailed;   6
And when a woman woos, what woman's son
Will sourly leave her till she have prevailed?
Ay me, but yet thou might'st my seat forbear,   9
And chide thy beauty and thy straying youth,
Who lead thee in their riot even there
Where thou art forced to break a twofold truth: 12
    Hers, by thy beauty tempting her to thee,
    Thine, by thy beauty being false to me.

The mood has changed: lightly and companionably, the speaker brushes his own hurt aside, to take his friend's part. In a finely-knit octave, as if with a smile and a shrug, Shakespeare grants his friend all the leeway in the world. 'She' in line 8 is printed 'he' in Q (the First Quarto, the original printing). Malone in his edition of 1780 says, 'The Lady, and not the man, being in this case supposed the wooer, the poet without doubt wrote . . . *she*.' Dover Wilson (1966) wrote, 'Nearly all editors agree with Malone, but male readers, except those who know less about sex than Shakespeare, will agree, I think, with Q .' Booth follows Dover Wilson and quotes him approvingly – it is the one amusing thing in Booth's commentary, if unintentionally so. I go the way of ignorance and assume a misprint.

    The tone becomes more urgent as the speaker allows himself to feel his smart. One can imagine his dismay as he reminds the youth of the outlandishness of his offence. Quite simply, he has slept with the poet's mistress. ('I do suspect the lustful Moor hath leap'd into my seat,' says Iago of Othello.) In the most hurtful of developments the young man has taken the older one's place. Suddenly much becomes clear.

'Truth' in line 12 is 'troth': and the couplet outlines the double betrayal. It seems to me that the initiative is all the woman's, in the speaker's mind, until line 9, when he almost reluctantly suggests the young man might have thought twice; and the focus stays upon him, and the increasingly clear fact of his own responsibility, till the end. Yet the tenor of a forgiving heart, that is sounded early on, never goes, even as it absorbs the note of hurt, and the overtone of accusation. In virtually every one of the Sonnets there is a chord of a play of feelings to be struck.

Here the couplet is again a tad too outspoken, to my mind. I see that in Q the spelling is 'beauty . . . beautie', the permissible variation needed perhaps to avoid a slight thumping note.

The story moves on, the figure of the poet more recognisable, but still the same man.

That thou hast her, it is not all my grief,
And yet it may be said I loved her dearly;
That she hath thee is of my wailing chief,   3
A loss in love that touches me more nearly.
Loving offenders, thus I will excuse ye:
Thou dost love her because thou know'st I love her,   6
And for my sake even so doth she abuse me,
Suff'ring my friend for my sake to approve her.
If I lose thee, my loss is my love's gain,   9
And losing her, my friend hath found that loss;
Both find each other, and I lose both twain,
And both for my sake lay on me this cross.   12
　　But here's the joy, my friend and I are one.
　　Sweet flatt'ry! Then she loves but me alone.

After the first quatrain Shakespeare (as in 35) seems more and
more to be talking to himself, playing a mind-game to come to
terms – any kind of terms – with the situation. From line 10
there is no direct address. It is interesting that to distinguish
between his two loves, the woman becomes 'my love' and the
man, if by far the dearer, 'my friend'. One's sense is that the
speaker hardly knows where to go with the facts of the matter
– at once preposterous and appalling – which may account for
yet another somewhat weak ending. After a delicately pointed
reference to his hurt, in the final phrase of the dodeka, he turns
aside from it, where in poetic terms he might have done better
to advance. The self-flattery he indulges in at the end, the
familiar trope leading to an open illusion, seems rather to deal
with the business for the time being, than to seal off a poem.
Purely as a piece of rhetoric, however, it works well enough.

　　The first four lines really say all he has to say for the moment.
The second line recalls the second of sonnet 14 in its incidental

matter-of-factness. (I feel no implication that his love for her is fading.) He is compelled to order his thoughts, in this tangle, and to keep the banner of his ideal love flying. He is committed to the ideal as to the person behind it; in a situation where suddenly another kind of love sharply intrudes, he makes the priority clear. The later sonnets (from 127 on) that are addressed to or in some way about the woman, and at least some of which may have been written at the same time as 40–42, show a love that is as far removed from that for the young man as it is possible to imagine; and every bit as real. The drama of friendship, love and betrayal is a compelling one (even if it only ever existed within the sonnets themselves). Beneath a certain plangency on the speaker's part, over the sequence as a whole, lie the shards of a true pathos. Virgil's line, 'Sunt lacrimae rerum et mentem mortalia tangunt' ('Matter has tears, things mortal touch the mind'), seems to speak to it; as elsewhere in the poet's work. The somewhat haphazard progression of the whole reinforces the sense of a spontaneous reality, at least so far as a love triangle is concerned. It still remains a bit of a puzzle.

The love for the man is both painfully real and a phantom. Perhaps there are two kinds of love, and this is one. As we come back to the woman in the later section, we will be able to consider whether that is a fair – or dark – representation of the other.

When most I wink, then do mine eyes best see,
For all the day they view things unrespected,
But when I sleep, in dreams they look on thee, 3
And darkly bright, are bright in dark directed.
Then thou, whose shadow shadows doth make bright,
How would thy shadow's form form happy show 6
To the clear day with thy much clearer light,
When to unseeing eyes thy shade shines so?
How would (I say) mine eyes be blessèd made, 9
By looking on thee in the living day,
When in dead night thy fair imperfect shade
Through heavy sleep on sightless eyes doth stay? 12
    All days are nights to see till I see thee,
    And nights bright days when dreams do show thee me.

It may be partly because this unhistrionic sonnet comes after an outspoken and at times declamatory patch, or that in its way it is perhaps the quietest in the whole series, that I like it so much. But in part it is simply for its texture, in itself a commentary on its setting. The soft shade of night permeates the lines, word-patterns mix and echo, an underlying calm absorbs the restlessness of sleep's images. And there is a final effect that unaccountably stays in my mind.

In the first line 'wink' is 'have the eyes closed'. 'Unrespected' in line 2 has a fine accuracy, with the sense of details passing by in a kind of blur, together with a lack of need to regard them as of any worth. The soft agitation of the echoes and reversals of the next lines lends the octave a kind of thrill, like dreams passing under closed eyes. A rhetorical questioning in 9–12 is closer to a waking consciousness, the speaker almost ready to look about for the vivid reality of his sleeping thoughts; and the couplet settles back into a steady state that is neither sleep nor waking but merely, I feel, the consciousness, that is at some level always switched on. Its twenty monosyllables seem to indicate a ticking-away, as if of time in the mind.

This is a fanciful interpretation, but art encourages such, beside whatever signposts it may leave as to a more direct receptive process. To put differently what attracts in this piece, it is that as well as saying what it says, it can function almost as a piece of pure music.

The theme of absence from the loved one for a moment finds a new voice. On occasion an unresolved syntactic complex adds to the sense of words as sounds. In line 6 'form happy show' both runs as it looks and in reverse (the latter aided by 'To the clear day' that follows); one need make no decision as to which. The same goes for the final phrase, 'show thee me'. Beyond the speaker's seeing the other ('show thee [to] me') there is a hint of the reverse, with its magical focus; but it is not finally said. It is an implication, that we may be more or less aware of, or not at all. (As in the very first line, when 'wink' can suggest turning a blind eye to something it would rather not see.) Less given than many to a sweep of rhetorical power, more to musical suggestion, the piece appears perfectly formed, a jewel of poetry's deftness.

The effect that stays with me, that lightly haunts me, is the 'bright days' of the ending. One could find a detailed explanation of why it is so; but it would fall away, the two-word phrase, to my mind at least, beyond the sum of its parts. There is a time when explanation has to stop.

If the dull substance of my flesh were thought,
Injurious distance should not stop my way;
For then despite of space I would be brought   3
From limits far remote, where thou dost stay.
No matter then although my foot did stand
Upon the farthest earth removed from thee;   6
For nimble thought can jump both sea and land,
As soon as think the place where he would be.
But ah, thought kills me that I am not thought,   9
To leap large lengths of miles when thou art gone,
But that, so much of earth and water wrought,
I must attend time's leisure with my moan;   12
    Receiving nought by elements so slow
    But heavy tears, badges of either's woe.

A variation on the theme of absence, this goes with the next
sonnet. The theory of the four humours or temperaments in clas-
sical, mediaeval and Renaissance thought is still with us, for
example in the work of Rudolf Steiner and Hans Eysenck.
Shakespeare adapts it simply and effectively to express melan-
choly. I find the first two lines memorable for their precise
statement, that balances blunt monosyllables ('dull', 'flesh',
'thought', 'stop', 'way') against a lingering 'injurious'.
'Substance' and 'distance' are also held together and contrasted.
Line 9 with its accelerated awareness, given as it is to paradox,
is arresting; and more than that, somehow devastating. It is yet
another example of the poet's extraordinary facility, a *cri de coeur*
arising from a conceit. Line 12 is strangely dreary; and the pace
slows right down to the final full stop. The earth's heaviness,
the water's tears charge the poem; that is how well (in part in
retrospect) the image works. But why 'badges' works so well I
cannot say.

Instead I will digress for a moment on an aspect of the sequence that, a quarter way in, may need comment. To follow the same form repeatedly is inevitably a technical exercise to a degree. I take the poet as using a prosaic theme – live on by propagation – in sonnets 1 to 17 to "find his feet" with his chosen version of the form; after which he is free to explore his true theme – love – to his heart's content. Often one is aware of enjoying the sonnet for its own inner melody, the musical sense in advance of the lexical: some lines of the above poem can be taken as an example. Yet each piece has an argument that holds good within itself; nor does the exploration cease till the very end. (There are a few poems of a more trivial sort to come later that are an exception, if they are Shakespeare's.) In sonnet 76 the poet asks why he should not go 'to new-found methods and to compounds strange'. His answer, that just as his love does not change, 'all my best is dressing old words new', is only partly convincing.

He is also in love with his form. There is a modern example of the condition. Vikram Seth in 1986 published a novel in verse, *The Golden Gate*. In 594 verses in fact, including one each for the biodata, the acknowledgements, the dedication and the contents. And the verse-form in question is one of the most complex there is, the 14-line stanza of Pushkin's *Eugene Onegin* with its unvarying rhyme-scheme and feminine endings. In Seth's hands it may be something of a dry well, so far as poetry is concerned. The versification is lucid, but appears to take centre stage, too much of a character in itself. Yet in terms of its own technique it is one of the wonders of the modern poetic world. (*Pearl*, already mentioned in the note to 34, is at the opposite end of the scale, a repeated form of 101 stanzas of as rich a poetry as can be.)

Reading Shakespeare's sequence is also to read an exercise. It may be worth a mention.

The other two, slight air and purging fire,
Are both with thee, wherever I abide;
The first my thought, the other my desire,   3
These present-absent with swift motion slide.
For when these quicker elements are gone
In tender embassy of love to thee,   6
My life, being made of four, with two alone
Sinks down to death, oppressed with melancholy;
Until life's composition be recured   9
By those swift messengers returned from thee,
Who even but now come back again, assured
Of thy fair health, recounting it to me.   12
    This told, I joy, but then no longer glad,
    I send them back again, and straight grow sad.

There is something a little odd about this. 'Oppressed with melancholy' (line 8) is unwieldy metrically; and the rhyme of 10 and 12 repeating that of 6 and 8 is flat and unShakespearian. One could argue that 'melancholy' is 'metrically oppressive', as Booth has it; and the line in itself is a good one. But it is an unlikely rhythm, even as the sinking-down is suggested. The other matter is more clear-cut. In no other sonnet does Shakespeare permit his rhyme a bathetic effect by repetition. Where a rhyme is repeated it is counter, in the quatrain, the odd lines as against the even; or it is in the couplet, from which its energy is renewed (as in the next sonnet). The one exception is 135, a deliberate frivolity where the repetition adds to the effect, such as it is. The comparative weakness of 'recounting it to me' in line 12 also makes me wonder if this was a rough draft the author did not return to.

    That said, there are moments of the poet's authentic touch, in line 4 (how well the old physics here fits with the new); and in the hidden switch to a deeper realisation in the final few words. This last, a feature especially of the first series, is a sonnet-effect that may be unique to Shakespeare.

The 'purging fire' (1) of 'desire' turns out to be satisfied with a kind of telepathic visit to ascertain the good health of the beloved. At which the cycle starts again. The poet's harnessing of the courtly convention seems to creak somewhat; but the ending restores the reader to the matter of the moment, which is not that of 'life's composition' (9), which is healed or recovered ('recured'), but purely the sadness of separation.

The Bengali poet Rabindranath Tagore (1861–1941) makes great play with the concept of *biraha*, separation from one's beloved, which he uses in a religious context. He read Shakespeare but may not have made this connection. However in some respects they are two of a kind. In his *Gitanjali* (*Song Offerings*), in which the idea of *biraha* is to the fore, and which consists of 157 short poems, again and again the voice is the same as that in the Sonnets. The ego is at once altogether there and not there. Tagore is the Shakespeare of Bengali poetry. In his sonnets Shakespeare is the Tagore, on an all too human level, of the poetic properties of *biraha*.

It is strange how close the two poets seem. Shakespeare is a far more restless character on the surface. The storm-tossed persona of the sonnets could be a character from one of the great plays. But Tagore too was beset and torn by the opposites, joy and despair, claim and renunciation. Throughout the two collections of personal poems is one voice. It is a kind of errant nobility that speaks: the self-denying acceptance of one who knows the human universe.

Mine eye and heart are at a mortal war
How to divide the conquest of thy sight;
Mine eye my heart thy picture's sight would bar,   3
My heart mine eye the freedom of that right.
My heart doth plead that thou in him dost lie,
A closet never pierced with crystal eyes;   6
But the defendant doth that plea deny,
And says in him thy fair appearance lies.
To side this title is impannellèd   9
A quest of thoughts, all tenants to the heart;
And by their verdict is determinèd
The clear eye's moiety, and the dear heart's part: 12
    As thus – mine eye's due is thy outward part,
    And my heart's right thy inward love of heart.

This and the next make another set of two. The eye-and-heart motif of 24 I find more interesting; but Shakespeare has turned to a more common opposition here to offer an act of reverence – and, as I think, to practise writing sonnets. He may have poems in mind of Henry Constable (*Diana*) and Thomas Watson (*Tears of Fancie*) at this point; at other times he echoes other 16th-century sonneteers, among them Sidney, Spenser, Daniel, Barnes and Wyatt. The last-named is credited with introducing the sonnet into English literature, taking it from Petrarch and others, but with a more flexible approach as to rhyme, This may have allowed in a certain argumentative force, that in turn led to the sonnet's semi-emergence from the mediaeval mist of devotedness, a stage we find in Shakespeare's use. It was still a love-poem, still attached to the courtly ideal; but beginning to clear its head with a vengeance. Its history down the ages is a particularly interesting one.

    The picture of the eye and heart at odds in a petty children's quarrel, then reconciled (47), is droll. The reader cannot take it seriously; but rather appreciates the deftness of the reasoning (by now with the taste of a connoisseur), the occasional phrase or image (line 1 or 6 or 10 . . .), the courtroom setting, the music and the movement of the whole towards a conclusion, all with a kind of tolerance. And then the ending has a penetrative existence of its own. The lovely balancing act of line 12 sets up a verdict that leaves the sides with honours even; and the suggestion of a further honouring in the final line. Again a double reading, that happens without our knowing it, makes its own conquest. We have a hint (a statement, a suggestion?) of the speaker's standing (actual, desired, either, both?) in the other's affections. It is conveyed in a way that is too complex entirely to unravel, fortunately, for it would be a shame to do so.

The 'closet' (6) is a box or cabinet. 'Moiety' (9) is 'part' or 'portion'. 'Side' (9), that some editors give as ''cide', was probably a transitive verb, to award to one side or the other (or both). A quest (10) is a jury. Whatever distance a vocabulary over four hundred years old may sometime impose, the last line always seems to leave the reader with a sense of no distance at all.

Betwixt mine eye and heart a league is took,
And each doth good turns now unto the other.
When that mine eye is famished for a look, 3
Or heart in love with sighs himself doth smother,
With my love's picture then my eye doth feast,
And to the painted banquet bids my heart. 6
Another time mine eye is my heart's guest,
And in his thoughts of love doth share a part.
So either by thy picture or my love, 9
Thyself away are present still with me;
For thou no farther than my thoughts canst move,
And I am still with them, and they with thee; 12
    Or, if they sleep, thy picture in my sight
    Awakes my heart to heart's and eye's delight.

Since writing the last I have read J. Dover Wilson on the Sonnets and my eyes have been opened. 46 and 47 would seem to refer to an actual portrait of the youth that the poet loved to gaze at. (It may also be indicated in 16.8, where a child is suggested as continuing his beauty, 'Much liker than your painted counterfeit'.) The middle-aged humanist Hubert Languet commissioned a portrait of the youthful Philip Sidney, with whom he had a passionate correspondence, by Paul Veronese. The practice does not seem to have been anything very exceptional; and the likelihood gives added point to this pair of poems. (I have not re-written my note on 46; nothing in the poem seems to change with the presence of the imagined catalyst, apart from a clearer focus, and the touch of urgency behind it.)

In this one I had thought 'thy picture' in line 13 spoke of dreams; with the portrait to hand all is clearer, and the last line marvellously awake. The 'league' (1) or alliance between heart and eye, that on one level is a plaything of the mind, to forge a new compliment, on another suggests a personality refreshed and made one. Delight has the last word.

How far the act of homage behind an Elizabethan sonnet-sequence was "real" and how far "conventional" is itself an unreal question in a way, though in one form or another it is liable to persist, at least with a modern reader. Dover Wilson quotes T.G.Tucker, who edited the Sonnets in 1924, to illuminating effect:

'Shakespeare was the poet in 'service' or 'vassalage' to his 'lord', and in the recognised manner of sonneteers, supposed himself bound to write piece after piece to the beloved with a certain continuity of production and with as much variety of 'invention' as possible upon his adopted theme. Any intermission of greater length than usual, any omission to keep up the regular supply of offerings at the altar, would call for self-reproach and apology; it would even supply the poet with matter for the next effort.'

Sonnets were the rage. It is reckoned that 300,000 of them were produced in Western Europe in the 16th century, spreading from Italy to Spain and France and England. Tucker's 'lord' was more often a lady; but the word usefully reminds of a touch of the feudal spirit at the back of it all. 'Lord of my love, to whom in vassalage / Thy merit hath my duty strongly knit', begins 26. It was a way of writing, and a way of being for a writer. In Shakespeare's case it was also a way to lay bare, through the insubstantiality of the convention, a vein of the richest mineral.

How careful was I, when I took my way,
Each trifle under truest bars to thrust,
That to my use it might unusèd stay   3
From hands of falsehood, in sure wards of trust!
But thou, to whom my jewels trifles are,
Most worthy comfort, now my greatest grief,   6
Thou best of dearest and mine only care,
Art left the prey of every vulgar thief.
Thee have I not locked up in any chest,   9
Save where thou art not, though I feel thou art,
Within the gentle closure of my breast,
From whence at pleasure thou mayst come and part;   12
   And even thence thou wilt be stol'n, I fear,
   For truth proves thievish for a prize so dear.

In line 5 'to whom' is 'compared to whom' rather than 'in whose estimation'. Line 14 has more of a planned double meaning: truth itself will lose its virtue, its hands as thievish as falsehood's (line 4), for such a prize; and (conversely), if I am to speak the truth – I shall lose you. Much goes on under the scenes in a swift two beats ('truth proves thievish'): as one reads one knows what one does not know, or does not want to know. The line remains a direct one, conspiring with the reader to accept the first of the meanings on offer, in terms of a playful personification, so to let the full import enter later. It is a tender poem, born of a tender hurt.

   To know the householder is to know the man. The vast mass of contemporary sonnet-writing, the "sonnet blob" to coin a term, puffed with knight-errant ardour, is off on a journey in another world. There are wonderful lines here and there, appealing snatches of feeling, memorable poems, as Sidney's to the moon . . . but in the main the speaker is hardly *knowable*.

Michael Drayton is an exception. A sonnet from his *Idea* robustly begins, 'Since there's no help, come let us kiss and part – / Nay, I have done, you get no more of me . . . ' Sidney's celebrated line at the end of his introductory piece to *Astrophel and Stella* is similarly direct. He is unable to write, 'great with child to speak . . . beating myself for spite', when, ' "Fool," said my Muse to me, "look in thy heart and write". ' But the drift is always towards a story-book stage, where the scenery is ready-made.

Perhaps we have a clue here as to Shakespeare's extraordinarily idiosyncratic way with the props. The love story he tells uses the old materials but is played out on his terms. The development of poetry itself is a part of a great poet's concern, whether consciously or not. The writing persona is given a lead, as into a freer air, a more open land, a voyage in less constrained waters.

Lines 7 and 10–11 are dear to me. How easy Shakespeare makes it for us to accept his presence, as at the other side of the table; to feel something of his 'greatest grief' (6). The loudest love is the softest.

Against that time, if ever that time come,
When I shall see thee frown on my defects,
Whenas thy love hath cast his utmost sum,   3
Called to that audit by advised respects;
Against that time when thou shalt strangely pass,
And scarcely greet me with that sun, thine eye,   6
When love, converted from the thing it was,
Shall reasons find of settled gravity;
Against that time do I ensconce me here   9
Within the knowledge of mine own desert,
And this my hand against myself uprear
To guard the lawful reasons on thy part.   12
    To leave poor me thou hast the strength of laws,
    Since why to love I can allege no cause.

This is one of the great sonnets. There is a kind of knowledge that has its own logic, that is not up for discussion, and by which a person is defined. The tenor of these lines has such a depth. C.S.Lewis noted the 'unembittered resignation' to be found in the Sonnets, but it is more positive than that: a love that acts and not merely accepts. Its own interests are nowhere when the other's are threatened.

The structure is a model for the form: the three quatrains with a repeated introduction presenting a view of an increasing power, and the couplet responding to the mind-set so outlined, with the final line both representing and re-presenting the whole. 'Against' is finely echoed in line 11 with the more usual meaning lending an added thrust. He is raising his hand in court, to swear as a witness against himself, as well (as it were) as being about to attack himself more directly; and the court-room metaphor, taking over from the financial, itself adds an air of finality. Yet the solemnities of court are overturned at the end.

One sees or hears the speaker using the key-words of either metaphor with an increasing ironic emphasis, veiled or not according to the reader's whim. 'Reasons find of settled gravity' could be tapped out on the table; 'lawful reasons' could be almost shouted out; or either, as other terms, quietly stressed. But the final line has no need to draw any more attention to itself than the mere utterance of the words.

There is no reason why the other should love him. When finally reason and love have nothing to do with each other, his own argument (by implication) is subverted. There is only his love to make any kind of case at all; the naked persona is before us, frail and strong. The terminology of 'allege no cause' is beautifully used against itself as all deliberative and legal apparatus is thrown out. There is no reason why the other should not love him also.

To an extent as one reads the last line this is subterranean. The broad sense is taken; it is enough; the rest contributes and fits in indefinably. The contrast of the ending with the rest states its own case; and at a level that may vary with every reader or reading, it has its effect.

'No cause, no cause,' weeps Cordelia as her father, 'bound upon a wheel of fire', says she has 'some cause' not to love him. Cordelia exists behind the Sonnets; all the major characters of *King Lear* are there, from Edmund to 'poor Tom', Goneril and Regan to the loyal Kent, from the Fool to the King himself. And so with all the plays. The spontaneous, and unaccountable, intermingling of energies that crackles to life on the stage, is present in its nuclear potential in the personal poems. Even the goodhumouredness of the "low-life" scenes is there in the easy sense of the natural person; and the wit of Falstaff, as it may be, in a punning tendency beneath the sonnets' surface; and the driven tide of them all.

How heavy do I journey on the way,
When what I seek, my weary travel's end,
Doth teach that ease and that repose to say,   3
'Thus far the miles are measured from thy friend.'
The beast that bears me, tired with my woe,
Plods dully on, to bear that weight in me,   6
As if by some instinct the wretch did know
His rider loved not speed, being made from thee.
The bloody spur cannot provoke him on   9
That sometimes anger thrusts into his hide,
Which heavily he answers with a groan,
More sharp to me than spurring to his side;   12
    For that same groan doth put this in my mind:
    My grief lies onward and my joy behind.

This and the next create another linked pair, harking back to 44
and 45 in a suggestion of the quick and the slow elements. These
two, relatively uninspiring as poems, are not without their own
charm. I think Shakespeare may have composed them both on
a tired journey, and whether or not they were sent to his friend,
the poet did not get around to polishing them up (or rejecting
them). We do not know how Thomas Thorpe got hold of the
sonnets but it does not seem likely that Shakespeare oversaw
their publication: too many anomalies in their order and here
and there in the poetic standard argue against it. This one in fact
would stand well in any other sonnet-sequence of the time. It is
clear, and in its slow weary tone, altogether convincing; but its
substance, derived solely from the occasion, has little further
reference. Yet its very simplicity helps us to know its author
better.

    'Dully' in line 6 is 'duly' in the printed original; as either
word could be spelt either way, and either works, the more

evocative seems the better choice. In line 12 the horse's groan (I am told it can signify pain) hurts the speaker more than the spur the horse. My sympathies are the latter; at least the animal is not partly making things up. (Though with the pathetic fallacy in operation one never knows.) 'Tired' in line 5 probably means 'attired' or 'burdened' as well as 'wearied'.

For all its halting gloom, it is an oddly light piece. Yet the last line is moving in its way. The two nouns raise the stakes: at that moment all his life is involved. Apart from a touch of double meaning in the very last word (in its temporal sense delivering all to a bleak outlook), the poem-statement is, at every point, merely what it says. I cannot help seeing it as an effect of physical tiredness on Shakespeare's mind. The final line makes for an interesting comparison with so many concluding lines in the sequence, and has something to be said for it. But its plainness, to me, is not the true Shakespeare.

Thus can my love excuse the slow offence
Of my dull bearer, when from thee I speed:
'From where thou art, why should I haste me thence?   3
Till I return, of posting is no need.'
O what excuse will my poor beast then find,
When swift extremity can seem but slow?   6
Then should I spur, though mounted on the wind –
In wingèd speed no motion shall I know.
Then can no horse with my desire keep pace;   9
Therefore desire, of perfect'st love being made,
Shall nigh no dull flesh in his fiery race,
But love, for love, thus shall excuse my jade: 12
   'Since from thee going he went wilful slow,
   Towards thee I'll run, and give him leave to go.'

After the leaden footfall of the last, the poet strives for something more uplifting, Ariel-like; but the effort shows. The final lines reach little more than a confusion (if one that can be puzzled out). The octave has a light whirl to it, as if the poetic spirit had a second wind; but the resolution needed sleeping on. It seems rushed to me.

'Dull' in lines 2 and 11 confirms 'dully' in 50.6. 'Posting' (4) is 'hurrying'. The poet's love speaks: imagining the next journey to the beloved, its 'fiery race' (11) of desire will exceed mortal speed. 'Nigh' (11) is 'naigh' in the original and generally taken as 'neigh'. But desire neighing, a horse of no dull flesh, is a little too wild and wonderful, when there's a fair chance of 'naigh' meaning 'nigh' as a verb, here 'linger near' (a similar spelling staying in 'neighbour'). No comma comes after 'naigh', and the transitive verb makes for a stronger line and a more assured passage altogether. Desire, made up of perfect love, will outrun any horse. In line 12 the poet's love returns as excuse-maker for the poor nag from line 1. 'For love' suggests its/his affection for what he now calls his 'jade', a disreputable woman as well as a worn-out horse: a rough affection, not dismissive in context; and by contrast lightly drawing attention to the purity of his true love. Perhaps the first 'love' in line 12 is for the beloved and the second for the good old horse. The final two lines, as 3–4, are love's imagined words. It will dart ahead while the horse is allowed to walk ('go', as in 130.11) at its own slow pace, in the magical journey back, yet to happen.

That's how I see it. But there has been quite a variety of interpretations, including Shakespeare outrunning the horse at the end, which with desire neighing, gives us a page from an Elizabethan Comic Cuts. Another has the horse thinking aloud, about how love neighs for love (a fancy not unworthy of Shakespeare); and how it will gallop its hooves off to get the rider to his friend (make it possible for him to go).

There is a condition, like rust in plants, that I propose to refer to as 'goldengate' (see the note on 44). It's when you can't stop writing in the same form; and a certain deterioration sets in. Chaucer's *Troilus and Criseyde* has 1177 stanzas in the 7-line *rime royal* manner and never seems to nod off; but while both authors had a prodigious work-rate, Shakespeare seems to have been the more tempestuous and possibly the more erratic character. In the Sonnets, semi-private in conception as they are (and as the plays are not), the slightest trace of professional torpor, the writer's fungal infection, may lurk at times. At any rate he shook it off at will.

So am I as the rich whose blessèd key
Can bring him to his sweet up-lockèd treasure,
The which he will not every hour survey,   3
For blunting the fine point of seldom pleasure.
Therefore are feasts so solemn and so rare,
Since seldom coming in the long year set,   6
Like stones of worth they thinly placèd are,
Or captain jewels in the carcanet.
So is the time that keeps you as my chest,   9
Or as the wardrobe which the robe doth hide,
To make some special instant special blest,
By new unfolding his imprisoned pride.   12
        Blessèd are you whose worthiness gives scope,
        Being had to triumph, being lacked to hope.

Back to absence. But after a graceful presentation, the sonnet seems to judder at the close, both in a sudden paucity of feeling, and in the ungainly repetition of 'being' with an extra syllable to it. I have my suspicions of Thorpe's editorial interference on occasion, and I wonder if he was not missing a last line or two here. In the case of 96 he is not averse to using the couplet from 36 to finish things off, as it appears; and there are a few other questions of authenticity to arise along the way. Here the lack of negativity, in the form of a more or less veiled accusation, or simple suffering on the speaker's part at the separation from the other, gives us something of a forced smile to end on: a stiff upper lip, that punctures the poem's true resolution. Or again it may be merely an unrevised ending.

   The first twelve and indeed thirteen lines have a fine sweep to them; though the thirteenth is a little startling. 'Worthiness' suggests both outward value (as of line 7) and inward worth. Perhaps the final phrase of line 14 indicates the latter, an appeal to the youth's better side. Still the ending, while it has "body" in the Shakespearian way, scarcely has the reflective depth we have become accustomed to, and that the lead-up seems to prepare for. Perhaps it was written by the poet at a later time; or perhaps I am simply grasping at shadows.

'Carcanet' (8) is probably an ornamental collar, laid away as it may be with a rich necklace suggested by line 7. The third quatrain has a secretive air to it, with the repetitions in lines 10–11 volunteering an idea of concealment, something within.

It is a moment to celebrate the marvel of the sonnet-line in Shakespeare's hands, that gives us so much of a good poem above. In his plays the pentameter is employed in blank verse to make the strongest substance I know of on Earth. In the Sonnets the energy of the five beats is at once unleashed and held in check, not so much by dramatic interplay (though there is more than a touch of that), as by a supple rhyme, and the rhetorical power of what I term the sonnet-sentence. The three quatrains, each interwoven by rhyme, build and develop a thematic structure, that the couplet sums up, and as if from underneath, takes to a new level. The conclusion it presents, that involves a shift or deepening in the reader's perception, and is underlined by the closing rhyme, takes one back to the consciousness of the speaker at the start, now fully informed. It is the sense of completeness of this information, and the depth of its discovery, that enlightens us, not only as to the local sonnet-context, but as to what we may know in life, and take from it. Time and again a resonance of this sort is with us.

What is your substance, whereof are you made,
That millions of strange shadows on you tend?
Since every one hath, every one, one shade,   3
And you but one, can every shadow lend.
Describe Adonis, and the counterfeit
Is poorly imitated after you;   6
On Helen's cheek all art of beauty set,
And you in Grecian tires are painted new.
Speak of the spring and foison of the year;   9
The one doth shadow of your beauty show,
The other as your bounty doth appear,
And you in every blessèd shape we know.   12
    In all external grace you have some part,
    But you like none, none you, for constant heart.

This too is innocent of any distress. One wonders if such pieces were composed before complications disturbed the even tenor of the relationship; or perhaps after a reconciliation. The beginning is one of Shakespeare's wonders. As with the first four lines of 19, the first two here are of such a nature, a poetic outburst, as to enrich the entire word-mongering business. The excitement is intense, even as the question of the first line is part-answered in the quick amassing texture of the second. One can almost touch the Platonic ideal. And then, extraordinarily, the rest of the dodeka descends to little more than an accomplished tum-ti-tum. The argument is followed through: all that we term beautiful is but the shadow of a further perfection (the youth). But compared with the opening the writing is mechanical. The couplet injects a freshness of a sort, with the last line by contrast (the heart's substance as against the body's) carrying its own reminder of what is special in love. It lacks comparisons. Nevertheless, after line 2 all is unconvincing to a greater or lesser degree; one feels the poet has discharged a duty as much as anything else. Still the astonishment of the opening lingers.

The gender-equal reference to beauties of the past recalls the 'master-mistress of my passion' of 20. When one considers this together with the hyperbole the poet is content to use in talking of the man's attributes but scorns (see 130) for the woman, it is hard not to see the sonnets to the man as on some level above gender. At the back of the whole of the first sequence 1–126 there would seem to lie the ideal of all a pure love can encompass. That it is a man the writer knows and loves who enables the poet's quest, so to speak, provides its own tensions and particular story. The sequence 127–154 is of a less ambitious nature; and as we shall see, in more than one way a deliberate contrast.

'Foison' (line 9) is 'rich harvest'. 'Counterfeit' (line 5) is 'portrait', with the suggestion of sham. In the youth is beauty in its pure form, so outshining any possible representation of Adonis or Helen. (I think line 7 must suggest a painting of the latter's face, with a touch of both senses to it.) He is no imitation but the substance itself. It is difficult to see the poet intending any kind of literal "take" on line 8 (where 'tires' is 'attire'). The young man is less a man than a human, a vehicle for the writer's thoughts to take wing. And yet it must be admitted that in 20 there is a very real sense of the feminine and masculine in one form, and that the physical glow or shimmer of the young man may carry Shakespeare away here too. The particular operates together with the general it leads to. It is not always an ideal marriage.

O how much more doth beauty beauteous seem
By that sweet ornament which truth doth give!
The rose looks fair, but fairer we it deem   3
For that sweet odour which doth in it live.
The canker blooms have full as deep a dye
As the perfumèd tincture of the roses,   6
Hang on such thorns, and play as wantonly,
When summer's breath their maskèd buds discloses.
But for their virtue only is their show,   9
They live unwooed, and unrespected fade,
Die to themselves. Sweet roses do not so;
Of their sweet deaths are sweetest odours made.   12
    And so of you, beauteous and lovely youth,
    When that shall vade, my verse distils your truth.

Again there is something of a perfunctory touch to this. The conceit is almost laboriously worked, at the expense of the refreshing influx of a new or parallel approach. Similarly the repetition of 'sweet' hammers out the essence of what the poem has to say almost into thin air. Its further "truth" is caught only at the end, with the true point, which is not the youth's beauty but the poet's poetry. As such the piece is representative of an important distinction within the layers of the poet's intention, which is generally less apparent than it is here.

That said, he cannot help writing quite charmingly as the mood takes him, as at the end; and also mid-poem, where the rhythm and graduated pace somehow reveal the 'canker blooms' (dog roses or wild roses that have no scent) dallying in the air. Lines 7–8 play as wantonly as the buds they disclose. Line 9 means, 'But because their only virtue is their show'. 'Unrespected' (10) is 'unheeded'. The more one enters this poem, or at least the main body of it, the less one believes it.

But it is all for the end, where with a rush the poet speaks truth – his own, not the boy's.

The irony of this and of so many sonnets preserving virtually nothing of the loved one, beyond an idealised surface, is never deeply felt. Somehow the reader knows it is a surface issue only. The loveliness of the poetry is the deeper justification. Yet one cannot doubt that at least so far as the sonnets have a life of their own, the writer's affection for the young man is a real thing. It is not poetry for poetry's sake, but for love's sake; and the burden that love carries. Gradually the sequence unfolds whatever Shakespeare has to say on the subject from a viewpoint that is always lodged in the personal and immediate. It is not a tidy process; nor could one expect it to be.

'Vade' in the final line is 'depart' or a form of 'fade' (or both). 'My verse' in the original is 'by verse' but while that works after a fashion, I have assumed the misprint, as others do. As regards the bottling, so to speak, of the idea of perfumery, sonnet 5 with 'a liquid prisoner pent in walls of glass' goes about it in a way that is swifter and altogether more striking. Yet through the languorous play of all the lines above I can see the roses bobbing. Each poem to its own.

Not marble nor the gilded monuments
Of princes shall outlive this powerful rhyme;
But you shall shine more bright in these contents   3
Than unswept stone, besmeared with sluttish time.
When wasteful war shall statues overturn,
And broils root out the work of masonry,   6
Nor Mars his sword nor war's quick fire shall burn
The living record of your memory.
'Gainst death and all oblivious enmity   9
Shall you pace forth; your praise shall still find room
Even in the eyes of all posterity
That wear this world out to the ending doom.   12
    So till the judgement that yourself arise,
    You live in this, and dwell in lovers' eyes.

The war with Time that Poetry wages, first in sonnets 15–16, more deliberately thereafter, is centre stage. After this piece, a quite magnificent stroke on its behalf, it is again addressed circuitously. But every now and then (as in 19) the poet lets himself go. Horace's tribute to his own poetry was famous in Renaissance learning, *exegi monumentum aere perennius*, I have finished a monument more lasting than bronze; and whether from this or the slightly later Roman poet Ovid who voiced a similar sentiment, the reference would be familiar to many of Shakespeare's readers. But he makes the statement his own, not only by the sheer power of his verse, but by the delightful conceit in the final phrase. The idea that lovers will read his verse, and so through their understanding his love will stay alive, is the justification (elsewhere implicit) that lies behind the claim such as at the end of 18, 'So long as men can breathe or eyes can see, / So long lives this, and this gives life to thee.'

    It is a love poem. But what is it that lovers who read it under-

stand? It is not to do with the young man as such: but that a
need to praise the loved one has led to a tribute such as this. Love
is resistless. Whether the force of Shakespeare's love created the
poetry more than *vice versa*, the power of the writing arm
somehow expanding the theme to realise its own true strength
(in the terms of a personal poem), is unanswerable, and prob-
ably an illegitimate question. The poem exists, the sequence
exists; and there are members of it that, to my mind, say even
more.

The reference to Doomsday in lines 12–13 is a little
intriguing: one would like to know if the poet "believed" in it.
And even as one poses it it becomes another illegitimate ques-
tion. He used the idea, as here and there in his plays. A true
literary appreciation does not ask the wrong questions – easier
said than done.

And perhaps it does not enquire too deeply into the genesis
of what lies before it. I cannot bring myself to apply a micro-
scope to these lines. I shall merely observe that behind the
rhetorical sweep, so finely controlled as so often, lies a voice like
thunder. But whether it whispers, speaks at normal volume or
louder, is entirely up to the reader. It is a licence enjoyed by
every reader of every poem, however light, however lasting.

Sweet love, renew thy force; be it not said
Thy edge should blunter be than appetite,
Which but today by feeding is allayed,   3
Tomorrow sharpened in his former might.
So love be thou; although today thou fill
Thy hungry eyes even till they wink with fullness,   6
Tomorrow see again, and do not kill
The spirit of love with a perpetual dullness.
Let this sad interim like the ocean be   9
Which parts the shore where two contracted new
Come daily to the banks, that when they see
Return of love, more blest may be the view.   12
    Or call it winter, which being full of care,
    Makes summer's welcome thrice more wished, more rare.

Again to absence. Shakespeare chooses a new angle to target the
theme, addressing love in the abstract, personifying the feeling.
A gentle yearning seeps through the first quatrain; a sense of
heavy satiety lingers in the second (with lines 6 and 8 them-
selves replete with a 'fullness' of syllables). Lines 9 to 12 occupy
a special place in my knowledge of love poetry.

Now and then the sestet has the feel of being written at a
different time from the octave, if for the same occasion. A
notable example is 94. It seems to me Shakespeare has come
back to this sonnet with a fresh thought, a clear head; and in a
no-man's-land between love's satisfaction and anxiety for
renewal, so to speak, has crystallised, in passing, a moment of
acceptance. It is a magical image. The story of Leander swim-
ming the Hellespont to be with Hero, a priestess of the Goddess
of Love, would have come to many then (to relatively fewer
now); but the picture is as timeless as the ocean, the land, and
la condition humaine. I would love to know what Rabindranath

Tagore (note on 45) made of this passage, if he read it. The two separated lovers wait, not passively yet acceptingly, for 'return of love', that is presumably the arrival of one on the same shore as the other. But to say that would be somehow banal. Instead it is implied; and for me at least, something other is in the offing, a stronger part of the half-seen picture, which on face value contradicts the first effect. For my mind has a glimpse of the freshness of the ocean rolling, both before them and between them, "they" are not positioned, only the pristine majesty of Nature's wave, itself in its newness signalling 'return of love'. Ridiculously, from the logical point of view, I see dry land, between or before the lovers, converted to a tremendous surge of the waters. It is not difficult to reconcile such a sequence with a 'sad interim' and its passing. Indeed, my personal "take" on lines 9–12 has always been the aftermath of a quarrel and a subsequent reunion. By not saying too much the poet has said more. Poetry has its miracles; here is one.

After such an effect it may have been out of place to move on to a complex conclusion. 'It' (line 13) is the interim; "summer" with its promise of happiness, that is wistfully awaited, is the keener in the appreciation. 'Welcome' is a word well chosen; and 'rare' too has the touch of a double reference, linking to the idea of appetite as well as to the space of days. Otherwise the fade-out could scarcely be a simpler one. Quietly lucid, it is apt to the occasion.

Being your slave, what should I do but tend
Upon the hours and times of your desire?
I have no precious time at all to spend,   3
Nor services to do till you require;
Nor dare I chide the world-without-end hour
Whilst, I, my sovereign, watch the clock for you;   6
Nor think the bitterness of absence sour,
When you have bid your servant once adieu.
Nor dare I question with my jealous thought   9
Where you may be, or your affairs suppose;
But like a sad slave stay and think of nought
Save where you are how happy you make those.   12
    So true a fool is love, that in your will,
    Though you do anything, he thinks no ill.

The opposition of slave or servant and sovereign is the fancy here, a rueful exaggeration of the situation he has no choice but to accept. The personal note in line 3 is all Shakespeare's own; again he is simply there, before us. 'World-without-end' (line 5, separate words in the original) may come from a sentence of morning prayer, 'As it was in the beginning, is now, and ever shall be, world without end'. The words telescope the infinity of waiting. It seems less likely there is an echo of the evening prayer in line 8, 'Lord, now lettest thou thy servant depart in peace . . . ' so far as the author is concerned; but the balance if it is there is an interesting one, for the more God-fearing time; and certainly a reader now can allow in a hint of the further fiefdom. It adds to a flicker of self-mockery beneath the hurt. The servant-master tie is drawn to an anguish of not seeing and seeing in 11–12. On the one hand he thinks of the innocent delight others find in the company of his friend. On the other there is the overriding thought of a pleasure that is far from innocent. The latter is alluded to in the couplet, a masterpiece of artlessness and art.

It is extraordinary that Shakespeare time after time is able to present a couplet that satisfies the reader on a straightforward level, so that one is not stopped in one's tracks; and at the same time offers a statement not unlike an underground burrow. 'In your will' has three clear and separate meanings, that involve different readings of the last line. The natural one is where 'will' means 'wish' or 'whim'. Then there is 'will' as the sexual organ, with a far more trenchant final line. Then there is the poet's name, Will, that is to be introduced a good number of times later on under the guise of another meaning, and once or twice as itself. Here it can even occasion a new 'he' in the final phrase, not love but Will himself. The natural reading however ushers home the poem to the understanding, other tones of the mental picture merely deepening the whole, hues in a painting, rather than rendering it incomprehensible. Such ambiguities are or are not, or are partly, registered in passing; and the fine security of the whole, the phrasing, the poetic structure, and the controlled rhetorical progression, cannot do other than invite the reader's acceptance. And underlying all the art, and more than all else linking with the reader's intuitive experience, is the sense of an artless journey of the heart. The speaker may point a finger. But he will not condemn.

That God forbid, that made me first your slave,
I should in thought control your times of pleasure,
Or at your hand th'account of hours to crave,   3
Being your vassal bound to stay your leisure.
O let me suffer, being at your beck,
Th'imprisoned absence of your liberty,   6
And patience tame, to sufferance bide each check,
Without accusing you of injury.
Be where you list, your charter is so strong,   9
That you yourself may privilege your time
To what you will; to you it doth belong
Yourself to pardon of self-doing crime.   12
    I am to wait, though waiting so be hell,
    Not blame your pleasure, be it ill or well.

This links with 57 in theme, metaphor and ending. It feels rushed, switching from tightly compressed language to freer construction a little unevenly. 'That God forbid' is probably 'Let God forbid that . . . ' rather than suggesting one of a number of gods (the original has the capital but editors tend to take it out). Line 6 is almost painfully compact: a memorable phrase whose meaning is more or less clear. (I am in the prison of the absence of your person that is in every way free.) The next line needs the two commas of the original which I keep, though the practice seems to be to dispense with at least the first. I must tame, refine my capacity for patience, and accept each restraint on my 'sufferance'. Here Shakespeare may have a legal sense in mind. The Oxford English Dictionary gives for the sixth meaning of 'sufferance', quoting usage of the time, 'The condition of the holder of an estate who, having come in by lawful right, continues to hold it after the title has ceased without the express leave of the owner.' Line 8 follows better on this, 'injury' also drawing on the legal context. It needs to: the line feels too overt even so, too earnest an announcement of his own restraint. To take away the first comma of line 7, or to replace it after 'sufferance', and make 'tame' an adjective as in 'patience-tame' (!), as some do, is to lose the verbal build-up and reduce line 8 to a parody of a Shakespearian pentameter, with scarcely any force to it at all.

In the third quatrain the writer gains a second wind, an expressive energy; and line 13 has the person before us again (as at 57.3 and so often elsewhere). This is where we know our man. The final line, picking up from 57's ending, is a little flat in poetic terms. Shakespeare makes his point well enough, but if his intention is to commemorate his love (here surely the mental abstract) in immortal verse, it is ill served. The whole is an interesting example as I see it of a piece more or less dashed off by a hand of genius, that might have been re-fashioned to advantage. 'Pleasure' at the end neatly picks up from line 2 and reminds of the drama in the poems at this point, the vassal-lord motif. Such word-pageantry, that is half a playful thing, tells us all too well of the unevenness of the situation. 'Entre deux amants il y a toujours un qui aime et un qui se laisse aimer,' wrote la Rochefoucauld, not so long after Shakespeare's time. I suppose it is unlikely he saw the little Thomas Thorpe book; yet he was an accomplished nobleman. One never knows.

If there be nothing new, but that which is
Hath been before, how are our brains beguiled,
Which, labouring for invention, bear amiss   3
The second burden of a former child?
O that record could with a backward look,
Even of five hundred courses of the sun,   6
Show me your image in some antique book,
Since mind at first in character was done,
That I might see what the old world could say   9
To this composèd wonder of your frame;
Whether we are mended, or where better they,
Or whether revolution be the same.   12
    O sure I am the wits of former days
    To subjects worse have given admiring praise.

'There is no new thing under the sun,' we are told in Ecclesiastes.
The theory of history cyclically repeating itself is entertained,
to pay a new compliment: it cannot be. Yet one wonders if the
poet were not more interested in the philosophical idea than in
its refutation by the uniqueness of the young man's beauty.
There is a wondering tone to the first two lines that vanishes as
a kind of superb perfunctoriness takes over. The (brain)child or
concept of line 4, that amounts to any human creation, has been
born before. 'Second burden' is a bearing-again; nothing (now)
is original. The cycle needed for apparent novelties to run their
course might have been five hundred years. Shakespeare
proposes the existence of a portait of old (in poetry?) of a
matching excllence, so to conclude it cannot be. In a sense the
poem is the merest dallying with an idea. Yet it is turned well,
indeed one mght say perfectly; and so a spark is struck, the
tribute continued.

    Line 8 says a deal in a little. Speaking of 'Since' at its beginning ('From the time that'), Stephen Booth proceeds to characterise the rest of the line as 'the clumsy, unidiomatic, pseudo-primitive construction it introduces'. This is oddly harsh. Booth is precise on the niceties of grammar as on turns of expression, but he was risking his health with the Bard. I find the line deft, in the elliptical way poetry can be, and historically thoughtful. At some point people began to capture, and to continue, the mind's activity in writing. There are moments in the Sonnets when Shakespeare appears to take the great sweep of Time on board. This is not one of them; but one feels it touch his thought nevertheless. In every poet there is something of the philosopher.

Lines 9–10 are romantic, roguish almost. 'Mended' in 11 works as a synonym for 'better'. 'Where' (11) may be taken as a shortened 'whether', as 'whe'er'; or 'where', 'in which places'. It is probably the former but since the latter works well enough, and that is the spelling in the original text, let it remain. 'Revolution' (12) had the meanings it has now of turn and change: the line hints a paradox, change is no change. But a breath of common sense appears to return to validate the conclusion. Of course things change: and his friend is the living proof. Beneath the compliment, then, is a light sub-text. The theory of repeating patterns, that began with Pythagoras and his followers in the 6th century BC, is taken up and gently cast aside.

Like as the waves make towards the pebbled shore,
So do our minutes hasten to their end,
Each changing place with that which goes before;   3
In sequent toil all forwards do contend.
Nativity, once in the main of light,
Crawls to maturity, wherewith being crowned,   6
Crooked eclipses 'gainst his glory fight,
And time that gave doth now his gift confound.
Time doth transfix the flourish set on youth,   9
And delves the parallels in beauty's brow,
Feeds on the rarities of Nature's truth,
And nothing stands but for his scythe to mow.   12
    And yet to times in hope my verse shall stand,
    Praising thy worth, despite his cruel hand.

Still on a philosophical tack, Shakespeare speaks from the heart not of the temporal storm of the man but the eternal world of the artist. The arresting first lines attest to the influence of Arthur Golding's translation of Ovid's *Metamorphoses* (1567), a text the poet clearly knew well: both sonnets and plays benefit from it. 'As every wave dryves other foorth, and that that commes behynd / Bothe thrusteth and is thrust itself: Even so the tymes by kynd / Doo fly and follow bothe at once, and ever-more renew.' But trust Shakespeare to conjure up the incoming tide in the sound and the beat of the first line.

The fourth, remarkably abstract and accurate, again seems to correspond with what little we now know of the war within the atom. If the ages of man are bounded in a nutshell in 5–8, in 9–12 Time's art and power to create and destroy are to the fore. Shiva is present though Shakespeare knew him not. The economy and poise of the three quatrains, that still the chamber, so to speak, as one reads, are attributes of a deeper personality, the orator himself. And this is not Shakespeare so much as Man, whom he represents as at war with Time.

They are rivals. In a conflict first openly declared at the outset of sonnet 16, the poet now takes up the cudgels in full possession of their use and nature. So far from pleading with somebody to have a child, he sends his own offspring into the field. Art shall stand though all else fall, and the only cause worth fighting for is Love.

If Time reveals a touch of the artist (lines 9, 10) and connoisseur (11), a piquancy is added to the fray. There is no hidden dimension to the couplet (apart from the suggestive 'to times in hope' with its sense of an indefinable yearning). Only the bare battle is before us, as if on a frieze, 'my verse', 'thy worth', 'his . . . hand'. Yet the final phrase is as commanding as ever. Time's power sweeps through: despite 'despite', it has the final word.

Later in the Sonnets the speaker is concerned with a rival or rival poets, in whose verses the young man seems at least for a time more interested. But that is in the weather of the everyday world. His true rival poet is here.

As a teacher I have long appreciated the precision of line 9. There is a moment, it seems, when a young person passes a relatively amorphous stage and is stamped, almost branded, with a look that for a good many years is his or hers. It is not entirely facial expression; it is also gestures, a way of being, a vital outwardness, carried unknowingly like a banner. What better word than 'flourish'? Or 'transfix' for its catching and setting? What can this ever-living poet not say?

Is it thy will thy image should keep open
My heavy eyelids to the weary night?
Dost thou desire my slumbers should be broken,　　　　　3
While shadows like to thee do mock my sight?
Is it thy spirit that thou send'st from thee
So far from home into my deeds to pry,　　　　　　　　6
To find out shames and idle hours in me,
The scope and tenor of thy jealousy?
O no, thy love, though much, is not so great;　　　　　9
It is my love that keeps mine eye awake,
Mine own true love that dost my rest defeat,
To play the watchman ever for thy sake.　　　　　　　12
　　For thee watch I, whilst thou dost wake elsewhere,
　　From me far off, with others all too near.

We return to the everyday, to insomnia and desertion, and to
the frailty of one undergoing a hurt. The voice on entrance seems
to breathe shallowly, as if in a stumbling lethargy; after which
(from line 3) the speaker, roused by his own questions, devotes
the piece to finding an answer. As so often the opening has the
mood, that drives the pen to paper, the follow-up has more of
the mind, and the conclusion the touch (that can seem almost
physical) of a deeper insight or realisation. In 27 the poet sees
the other's shadow or form and cannot sleep. He states the situ-
ation, tellingly enough, of his mind's obsession; but here he
plays it over as in a dramatic scenario. Are the 'shadows' (4)
spying on him? No, nothing so complimentary: but he will keep
the other's image (1) in mind, to 'play the watchman' (12). I
imagine this is keeping an eye open on his friend's behalf, lest
he come into contact with any unsavoury companion. The line
of argument could scarcely be more tenuous: yet the speaker's
self-negation, where the other's interests are concerned, rings

true. At the same time there is an accusation waiting to be made. In the double meaning of 'my love' and 'mine own true love' (10 and 11) he edges towards it, and away from it; finally it is unequivocal; and yet the altruistic concern of the speaker is not dislodged. But he can do nothing. A light thing in itself, the sonnet in its way precisely reflects the vulnerability of the one who loves.

'Scope' in line 8 is 'target' (rather than 'range' as in 29.7); 'tenor' is 'purport'. The line has a Shakespearian roll to it, as in 'the hours and times of your desire' (57.2), or 'the slings and arrows of outrageous fortune' (from *Hamlet*). The poet to whom the pentameter became a second nature had a penchant for a hendiadys of nouns: good strengthening material for the line itself, it is apt to add point and force to the speech as a whole, as to the speaker. He was a man for nouns. Such linked pairs are everywhere in the plays, less so in the sonnets, no doubt reflecting the more decisive presentation of the former. The inner self is a tentative entity, uniquely captured at one remove in *Hamlet*, emerging direct in its way in the Sonnets. Its way is erratic, dream-chasing; passionate, weary (as when he cannot sleep); as raw as an exposed nerve; as resolute in love's service as any pilgrim.

Sin of self-love possesseth all mine eye,
And all my soul, and all my every part;
And for this sin there is no remedy,   3
It is so grounded inward in my heart.
Methinks no face so gracious as is mine,
No shape so true, no truth of such account,   6
And for myself mine own worth do define,
As I all other in all worths surmount.
But when my glass shows me myself indeed,   9
Beated and chopped with tanned antiquity,
Mine own self-love quite contrary I read –
Self so self-loving were iniquity.   12
    'Tis thee, myself, that for myself I praise,
    Painting my age with beauty of thy days.

There are certain things Shakespeare meets head-on. The idea of sex with a man (20), the fact of sex with a woman (151), ageing (*passim*), and further intimate reflections, of which this is one. By the poetic era he was born in, as well as by inclination, he was set down on the pilgrim's path of the mediaeval lover; yet being the realist he is, he dodges no issue in the quest. Selfless as love is, there is an element of self-love to be confronted.

And how well he does it. With an almost lascivious greed the octave lays claim to a new treasure in the sequence. Unexpectedly, in view of the self-obscuring aspect of the speaker that the reader is familiar with, an inner Narcissus is revealed, yet to no real surprise. The poetic ego, a declamatory assurance without which there would be no poetry, nor any other form of art, is pronounced from the first line of the first sonnet. Again and again the speaker cries aloud to the heavens, his own King Lear. But as with Tagore and his *Gitanjali* (45, note), the loudest claimant to love can be the quietest.

The obstacle to love is noted and cleared. That is it noted by way of a roaring hyperbole merely captures the nature of the beast. And in any case, to snuff the candle to any effect it must be let burn brightly. The breathtaking last line is more than word-play. It bears witness to the ability of the mind to evolve and look outwards. The lead-up to the switch shows the writer at his instinctive controls. After line 1, 'self' does not reappear till 11–12, three times. The emphasis prepares us for a different gloss on the word. This is finely discovered in 13 with the half-veiled further repetitions; after which the selfless final line emerges in a crystalline freshness. The reader is left with nothing to say, nothing to think, nothing to do except be.

We allow the poem to work its magic; and while at some level we are aware the candle-flame burns, that it is only wishfully extinguished, we accept the equation in some way is balanced. The flame of line 14, to which the previous five lines lead, matches that of the octave, less aggressive but as strong. And in reality, in love, neither flame can be out.

Line 10 is one of many in the Sonnets (including the next) to reflect the harsh artistry of age. This is exceptional in standing alone as such in the poem. As an individual effect I would also note the insidious sibilance in the first lines, with its echo in the repeated 'self', but quite absent in the finale. In the latter flame, gentle as it is, is something quietly triumphant.

Against my love shall be as I am now,
With time's injurious hand crushed and o'erworn;
When hours have drained his blood and filled his brow   3
With lines and wrinkles, when his youthful morn
Hath travelled on to age's steepy night,
And all those beauties whereof now he's king   6
Are vanishing, or vanished out of sight,
Stealing away the treasure of his spring;
For such a time do I now fortify   9
Against confounding age's cruel knife,
That he shall never cut from memory
My sweet love's beauty, though my lover's life.   12
    His beauty shall in these black lines be seen,
    And they shall live, and he in them still green.

Again the first two lines are full of poetry after which the writer seems to wait for a second wind. This comes a little before the sestet here; but in my view the piece never quite takes off. I find it strangely unconvincing.

The opening is marvellous. How much the writer felt the hand of Time on his own person! His forecast of a like effect on the person of his friend has no such intensity. Rather it is diluted by cliché, until momentarily at lines 7–8; and as a consequence, line 12 feels overdone. The couplet makes the point he is after well enough, though the metaphorical 'green' against the literal 'black' is not perhaps the happiest of oppositions. Lines 2 and 8 are beautiful however; and the whole is as always a statement of a cumulative rhetorical power. But despite the promising start, something appears to be lacking behind the rhetoric.

One has only the author's finer sonnets to compare with. Three of these come next: I know of no succession of poems at a similar level. Rather than anticipate them in their particularity,

I shall take the opportunity to look back and note such sonnets as we have already come to that seem to work perfectly, the whole in each case balanced and carried along by its own conviction (even if that depends on a conceit). This is of course a personal choice and readers will disagree and make their own. In part an act of homage, it is also a way of noting something of the poet's range.

Sonnet 8 for its music, 18 for its joy, 19 for its challenge, 29 for its escape from despair, 30 for its nostalgia, 49 for the absolute disclaimer, 55 for the epic touch, 60 for the continuing sense of the sea coming in, and 62 for its inward-outward knowledge.

The exercise clarifies something for me. Given that one's mind is turned to the magnet of the poem in general, by the attractiveness of its content, then one has an affection for a piece that has a personality of its own. There is a voice behind every poem, a personal reality behind the voice, an acquaintance to be made not merely with a series of thoughts and word-pictures; the more so, as a general rule, in the case of a poem in the first person. It is not the artist's but a personality in common, of giver, recipient and what is given, that one meets. It may be in this respect that art lives.

But there is a danger in aesthetic matters of too much theory, of bumbling about in loose sand when one should be treading a firmer path. I return to a detail of the above poem. 'Travelled' in line 5 is 'travaild' in the original. 'Travel' was sometimes spelt as 'travail' meaning 'toil': the context indicates the former in harness with the latter. And so we come to a moment, one feels, Shakespeare wrote the Sonnets for.

When I have seen by time's fell hand defaced
The rich proud cost of outworn buried age,
When sometime lofty towers I see down-razed,   3
And brass eternal slave to mortal rage;
When I have seen the hungry ocean gain
Advantage on the kingdom of the shore,   6
And the firm soil win of the wat'ry main,
Increasing store with loss, and loss with store;
When I have seen such interchange of state,   9
Or state itself confounded to decay,
Ruin hath taught me thus to ruminate,
That time will come and take my love away.   12
    This thought is as a death, which cannot choose
    But weep to have that which it fears to lose.

Again a strong Ovidian echo, through Golding's translation of *Metamorphoses*, is to be heard. 'Even so have places oftentimes exchaunged theyr estate, / For I have seene it sea which was substanciall ground a-late, / Ageine where sea was, I have seene the same become dry lond, / And shelles and scales of Seafish farre have lyen from any strond . . . ' From the Latin hexameter to the rare English heptameter to Shakespeare's pentameter the view is passed on of the inexorable exchange of the elements. Finally, in what must be one of the most finely-used literary inheritances, a vista of mortality is gained itself more than mortal.

But it is for the most human of purposes. The tremendous vision, a compression of human experience, brings home a single truth to the observer. With the simplicity of everyday speech (or song), the twelfth line reduces the grandiosity of the transforming world to one pure fact. In context the line itself is an epiphany.

In the couplet the awareness of the fact acts with its own force. The mind sees its own sadness. It is the thought (I take it) that weeps, that almost ceases to exist. The foreknowledge of what must be casts a chill over present happiness. It may be said the older person would scarcely anticipate the youth's pre-decease: but it is the realisation striking home that his friend will die at some point (taking the riches of the world with him), that surely lies behind the sadness, even as it is couched in directly personal terms. The sense of loss in the last line is instilled with a purity of tone that somehow detaches it from the need of the speaker, even as he announces it: and how Shakespeare does this I do not know.

In line 4 'eternal' goes back to 'brass', as an epithet deriving from Horace's words 'aere perennius' (55, note), as well as forward to 'slave'. Otherwise the language is clear and straight-forward, until the reflective sadness of the couplet. The first sentence (lines 1–12) takes us on a journey of perception, from the never-still forces of the outside world to the certain knowl-edge of the mind, as if with an evolutionary touch. On one level the observer can seem to speak for mankind: we see the use of inference and its consequences. At the end we have no more than an individual, no less than a tangible presence, in whom thought and feeling are one.

Once as a teacher at a comprehensive school in London I recited this poem during a talk on "change". Three years later a girl I had never taught approached me: could she study English for A level? She had remembered the last line and found it in her parents' copy of Shakespeare, and gone on from there on her own. She ended up at Oxford reading English, though I believe she went on to become a full-time musician. Maybe, in four hundred years, it will happen again.

Since brass, nor stone, nor earth, nor boundless sea,
But sad mortality o'ersways their power,
How with this rage shall beauty hold a plea,   3
Whose action is no stronger than a flower?
O how shall summer's honey breath hold out
Against the wrackful siege of battering days,   6
When rocks impregnable are not so stout,
Nor gates of steel so strong, but Time decays?
O fearful meditation! Where alack   9
Shall Time's best jewel from Time's chest lie hid?
Or what strong hand can hold his swift foot back?
Or who his spoil of beauty can forbid?   12
    O none, unless this miracle have might,
    That in black ink my love may still shine bright.

Having ended the last note with a personal recollection I'll start this with one. All his adult life my father would go through the words of this poem to himself when in the dentist's chair. If it worked for him . . .

While the "I" in 64 is almost oracular in vision, until reminded of the depth of its love for another, here a series of questions carries a sense of the narrator's apparent helplessness throughout the dodeka; and the couplet finds a recourse, again running contrary to 64 where there is none. The texture of this poem is wonderfully appealing, the humanity of the questioner, before us from the start, as it were battering back at Time; the vulnerability of his frail stance, as with all things beautiful, somehow holding out, until the poem's own material, its 'black ink' can leave its indelible mark. The process of the poem, intricate with the suggestion of its content, is itself part of the effect: as always to a degree, but never more tellingly. A cry is caught from an immortal battle-field.

Beauty's 'action' (line 4) is at first legal then military, the reference working back to 'plea' and ahead to 'siege', re-emerging again, as it may be, in the act of writing at the end. There is much to marvel at in the means of opposition the lines discover to highlight their protagonists, slightness and force; but more noteworthy, and individually Shakespearian, is the acceleration the poet has on offer at the *volta* (line 9). None of the other great sonnet-writers in English, Donne, Milton, Wordsworth, Keats, Hopkins, Auden, and there are others, is as drastic as Shakespeare often is at this point, nor in the sonnets of any other language have I felt such a hand at the controls. The acceleration is not in the rate at which one reads the words to oneself, but in the power of the mind to expand, to be one with the poet's mind, even as it reads. At this point in the sonnet, in the dynamic of the three quatrains, and above all (or below all) in the couplet, Shakespeare's authority is complete.

As an engineer of 'mind . . . in character' (59.8) he understood all a sonnet's capacity. Many users of the form are outspoken; it lends itself to apostrophe. But the energies of the mind, and the dramatic possibilities of the personality, probably find fullest expression in Shakespeare's verse. It is so too in the plays, where his exploitation of the pentameter in blank verse needs a study of its own. I can only hope that my drab musings in this and other notes do not blur the gleam of the 'black ink' (14) for any reader.

Tired with all these, for restful death I cry,
As to behold desert a beggar born,
And needy nothing trimmed in jollity,   3
And purest faith unhappily forsworn,
And gilded honour shamefully misplaced,
And maiden virtue rudely strumpeted,   6
And right perfection wrongfully disgraced,
And strength by limping sway disablèd,
And art made tongue-tied by authority,   9
And folly, doctor-like, controlling skill,
And simple truth miscalled simplicity,
And captive good attending captain ill.   12
    Tired with all these, from these would I be gone,
    Save that to die I leave my love alone.

To deal with a few minor points first. 'Disablèd' (8) can have a
hint of four syllables; it may be imitating a limping gait.
'Desert' (2) probably should suggest 'a well-deserving person'
rather than 'abandoned', as I took it on first reading; yet I am
not sure of this. 'Trimmed in jollity' (line 3) is 'decked out in
fine clothes', 'needy nothing' a 'needy-nothing', someone who
has everything, yet is given more. At first I took it as 'a needy
nothing', a no-one in desperate need who is trimmed, cut down
further in mere horseplay. But 'trimmed in jollity' cannot mean
that. It is an example of serious misinterpretation on my part (as
opposed to 'well-contented' in 32.1).

But a wrong reading or two scarcely matters in a list of such
power. The eye behind the plays looks round; and as man rather
than author, the observer can barely go on living. The last line
has been called a weak one but that may be to miss the impli-
cation. It is not merely that the loved one is left alone without
him; but that he is left alone in the midst of a moral hell, in

which love itself is barely to be supported. The poem is a statement of fact, unadorned by conceit: a damning indictment of the world, yet one with a tender voice behind it.

'And', the simplest word, takes on a searing force. As an explanation for the first line could more be said in the next eleven? Line 12 sums up the others (much as line 12 of 65). Otherwise each tells a tale of every society on earth at every time. I remember being taken aback by line 9 when I first encountered it in the early 'sixties. I later discovered something of the reach of the censorship of the arts in Shakespeare's England. There were other places on the globe of my own time to which the line immediately applied, as it does now.

Again, one may note the superb renewal of vigour as the *volta* is passed, here while continuing the main thread. Each aspect of the viciousness of the human race – not while at war but in the trail it leaves as it claws together in (so-called) civil society – presents itself as a separate detail and as part of a growing picture. That is always so in a list; but the visualisation here of the parts operates with a clarity that allows the underlying sense of the whole to build with an unrestrained intent. The separateness of each line leaves an effect of a world of evil that is continually met in this personal situation or that (somehow the personal example continues from line 2). It is to be countered only by love.

The list alone, that lays its own sonnet-structure, makes 66 stand out. I know of nothing like it. It may or may not be the most memorable poem. But I do think it tells us more of the man than does any other. The protective nature of his love is tendered with a difference. While 'my love' in 65.14 can be in part the feeling, here at the end it is altogether the person. It is a poem about people, as present as they are on stage, as real as in any of the Tragedies.

Ah, wherefore with infection should he live,
And with his presence grace impiety,
That sin by him advantage should achieve, 3
And lace itself with his society?
Why should false painting imitate his cheek,
And steal dead seeing of his living hue? 6
Why should poor beauty indirectly seek
Roses of shadow, since his rose is true?
Why should he live, now Nature bankrupt is, 9
Beggared of blood to blush through lively veins?
For she hath no exchequer now but his,
And proud of many, lives upon his gains. 12
  O, him she stores to show what wealth she had
  In days long since, before these last so bad.

After a trio of poetic moments of observation such as, in their different elements, to reflect the range and power of human insight, we are back to the business of compliments. In a display of gallantry that bids fair to out-Osric Osric, I half-suspect a mere competition with a rival poet, who has gained the young man's attention with sonnets made of delicate nothings (see 83.14 and elsewhere). And yet, even in the exaltation of his friend's excellence to absurd heights, Shakespeare is onto something quite serious to do with Nature and Beauty. It is a theme fully to be realised only in the last of the sonnets to the youth, 126.

This and the next are not as it happens addressed to him but in the third person (as are a few others). The opening two lines have a remarkable charm to them, chiefly of word-texture; there follows a fine iteration of hypothetical questions, as if with raised eyebrows, to prepare for an irrefutable answer. The poet's bugbear, the rage for cosmetics, is adapted to illustrate all that is second-hand, meretricious: all beauty, all virtue is leached from his paragon. It is all nonsense; except that something else is being said. The ideal that is only to be captured by the soul is somehow identified in Shakespeare's engagement, on paper, with this dearest of friends. Hyperbole, the poem seems to say, is acceptable, lying as it does in the language of love.

The wickedness of the present time, as compared to a Golden Age of the past, is a theme of writers of all times. It is used here in the process of a gradual crystallisation of 'nature's truth' (60.11). Just as we can allow dismissive over-statement to pass, in our capacity as readers at some level divining an underlying intent, so often we let by an ambiguity, or on occasion a lexical obscurity, securely set on a well-signalled if not well-defined route. Lines 9–12 may be paraphrased, 'Why should he exist, merely to keep Nature's account in profit, in these beggarly times?' (The question is finally answered, and the full account revealed, in 126.) 'Proud of many' may refer to Nature's fecundity; 'gains' may indicate the youth's reputation, see below. But it doesn't seem worth puzzling out the detail as the compliment, whatever it is, is essentially the same: and, it must be said, not meant. Or rather it is directed elsewhere.

The poet likes a financial metaphor. 'Bankrupt', 'exchequer', 'gains' (interest from capital) add to 'stores' and 'wealth' to imply the rather delightful picture of a cornucopian goddess with the beady eye of a magnate forever checking the Stock Exchange. Suddenly, with a Shakespearian sleight of hand, there she is, Dame Nature, volubly complaining in the couplet, shrugging expansive shoulders and shaking her head. And our object of holy reverence is a little boy in her hand. Sometimes I don't know what to make of Shakespeare. But he does repay the reading.

Thus is his cheek the map of days outworn,
When beauty lived and died as flowers do now,
Before these bastard signs of fair were borne,   3
Or durst inhabit on a living brow;
Before the golden tresses of the dead,
The right of sepulchres, were shorn away,   6
To live a second life on second head;
Ere beauty's dead fleece made another gay.
In him those holy antique hours are seen,   9
Without all ornament, itself and true,
Making no summer of another's green,
Robbing no old to dress his beauty new;   12
    And him as for a map doth Nature store,
    To show false art what beauty was of yore.

Line 1 is a minor wonder. The words say little, returning to the trope of 67 with an almost didactic 'Thus'. They offer the cheek (again), a touch of novelty in 'map' as 'epitome'; the same charm, the same impression of a 'ne-er-cloying sweetness' (118.5). Then why should the line drift unattached in my head half a hundred years? The lingering pace, the footfall ('cheek', 'map', 'days' crisper than 'Thus' and 'worn'), the dream-like quiet of the thought itself . . . a number of such lines, from the Sonnets and elsewhere, from this poet and others, have haunted me in this way. Some poetic thoughts are at once a reflection and a sensation, Keats' day that has glided by, 'e'en like the passage of an angel's tear / that falls through the clear ether silently'. At the same time the line has stood for something elusive in the link Shakespeare conceives between Nature and his love.

The second line too is fetching: I take the suggestion to be both of beauty's naturalness in the old times and its abundance. Then we have a ten-line rant against wigs. One can hardly imagine the youngster already bald or balding; Shakespeare simply works his slight obsession with 'false art' of this kind into the substance of the compliment, knowing that the literal level is no more than a catalyst for the true working of the poem.

Effortlessly, it seems, he palms timeless phrases, immortal lines out of the air. 'Holy antique hours . . . Without all ornament, itself and true.' There is what I call a Baron Munchausen effect in some of Shakespeare's finest verse, where he is assuming a situation that is not so, and presenting it, or aspects of it, as if in perfect sincerity. (A notable example is 147. 9–12 where he assumes madness.) This is the dramatist at work of course; but its appearance in a personal poem can be a little unnerving. But of course there is always something such lines are expressing that needs to be said. The 'holy antique hours' are of a prelapsarian innocence (to take the term not too technically). And at the end 'false art' turns the mind to a naturalness of being, all wigs and suchlike forgotten. Not only does the youth embody such virtue, present such a demeanour; but the reader may have a sense of an ethos of the past that takes a nobler attitude to the deed of life in general. The 'map' (now) is an instrument, a way to find a direction. There may, too, be a level at which the poet is castigating poor poems (of a rival?) that rely too much on artifice.

I rather like our man's irascibility at wigs and cosmetics. He is the more knowable for it. But what a paradox he presents, with his realism on the one hand and his uninhibited use of hyperbole on the other! Yet, it may be, in some form the same paradox has hold of us all.

Those parts of thee that the world's eye doth view
Want nothing that the thought of hearts can mend;
All tongues, the voice of souls, give thee that due,　　　3
Utt'ring bare truth, even so as foes commend.
Thy outward thus with outward praise is crowned;
But those same tongues that give thee so thine own,　　6
In other accents do this praise confound,
By seeing farther than the eye hath shown.
They look into the beauty of thy mind,　　　　　　　　9
And that in guess they measure by thy deeds;
Then, churls, their thoughts (although their eyes were kind)
To thy fair flower add the rank smell of weeds.　　　12
　　But why thy odour matcheth not thy show,
　　The soil is this, that thou dost common grow.

The poet moves from his friend's appearance to his character: not so lovely. To indicate 'in all sincerity' he has 'the voice of souls' (3): there, in a phrase, is what poetry can do. The poem is graceful as ever, with little intrinsic interest until the last three lines: the presentation is all an admirably clear preparation for an incisive closing metaphor. Gradually the finger is pointed. 'Common' (14) is a harder-hitting word than any other the poet uses against the young man (except one); and while mild in tone overall, the poem makes a devastating judgement. Yet balanced against the deserved accolades 'thy outward' (5) appears continually to garner, the whole can be still be seen merely as a warning, if one that does not mince its words. On the other hand it is easy to imagine the writer moved momentarily to anger by his friend's behaviour, and letting him have it with both barrels.

　　Somehow both attitudes are there, others no doubt as well, as Shakespeare creates a little more of his sonnet-story. Much in the sequence is built on shifting sand, but love, including its own nebulous basis, is the cornerstone forever holding it in place. The imagination simply flies off the handle in love, reality is overturned, superlatives march out and conquer the world. At the same time nothing is more real. In a way Shakespeare proceeds by stealth in 1–126, allowing the various moods that visit him, and levels of poetic energy, to draw him to a grail he cannot see or know; yet which is no more than to do his theme justice.

'Weeds' are used to effect elsewhere; and re-reading 94 I confirm there is a harder-hitting word than 'common'. 'Rank smell' (12) is harsh. 'Soil' (14) is marvellous. The original is 'solye', clearly a misprint; and all editors assume a reversal of the l and y. It is what it is, soil for plants to grow in, also 'ground' as in 'underlying reason', also something abhorrent; and 'assoil', a word for 'solution', may be there too. To pick over the meanings of the word with the mind's tweezers is both in the poem's interests and against them, for clear enough reasons. It is a cunning usage that works well with 'common grow'.

'Common' becomes both 'undiscriminating' (in choice and perhaps number of friends) and 'promiscuous', sexually, socially or both. One wonders, if Shakespeare gave this and perhaps others to his friend, whether they may have led to a rift, that in turn gave rise to an incomparable sonnet later (120), to do with the aftermath of a quarrel. Perhaps the youth showed his displeasure by appearing to enjoy another's verse-offerings more. All such local speculation attaches itself to the story on offer and breaks free. The scattered word-reality of the text itself is ineradicable (let us hope); a fact, like the Milky Way. As someone trying to respond to it in not too futile a fashion, that is sometimes the distance I feel.

That thou art blamed shall not be thy defect,
For slander's mark was ever yet the fair;
The ornament of beauty is suspect,   3
A crow that flies in heaven's sweetest air.
So thou be good, slander doth but approve
Thy worth the greater, being wooed of time;   6
For canker vice the sweetest buds doth love,
And thou present'st a pure unstainèd prime.
Thou hast passed by the ambush of young days,   9
Either not assailed, or victor being charged;
Yet this thy praise cannot be so thy praise,
To tie up envy, evermore enlarged.   12
    If some suspect of ill masked not thy show,
    Then thou alone kingdoms of hearts shouldst owe.

At once the poet turns the page on the condemnatory pose. While each poem reflects the mood of the moment, as we may suppose, the inconsistencies of a many-angled approach are to be seen as no obstacle, but rather as in the interests of a greater accuracy overall. To that extent the poet's aim is surely clear. 'Mark' (2) is target and blemish at once; and line 4 has the blemish almost humorously vivified and vigorous. If we take 'the ornament of beauty' (3) as truth (54, 1–2) then its misrepresentation by slander is carried off brilliantly. Otherwise it is clear enough from the context that it is reputation, which comes to the same thing. 'Wooed of time' (6) suggests the youth's good conduct (over a time) adds to his beauty to attract the envies of slander (the 'canker' or caterpillar revisiting from 35); and envy is always at liberty, at large, ever larger (12). One discerns a warning: 'So thou be good' (5). The 'suspect of ill' (13) is a burden the fair and good must carry, announces the speaker, for the moment forgetting his own suspicions and more. The uncompromising accusation of the last sonnet for the moment is deftly withdrawn. Yet the ending is a less than deft one.

Its surface does not carry the weight it should. Surely the poet imagines the 'kingdoms of hearts' as his loved one's right and due ('owe' is 'own'). The justification for the surface presumably is in its ridiculous aspect, the youth a giddy world-emperor of hearts; but since the literal level is not really a factor in the force-field of hyperbole that the poet surrounds the youth with, one is tempted to comment "Why not?" and the need for 'some suspect of ill' is undone. What has occurred, I think, is a too-close attachment to the previous sonnet (the last three words of the thirteenth lines are identical); and the unlikelihood from 69's angle of the youth's royal sway over the affections of so many, has entered 70 as a part of the background. But 70 is a different poem. I would call it an oversight by the author. While there is something cryptic about many of his closing couplets, the surface is not that of the modern cryptic crossword clue, where meaning often is mere misdirection: it has to hold. Only then is the consciousness of the reader more deeply informed. Here the stem of the last line, so to speak, wilts a little. Yet one accepts it. The poem is touching in its faith, graceful, charged, with its own memorable moments – as are so many. A phrase has stayed with me.

From the early 'sixties, when I came across it first, an undergraduate struggling to find my way, for decades later as father and teacher, now as grandfather and teacher, and all the time as anyone with half an eye on time and age and the young, a few words have summed up a mortal danger to my mind. Nothing is to be done about it; it is like the 'flourish set on youth' (60.9), a universal Shakespeare has plucked out of the air. While here (in the poet's heart, so to speak) the friend is untouched by it, elsewhere it is all too clear he has not escaped. Who has passed by 'the ambush of young days'?

No longer mourn for me when I am dead
Than you shall hear the surly sullen bell
Give warning to the world that I am fled   3
From this vile world with vilest worms to dwell.
Nay, if you read this line, remember not
The hand that writ it, for I love you so,   6
That I in your sweet thoughts would be forgot,
If thinking on me then should make you woe.
O if, I say, you look upon this verse,   9
When I perhaps compounded am with clay,
Do not so much as my poor name rehearse,
But let your love even with my life decay;   12
    Lest the wise world should look into your moan,
    And mock you with me after I am gone.

Thoughts of his own death possess the poet. 71–74 try out different ways of coming to terms with it, from the point of view of someone to whom his love is all the world. In one case an even tenor is established that bespeaks a perfect match of inner and outer, the poet's own deepest nature as at that moment, and the voice of the poem. In the other three the path travelled is less aware, more "correct" in a sense from the lover's point of view. Telling statements that conjure up poetry's magic each to leave a deep and lasting impression of its own, none of the three by comparison has the unifying touch of a great poem. In 71 the protective impulse, that so often directs the writer's poetic thought, is trumped by an element of self-pity.

Nevertheless, the chime of the funeral bell that seems to toll throughout is thrillingly measured. Nor do I find I recoil at the writer's self-concern. In self-pity there can be something noble. The quiet of Christina Rossetti's sonnet, 'Remember me when I am gone away', has a purity of tone that in part depends on a reference to an unutterable darkness only known to the speaker. (Her sonnet may well be descended from a reading of this one.) It is easy to sneer at a plea to forget that can mean "remember": thus Booth on 71, 'The narcissistic smugness of the speaker's gesture of selflessness is made ridiculously apparent by the logic of the situation he evokes: a survivor reading a poem about forgetting the deceased speaker must necessarily be reminded of him.' But this is not the sort of logic to apply to a poem.

'Surly' and 'sullen' (2) start the ringing. 'Vile' and 'vilest' (4) continue it; and the strong monosyllabic rhymes confirm the heavy spaced tones. A gentle increase in the urgency of the speaking voice in line 5 and again in line 9 mounts to a still-muted final imperative in line 12; and a dying-away in the couplet completes a poem of some beauty.

A sharp sense of unworth crosses the final stage. At several moments the writer pictures himself as 'in disgrace with Fortune and men's eyes' (29.1) and we do not know why. It may be the commoner all too aware of his lowly status; it may be outside vilification, the 'brand' his name has received in 111, apparently there because of his occupation; it may be anything and nothing. Hamlet's self-disgust, not altogether surprisingly, is apparent in the personal poems of his creator. 'What should such fellows as I do crawling between earth and heaven?' 'Sin of self-love' (62) is there too; and a deal of common humanity, self-less, selfish, far-seeing, blind. There is a sense in which the Sonnets are about only one person.

O lest the world should task you to recite
What merit lived in me that you should love,
After my death, dear love, forget me quite,   3
For you in me can nothing worthy prove;
Unless you would devise some virtuous lie,
To do more for me than mine own desert,   6
And hang more praise upon deceasèd I
Than niggard truth would willingly impart.
O lest your true love may seem false in this,   9
That you for love speak well of me untrue,
My name be buried where my body is,
And live no more to shame nor me nor you.   12
   For I am shamed by that which I bring forth,
   And so should you, to love things nothing worth.

Still dallying in mind with his own death, the poet deepens the note of self-cancellation. One recalls Hardy's Mayor of Casterbridge's instructions: '. . . & that no murners walk behind me at my funeral. / & that no flours be planted on my grave. / & that no man remember me. / To this I put my name.' Michael Henchard's disappointment is more than his life can support; Shakespeare's is a thing of mists and vapours. Yet while Henchard does glancingly mention his daughter, 'That Elizabeth-Jane Farfrae be not told of my death, or made to grieve on account of me,' our speaker here is less self-concerned. If resting on a self-indulgence of sorts, from first line to last the poem is a love-offering.

   With some editors I insert a comma at the end of line 2, so that 'merit' is the clear object of 'love', and both lines 2 and 3 have a certain definite presence, as I imagine the poet intended. Line 11 is a little startling: one almost sees the 'vilest worms' of 71 shredding the name's letters with the body's fibre. We are reminded of the shame by association the poet's name will bring, the world's mockery of the last sonnet, and are unexpectedly given a reason: it is his poor poems (line13). ('Bring forth' is used of poems at 38.11 and 103.1 and they seem at least the chief product in this case.) Modesty as to one's literary efforts was a convention of the time, and Shakespeare's adoption of the sentiment here carries little conviction, especially in view of his claims elsewhere. Yet who is to say he was not overcome, momentarily, by a sense of their trifling nature – especially if a rival poet's offerings were in favour? 'Things nothing worth' at the end are both his poems and, one supposes, things such as the poor wretch himself.

It is a flimsy piece, making play with the poet's vanishing sense of the centre of his own being. Perhaps an artist as committed as he was to the creation of a living surface, if art's process may be referred to in such inexact and crude terms, is the more apt at times to be out of kilter with his own. In the Sonnets is the playwright's raw nerve, in both senses. A vulnerable individual who speaks out is at their core; and so it is in the case of every dramatic character he created, and every last member of his readership and audiences. Even if it is only in 'the sessions of sweet silent thought' (30) that one gives vent to one's own thoughts and feelings, some would say that is what existence is for. As well as encompassing a kind of love, in his poems for the young man, the writer is offering a suggestion of a composite individuality. Taking up different stances, taking aim from different angles, making some kind of mark with everything from boss shots to bull's-eyes, he sketches out a personality – his own – of a composition we know only too well. With its frail edges and indelible if scattered defining lines, it has something of the self-portrait of us all.

That time of year thou mayst in me behold
When yellow leaves, or none, or few do hang
Upon those boughs which shake against the cold,   3
Bare ruined choirs, where late the sweet birds sang.
In me thou seest the twilight of such day
As after sunset fadeth in the west,   6
Which by and by black night doth take away,
Death's second self, that seals up all in rest.
In me thou seest the glowing of such fire   9
That on the ashes of his youth doth lie,
As the death-bed whereon it must expire,
Consumed with that which it was nourished by.   12
    This thou perceiv'st, which makes thy love more strong,
    To love that well which thou must leave ere long.

It is a little hard to believe that Shakespeare oversaw the exact positioning of this sonnet. Surrounded by 71, 72 and 74 it feels shuffled by an editor into a group. The others on his death are 32 and 81, neither surrendering to the ghost of a death-wish as do these four. But 73 is entirely different and separate from those around it.

It is one of those poems, entire in itself, that needs no commentary. The few ideas I offer are to be seen as if from a distance. Some of the poet's songs in his plays cast a spell; this too has a singing softness to it, enclosing it. At the same time it is undreamlike and clear-eyed.

I wonder if the poet had in mind the decline of his creative powers. As a secondary meaning it carries force, in the first quatrain where a knocking of the heart seems to touch the lines with its entrance; and in the third where a remarkable metaphor tumbles on the mind with a more insistent urgency. Nowhere does the author refer to an *oeuvre* rather than to writing as an activity (116.14); but it cannot be wrong to let oneself see a hint here, the question of definite intent set to one side.

Ageing is the deliberative theme: at a slow pace, a faintly hurried action, as of Nature's elements in their round, carries the sense of a quiet inevitability. The couplet is one of overlapping meanings. I take it the foremost is wishful, love me more while I am still here; while in the background a note of gratitude may or may not be overheard, my thanks for loving this ageing creature well.

What is so interesting, compared to the variety of approaches Shakespeare adopts elsewhere, is his acceptance of 'time's injurious hand' (63), the lack of ferocity in the recognition of its touch; and above all his simple request for love, rather than a (sometimes too) explicit demonstration of his own feeling. He has found himself in this sonnet. It is not an argument so much as a sketch of an inner landscape in which in some respect he is at peace. Keats' 'I have been half in love with easeful death' comes to mind, but this is a purer, or at least a less frantic knowing of what Nature has in store. The ghost of a death-wish is no more than a shade in the field of the living. And to call on his friend's affection, at a moment of such harmony, is somehow in itself a gesture of love for him as active as any in the more demonstrative poems. One could wish, perhaps, that the mind of the man had allowed its descriptive energies a little more room, in the work as a whole. But even as one wishes it one remembers that the pulsating analytical drive, that so much characterises the poet, created an overview of the workings of individuals and society, that has added its own element to the journey of civilisation. One knows, too, and this piece reminds us of it, that he never forgot the first requirement of poetry: to let the words carry a touch of beauty.

But be contented: when that fell arrest
Without all bail shall carry me away,
My life hath in this line some interest,   3
Which for memorial still with thee shall stay.
When thou reviewest this, thou dost review
The very part was consecrate to thee.   6
The earth can have but earth, which is his due;
My spirit is thine, the better part of me.
So then thou hast but lost the dregs of life,   9
The prey of worms, my body being dead,
The coward conquest of a wretch's knife,
Too base of thee to be rememberèd.   12
    The worth of that is that which it contains,
    And that is this, and this with thee remains.

The poet stands by his art. Assumed or felt, the revulsion of 72 is short-lived: his lines are the best of him and they are 'consecrate to thee' (6). For a moment the idea of the young man as a symbol of all his readership crosses the mind. In the logic of poetry it has every right to do so.

The image moves from Hamlet's 'fell sergeant, Death . . . strict in his arrest' to a financial setting the author often turns to ('bail' and 'interest' here), to a glimpsed idea from line 6 of a burial service. Typically the transitions are at once seamless and intellectually challenging; Shakespeare's verse makes a defter use of the imagination than anyone's. A series of quick-changing pictorial suggestions, some of which are left to linger and develop on their own, is his hallmark. Accompanied by a definiteness and clarity of tone, the whole governed by an immaculate use of the pentameter (and rhyme where applicable), his poetry does the opposite of bewilder. Rather it is a stimulus to a state of wakefulness the receptive mind is refreshed by, and otherwise not often in. It may not happen on first reading, but once one becomes familiar with a passage, something of that order I would hazard tends to come about. (I would except from this his early rhymed poems, *Venus and Adonis* and *Lucrece*, and a fair amount of the text of what appear to be the early plays.)

Of course one cannot sum up 'the worth of that' (13), least of all in the case of this poet. But given the poet's return of faith in his work, and the implied statement as to its complete importance in his inner life, it does not seem inappropriate to ponder the magic a little, yet again. Shakespeare is not so egoistic as to regard his poems as more than an expression of affection. It is his love that is his all, unyielding and undying. One way or another, a sonnet is an act of homage. In those days art had a purpose that could be defined. Nevertheless, for a modern reader the commitment to the work itself is also telling. He is empty without it.

'The coward conquest of a wretch's knife' (11) I take to be an example of the trivial cheapness that life can be forfeit to, rather than identifying 'wretch' with Death as some do. Shakespeare may have had Marlowe in mind, who died in 1593 after being stabbed in a lodging-house. Two extraordinarily gifted playwrights, they probably took a burning interest in each other's work. I would close by observing Shakespeare's play with pronouns in the couplet, with its indication of a semantic shift. There is a point to emerge from this method of resolving matters, a word-process I drew attention to earlier; but the perfect illustration is to come.

So are you to my thoughts as food to life,
Or as sweet seasoned showers are to the ground;
And for the peace of you I hold such strife   3
As 'twixt a miser and his wealth is found;
Now proud as an enjoyer, and anon
Doubting the filching age will steal his treasure;   6
Now counting best to be with you alone,
Then bettered that the world may see my pleasure;
Sometime all full with feasting on your sight,   9
And by and by clean starvèd for a look;
Possessing or pursuing no delight
Save what is had or must from you be took.   12
    Thus do I pine and surfeit day by day,
    Or gluttoning on all, or all away.

A gentle poem, a world removed from 118 where the idea of appetite and surfeit is used to express an altogether more violent state of mind. Each line here, at least of the first ten, has an easy, undemanding charm; the 'strife' of line 3 is barely felt. And yet, again, one can imagine it said with an agitation working itself up. The single sentence of the dodeka gathers an urgency that while never frantic, is expressive of the speaker's frustration; and it can be read either with that emphasis, or as still governed by the pure calm of the opening. Such a choice lies within the reading contract, so to speak, of every poem.

'The peace of you' (3) is an unusual venture for the author: imprecise, nebulously suggestive, dictated more perhaps by the minor role of the antithesis it sets up with 'strife', than by a clear meaning. And yet in itself it is a beautiful expression. An unexpected departure from the idea of refreshment in the opening similes, it still claims its place as if by right in the run of the lines. And surely the primary meaning – the contentment that is the gift of love – is clear to the reader of a love-poem, even if its borders are a little vague. Perhaps the image of the miser and his gold takes away any question-mark the phrase may raise; though for me an exclamation-mark (so to speak) at once balances it.

The miser, quick to usurp the writer's persona ('his treasure' . . . 'my pleasure'), has something of the comic about him; and yet, from what we know from past poems, lines 6 and 8 also carry a warning, to himself as much as to his friend. There are thieves about. But there is little enough of that: the poem is in essence the exposition of an idea, the possessive aspect of love; and despite the closing sketch of someone desperate to find a middle way, there is little sense of his actual suffering. An aspect of the sequence 1–126 seeks more to describe the condition than the experience. It does not happen with the sonnets to the woman.

It is a minor aspect; for the first series is shot through with the recall of some kind of experience of the neediness of love, its closeness and distance, the impulse to serve it gives rise to. There is something unreal in the presentation of it all, under the mediaeval canopy so to speak, the knight-errant's banner. But a driven engagement with reality is never quite absent, whether or not the scenario is true to life. Yet at the same time as recording the experience – whatever it was – the writer is doing something else. It could be put a number of different ways. He is describing an ideal. He is entering the gates of a garden of innocence. He is intent to show the blind shadow of an individual. (*Hamlet* and the Sonnets have more than a little in common.) Instinctively he is doing more than to record: he is always exploring, aiming at some kind of completeness. 1–126 is a voyage to map a far sea.

Why is my verse so barren of new pride,
So far from variation or quick change?
Why with the time do I not glance aside 3
To new-found methods and to compounds strange?
Why write I still all one, ever the same,
And keep invention in a noted weed, 6
That every word doth almost tell my name,
Showing their birth and where they did proceed?
O know, sweet love, I always write of you, 9
And you and love are still my argument;
So all my best is dressing old words new,
Spending again what is already spent. 12
    For as the sun is daily new and old,
      So is my love still telling what is told.

The poet may be thinking of revised and re-published sonnet-sequences of his contemporaries Drayton and Daniel, and commenting on his own dogged refusal to touch up or change his work. His own approach to publication, for whatever reason, appears to have been as much hands-off as hands-on. He is unlikely to be referring to the possibility of writing personal poems other than sonnets. Lines 7–8 may carry an allusion to his own sonnet style or stamp, three quatrains and a couplet, that perhaps in private circulation before publication had come to be identified with him. In 1598 Francis Meres wrote, 'As the soul of Euphorbus was thought to live in Pythagoras: so the sweet witty soul of Ovid lives in mellifluous and honey-tongued Shakespeare, witness his *Venus and Adonis*, his *Lucrece*, his sugared sonnets among his private friends.' At any rate he finds in his devotion to his habitual approach, whatever exactly he means by that, a new and rather charming compliment to pay his friend.

As we have seen there is any amount of 'variation or quick change' (2) in the content of his offerings. It is the outward form of his verse the poet seems to take as a metaphor for constancy. As a coiner of new words, new ways to present the action of a play, above all perhaps new sonnet-material, it is not enough to call Shakespeare inventive: he broke new ground as a condition of his being. But he was also a simple man, who followed a theme through to the end; and his sonnet-form quickly became integral to a quest more private and personal than the theatre dramas. As well as an expression of love this poem is also something of a sonneteer's credo. He stands by his method.

The opening question (or something like it) may have been put by his friend, as line 9 half-suggests. If so one would hope he treasured the reply. Lines 9–10 are surely moving in their 'simple truth' (66.11 and 138.8). Love is indeed his argument. Time after time the poet stands before us; we hear the voice of an unaffected human being. Time after time he is swept away, caught up in the overtures of gallantry, tucked away behind a compliment's gesture, near buried in a semantic ruse. But in every piece (bar a doubtful few) he reappears, never quite leaves the stage, and his presence stays in the reader's mind as if personally known to him or her. Such is the importance of lines like these (and there are many of them).

The simplicity of the couplet, that appears to work perfectly well without a second look, still carries a touch of cunning. At one remove the sun's brilliance is that of the friend's existence. The poet sees him 'telling', or going over, reading his 'old words new' (11). But it is also the light and warmth of the poems themselves ('my love' now the abstract concept). Nothing is routine in love, however much it appears so.

Thy glass will show thee how thy beauties wear,
Thy dial how thy precious minutes waste;
The vacant leaves thy mind's imprint will bear,   3
And of this book this learning mayst thou taste.
The wrinkles which thy glass will truly show
Of mouthèd graves will give thee memory;   6
Thou by thy dial's shady stealth mayst know
Time's thievish progress to eternity.
Look what thy memory cannot contain,   9
Commit to these waste blanks, and thou shalt find
Those children nursed, delivered from thy brain,
To take a new acquaintance of thy mind.   12
   These offices, so oft as thou wilt look,
   Shall profit thee and much enrich thy book.

                                      15

This can be taken with 122 as a delightful poetic account of a notebook given by Shakespeare to his friend for him to record his thoughts in, returned to the giver when so used for his appreciation – to be carelessly given away by the poet to somebody else! Though there are different interpretations this one appears to hold together perfectly well; and if accepted it offers an interesting sidelight on Shakespeare's way of viewing the friendship, when his mind is on the mundane.

    I imagine the poem was presented with the notebook (perhaps tucked in it). The book would have been finely-produced, something to treasure. The mirror and the clock tell the same harsh tale as always but the empty pages of this book offer the chance of a more deeply instructive lesson, one that one teaches oneself. The professional writer is anxious for his friend to profit from the craft himself, at an elementary stage. What better way than to compose and commit to paper thoughts you fear your memory will not hang onto, and in the process of deliv-

ering these children of the brain, after so nursing them, to find
they have an existence of their own, 'to take a new acquaintance
of thy mind' – ? It is a wonderful insight into the art of what is
known now as creative writing, which of course may include
maxims and suchlike. In fact from 122 we learn the poor lad
seems to have filled the book with his loving thoughts towards
our man, which makes the latter's oversight hilarious. But we
shall come to that in due course.

'Mouthèd' (line 6) suggests gaping, ready to take the body.
Line 8 is one of Shakespeare's immortal phrases, seemingly
effortless. One could write a page on 'thievish' and say nothing.
The 'offices' of line 13 are 'duties', that once undertaken will
reward the young writer more and more, when he returns to look
over his efforts; and naturally will make what will now truly be
his book, something of real value.

The dial of line 7 may be a sundial but a clock's hands may
have cast a shadow too. The direction of the poet's thoughts is
clear enough; and is it not marvellously different from his usual
line? The older man is an instructor, taking the younger under
his wing, passing on a treasured hint, about no less than how to
think, in a writer's terms. At the same time there is a lightness
attached to the occasion, a pleasure of the moment; it is some-
thing transient, everyday, the offering of a gift. The poet's head
is very much in the here-and-now. This is reflected in his real-
istic words as to what one finds in the mirror. In sonnet 3 'thy
glass' shows a 'golden time', a face of such youthful beauty as
must needs be almost magically reproduced in another. But this
poem is in a different vein.

So oft have I invoked thee for my Muse,
And found such fair assistance in my verse
As every alien pen hath got my use,   3
And under thee their poesy disperse.
Thine eyes, that taught the dumb on high to sing,
And heavy ignorance aloft to fly,   6
Have added feathers to the learnèd's wing,
And given grace a double majesty.
Yet be most proud of that which I compile,   9
Whose influence is thine, and born of thee.
In others' works thou dost but mend the style,
And arts with thy sweet graces gracèd be;   12
    But thou art all my art, and dost advance
    As high as learning my rude ignorance.

Momentarily in 77 at a remove from the convention of the humble lover and the imperious beloved, the reader is soon returned to the pageantry that defines the personal poetry of the time. In this and the two following poems, and again later, Shakespeare takes up the issue of rival outpourings, to further reflect on and set out his own position. While one does not doubt the poet speaks with 'the voice of souls' (69), at the same time one sees a slighted man take refuge in a practised asylum. Self-effacement is his strong card.

It has its own truth. Whether inspired by the speaker's own abundance of verse or directly by the generous interest of his youthful muse, others are crowding him out of his niche, as it seems. With a striking tribute to the divine power of the beloved (lines 5–6), he contrasts his simplicity with his rivals' sophistication, his artlessness with their art. Lines 9–10 speak from the heart – how else can one take it? – and the figure Shakespeare adopts for his knightly quest, where the young man represents an unattainable goal, is also an ordinary fellow in the privileged position of a dear friend. As such he is able to represent the very substance of love, all gloss discarded.

This is the paradox: the mediaeval quest, and the untidy everyday journey of disappointments and delights, reach one and the same noble conclusion, even though one can have no conclusion and the other no nobility. The two concepts feed each other, merge and separate; and the passionate pilgrim, a literary child of the age, supplies the ardour for a loving persona that is ageless.

There is a suggestion of a swooping movement in the lines: 'disperse', 'on high', 'aloft to fly', 'wing', 'as high as learning'. The opposition of learning and ignorance lingers too, of graceful and gauche; and even if one does not know of the plays, one suspects the speaker is not unlearned; and one knows his words can soar and his lines gambol with an inimitable grace. Poetry is made of paradox, a hesitancy catches at its boldness, all the confidences it shares with its readers are subject to a second reading, as a new creation of the mind touches down on firm ground. It can all happen very quickly; but ambiguity is always there, in some way or ways, to play its part.

And so the Shakespeare of the Sonnets is an ambiguous figure. Nor are any of his dramatic characters cardboard cut-outs. But there is someone we can know, a voice speaking from paper one can almost be in touch with through one's life. In these poems one makes the acquaintance of an unusual individual, but one whom it is a privilege as it were to visit and be visited by. And unlike someone in a play – and however much an invention – he is someone on our level.

Whilst I alone did call upon thy aid,
My verse alone had all thy gentle grace,
But now my gracious numbers are decayed,   3
And my sick Muse doth give another place.
I grant, sweet love, thy lovely argument
Deserves the travail of a worthier pen;   6
Yet what of thee thy poet doth invent
He robs thee of and pays it thee again.
He lends thee virtue, and he stole that word   9
From thy behaviour; beauty doth he give
And found it in thy cheek; he can afford
No praise to thee but what in thee doth live.   12
    Then thank him not for that which he doth say,
    Since what he owes thee thou thyself dost pay.

So far from reflecting anguish, now his verse is out of favour, the sonnets that arise from the situation amount to little more than a light shrug. The piercing sadness of separation we have seen before, and that is to haunt him again, is absent. It may be his person is welcome but his poetry less so. Meanwhile he finds ways to chide his friend, to advance his cause or to run down a rival's, and the sequence has a new angle to play its poetic turns upon. The knight has a further opportunity for gallantry; the quest is continued. Though he calls his lines ('numbers') 'decayed' (3), this poem appears as much as any to exhibit its own 'gentle grace' (2), and to delight in so doing. Perhaps he is making a point.

    Mellifluous repetition ('alone . . . alone', 'grace . . . gracious', 'love . . . lovely'), internal rhyme ('call . . . all') and inversion ('of thee . . . thee of') perform a pretty dance. Indeed the poem is an example of little more than a labyrinthine prettiness, for the exceptional paucity of the immediate argument more or less denies any serious intent. The whole is both intricate and charming, with a certain yearning for recognition at its root, and almost openly trite. The poet loves to practise his art; the Platonic ideal presents him with a new opening. And still 'thy lovely argument' (5; and see 76.10), the lodestar to a long voyage, is not forgotten.

If the rival has been presumptuous in his writing (lines 7–12) the speaker can hardly criticise him for it. 'The raven chides blackness', says Ulysses in *Troilus and Cressida* when Ajax comments on Achilles' pride, in a striking forerunner of the pot and the kettle. But of course that praise is a robbery is the merest conceit. It is all a sweeping compliment, meaningless in its exterior; and yet the light loveliness of the verse says something more.

It is a moment to consider what Shakespeare means when he first announces, in 18, 'So long as men can breathe or eyes can see, / So long lives this, and this gives life to thee'. It is clear enough that it is not the personality of his friend that we meet as a living presence in the Sonnets; nor is it his physical appearance, which is paid court to in such superlatives as the poet himself ridicules, notably in a poem to the lady later on. One may say it is the poet's own love, stored beyond the body, that later lives can bring to life; and there is truth in that. Art is an awakening of the potent within the artist, a seed that others bring to fruition. But it is not all about the artist. There is an apprehension of beauty, in art, and of a deeper meaning than the practical side of life tends to have time or room for. Usually it is at once associated with the subject-matter. The link is less immediate in the modern approach (but no less valid); and so it is with the Sonnets, four hundred years back. The brilliance of Shakespeare's lines brings to light love's condition. Both characters are illuminated, the one by his feeling and the other by his being. The latter is at the back of it all: so the young man lives.

O, how I faint when I of you do write,
Knowing a better spirit doth use your name,
And in the praise thereof spends all his might,   3
To make me tongue-tied, speaking of your fame.
But since your worth, wide as the ocean is,
The humble as the proudest sail doth bear,   6
My saucy bark, inferior far to his,
On your broad main doth wilfully appear.
Your shallowest help will hold me up afloat,   9
While he upon your soundless deep doth ride;
Or, being wrecked, I am a worthless boat,
He of tall building and of goodly pride.   12
    Then if he thrive and I be cast away,
    The worst was this: my love was my decay.

A touch of writer's block, that is made more of later, itself provides the material for a fresh approach. How is it to be explained away? The author is generous to his rival, 'a better spirit' (2). The metaphor he adopts for the three of them is rather wonderful, the broad ocean and the two vessels, one with little defence, at the mercy of the elements. Shakespeare may have had in mind 'the small, mobile ships used by the English at the time of the Spanish Armada and the larger, more impressive and more heavily armed Spanish galleons' (Duncan-Jones). The implication of the other's victory is a double-edged one in context. The poet's customary deference, in part a convention, in part a port of convenience so to speak, from which to conduct operations, has a truth to it of more moment than any artificial aspect. A relinquishing of selfhood we know by now is one of the deepest impulses of the man. To be at one with himself he has to lose himself. It is a characteristic, perhaps, of a kind of person hesitatingly revealed, over 1–126, in the writer's self-presentation.

To know such a call, at times to heed it, is in the nature of the lover; as it surely is, no less compellingly, in the related position of the artist.

Here his poetry (he says) is enfeebled by the mighty appearance of the other. But still he is able to write. A self-deprecating humour in the image of the 'saucy bark', as it bobs its way through the lines, is an attractive touch. One hopes the echo of the poet's name in the first syllable of 'wilfully' is accidental (8), but rather fears it may be a too-deliberate attempt to raise a smile. The play in a couple of later sonnets with the name and its homonyms reaches a desperate level. 'Soundless' (10) is both 'unfathomable' and 'silent', a lovely reflection on the youth and his status within the metaphor. Line 12 surely led T.S.Eliot indirectly to his closing lines on Phlebas the Phoenician, in *Death by Water* in *The Waste Land*. 'Gentile or Jew, / O you who turn the wheel and look to windward, / Consider Phlebas, who was once handsome and tall as you.' Eliot aside, the picture the line offers, including the contrast with the 'worthless boat' (11), takes us momentarily into the realm of epic.

The couplet finely disengages from a panoramic scene with the double meaning in 'cast away' (13, 'wrecked' and 'abandoned'), and the neatly weighted double sense of the final phrase. 'My love' as the feeling leaves the responsibility with the speaker; as the person, with the first reader of the lines (as we presume). One wonders, sometimes, what the young man made of these song-offerings (assuming he existed). It is hard to believe he really preferred the verses of another . . . and yet, considering the ready appeal of cliché to so many readers of poetry, all too easy to imagine it may have been so.

Or I shall live your epitaph to make,
Or you survive when I in earth am rotten;
From hence your memory death cannot take,   3
Although in me each part will be forgotten.
Your name from hence immortal life shall have,
Though I, once gone, to all the world must die.   6
The earth can yield me but a common grave,
When you entombèd in men's eyes shall lie.
Your monument shall be my gentle verse,   9
Which eyes not yet created shall o'er-read,
And tongues to be your being shall rehearse
When all the breathers of this world are dead.   12
    You still shall live, such virtue hath my pen,
    Where breath most breathes, even in the mouths of men.

Though the next poems 82–86 continue the rival poet theme of 78–80, this a little surprisingly returns to the deepest and dearest motive behind all his lines to the young man. In the constitution of art it is an article of faith that it shall supersede the merely temporal; but few artists "dig this out" of what they are doing, to announce it at large. They may do to themselves; but to Shakespeare there was no dividing-line, in the genesis of his personal poetry, between what he said to himself and what he said to the world. A necessary explicitness led to the declaration that for love he wrote, and he wrote to preserve his love's being. The 'sick Muse' that gives rise to verses that are 'decayed' (79) is forgotten; here is no 'worthless boat' (80); he has all the confidence he had when he was first able to reveal his true motive for writing (18). Yet there is no contradiction, but rather a writing as from different levels, that the various poems reveal.

    One may find one aspect of the position he adopts baffling, and accuse the writer of being disingenuous, in claiming line 5 after line 4. The author's name is likely to be remembered too. But to set out the proposition in such terms is to betray it. He is simply unable to intrude upon the space he is making for his loved one. There is no balancing of an equation, he is nothing, his love, his art, his other self is all. In the same way 'your name' in line 5 is no name, at least none that we can be sure of; it is the being, made tangible in the poetry, of the invisible person. Whereas the poet's name may or may not continue – no doubt here he thinks not – but as a term for something ever-fresh and cherished in its perfection, it will fall away and die.

Line 9 is one of my most treasured lines of poetry. Supple and clear in intent, it has its own nobility. Again we see the kind of nameless memorial that Shakespeare envisages. The tomb, the monument, even the second hearse (in 'rehearse', 11) catch at an idea of a new form of the journey of death. To state it openly, as a re-entrance to life, would not have worked; instinctively the poet leaves it to act as a kind of subliminal suggestion. In this as in other ways, in 1–126, he lets us know what his poems are for.

On the deepest level, then, he has no thought for himself, and his claim is not a boastful one ('such virtue hath my pen', 13). But we are never solely at one level. The self is mixed with the selfless; and we may even enjoy the ego of the writer, his self-belief. Everywhere in the poems there is a touch of paradox. But we remember 'the worth of that is that which it contains' (74.13). In the writer 'each part will be forgotten' (4) – and so far as the biography is concerned, by and large it has been. He exists in his work as a whole, rather in the same way that his loved one exists, in the sonnets to him. The name does not matter.

167

I grant thou wert not married to my Muse,
And therefore mayst without attaint o'erlook
The dedicated words which writers use   3
Of their fair subject, blessing every book.
Thou art as fair in knowledge as in hue,
Finding thy worth a limit past my praise,   6
And therefore art enforced to seek anew
Some fresher stamp of the time-bettering days.
And do so, love; yet when they have devised   9
What strainèd touches rhetoric can lend,
Thou truly fair wert truly sympathised
In true plain words by thy true-telling friend;   12
    And their gross painting might be better used
    Where cheeks need blood; in thee it is abused.

There is a fascinating difference here between octave and sestet. Beneath the surface, courteous and tolerant as it is of the youth's interest in the poems of others, a certain anger waits to make a clear point. The poem may be a reply to a complaint of the youth as to a lack of sincerity in Shakespeare's poetic style. That would fit the sense of a mounting irritation at what is felt as an outright injustice, and the insistent repetition in lines 11–12. It is one of the sonnets in which the relationship comes to life a little more.

The meaning takes a little sifting-out. The speaker admits his friend need have no special attachment to his own poetic approach, and may quite properly ('without attaint', 2) read the admiring words of other writers, exclaiming delightedly over every sheet of paper (for 'book' as such see 23.9). So far, so fair enough; but the second quatrain stretches the opening smile to something a little more forced, in its palpably thin argument. Your knowledge or wisdom, as fine as your complexion, tells you my words will never accomplish a fitting paean of praise, and so you must look elsewhere. A new generation of poets, more talented than those of my time, will no doubt furnish what you are looking for. ('Stamp' may add the suggestion of a printed book.) One wonders what the recipient may have thought of the assumption as to his character here; but as always it is a not quite relevant question. The biography piques the interest; but it lies outside the life the poems let us know of. The majestic presence, the god requiring worship, is all too clearly a part of a convention.

What we do know of is the writer's own pique. At the start of line 9 I take 'love' to be a vocative, not a verb, and insert a comma before it. An affectionate voice is with us a moment; and then we hear what he really thinks. As against the ridiculous hyperbole of other poets his verses tell the truth, in their simplicity showing the beauty of the subject. ('Sympathised' is 'depicted' as well as 'understood'.) No cosmetics are needed; they may prettify others but make your cheeks ugly. The metaphor is of a purity to conceal which is a crime.

The beauty of the natural state is at stake here. The writer's own hyperbole, as a way of expressing admiration, is born of a convention, to an extent a means to an end. His need to draw the reader's attention to the idea of an unvarnished essence makes that clear. The physical beauty he lauds is always at some level a picture of the soul. What he abhors in other writers is the simplistic adherence to a surface description, the inability to tell means from end. In almost every sonnet that mentions the subject's looks something beyond them is at the heart of things. (99 is an exception, which we shall come to.) No doubt he is also wearied by his rivals' less inventive art in general, and most of all by the boy's interest in it. At the end of the poem, as here and there in other sonnets, a note of reprimand lingers to be overheard.

I never saw that you did painting need,
And therefore to your fair no painting set;
I found (or thought I found) you did exceed 3
The barren tender of a poet's debt;
And therefore have I slept in your report,
That you yourself, being extant, well might show 6
How far a modern quill doth come too short,
Speaking of worth, what worth in you doth grow.
This silence for my sin you did impute 9
Which shall be most my glory, being dumb;
For I impair not beauty, being mute,
When others would give life and bring a tomb. 12
    There lives more life in one of your fair eyes
    Than both your poets can in praise devise.

Whether or not the last poem was in response to a comment from his friend, this one is, as he gives us to understand (9); and here it is his silence he is defending. Line 4 has haunted the poet in me. Shakespeare seems to imply that no writer can do justice to such a subject (with a faint thrilling suggestion of a double sense in 'tender' of 'offer' and 'tenderness'). But as with the 'deep-sunken eyes' of sonnet 2 the phrase has revealed an added intent, though to what if any degree it was the writer's one cannot tell. The line that one would cross in the making of a poem, if one is rash enough to think about it, can seem all too far away.

The natural touch of the parenthesis in line 3 brings the speaker closer, to us as to his friend. The spontaneous voice is key to the whole. 'Modern' (7) is 'commonplace', 'trite'. The poem touches on what it is, to 'give life' (12) to a subject. Here it is seen as an impossibility, at least for this subject; but in 81, and over 1–126 as a whole, the poet has the courage of his conviction. A "modern" phrase in itself, in such a context to 'give life' can be seen to require a commitment of a certain bravery. One begins to grasp a little more securely the nexus between love and art within the sonnets to the young man.

Sometimes we are aware of a number of rival writers but there would appear to be one in particular, as here. In a nice symmetry the couplet has the two poets as one in their unavailing artifice, and an eye of the subject standing for both eyes and his full living being. One feels Shakespeare is slowly allowing the aim of these poems to come into his grasp, not too far ahead of his reader. I have used the word "quest" before and gradually behind that a clearer idea of the journey may be beginning to emerge. It depends on the poems before us and is not something that can be hurried.

A long sequence of verses in the same form is more than likely to succumb to a kind of prettiness at some points, a form of 'goldengate' (51, note), that if not looked at too carefully by the reader can be easy on the eye; but that robs the petal of its colour and the leaf of its sting. Sonnet-sequences are fertile ground for this fungus. Shakespeare's lines occasionally take a spot or two; but the inner vitality, the life that is given them to give, is resistant. It is a strain of being altogether rich and rare.

Silence is a part of it. A facility such as the poet's with line and rhyme breeds its own dangers. The last thing on earth he would want to do is 'bring a tomb' (12). A discussion in this vein on lines as light as these may miss the immediate point of the poem, which is to develop and continue one theme of a number; and it runs the risk of taint by repetition and circuitousness. But that is a risk it shares (if less successfully) with its subject.

Who is it that says most? Which can say more
Than this rich praise, that you alone are you?
In whose confine immurèd is the store   3
Which should example where your equal grew?
Lean penury within that pen doth dwell
That to his subject lends not some small glory;   6
But he that writes of you, if he can tell
That you are you, so dignifies his story.
Let him but copy what in you is writ,   9
Not making worse what Nature made so clear,
And such a counterpart shall fame his wit,
Making his style admirèd everywhere.   12
    You to your beauteous blessings add a curse,
    Being fond on praise, which makes your praises worse.

In the original the three question-marks are all commas. There is often a need to update the punctuation in Q, Thomas Thorpe's printed edition and the first text we have; but generally, while editors may differ, the issues raised are minor and uncontroversial. Here the choice to be made is more significant, as the tenor and shape of the sonnet come into play.

The crux lies in the emphases of the first quatrain. As I take it the speaker follows on from the close of 83 to ask which of the two poets is the more expressive. The rest of the poem answers the question, with a barb at the end for the fair youth: it is one of those moments when he is on our level. But up to the last line he is the paragon.

As such, is the store 'which should example where your equal grew' (4) locked away ('immurèd', 3) in him, or is it rather not to be found in the speaker, his rival or indeed any poet? It depends on whether 'whose' of line 3 is read as interrogative, as in the text above, or as relative with 'you' of line 2 as antecedent.

Either way, lines 3–4 carry an interesting concept, that of the wherewithal to create a proper account of the subject's excellence. If located in the young man, it is the collection of qualities that constitute his uniqueness, and that no outside agency can parallel, by way of some kind of poetic description. If as above, the suggestion is that the task is theoretically possible. Following on that, the required quality in the writer's 'store' can only be that of an exact and unpretentious accuracy. (130 has the other side of the same coin.) The implication in the speaker's favour is clear. In addition, the text as above conveys a stronger sense of astonishment at the non-pareil.

The second two quatrains seem to develop the idea of a 'store' as the poetic imagination. The only way to success is not an effort at fine portraiture that must fail, so 'making worse what nature made so clear' (10), but simply to state, and by so doing to celebrate, 'that you alone are you' (2). This is to 'copy what in you is writ' (9), to make no false comparison, and to remark truly upon that uniqueness, impossible otherwise to grasp. To make such a 'counterpart' (11, 'copy') will bring fame, underlined in a faintly otiose line 12.

The speaker seems to come to the end of his latest bout of magniloquence, and to render the god human in the couplet, almost with a sigh of relief. 'Being fond on praise' (14) is one of a very few personal touches, that as each occurs make it hard to believe there was no historical young man of the Sonnets. As often the final phrase packs a punch. The youth's vanity makes the praises that are heaped on him less accurate. And a flicker of "double-take" enters the whole: is not the encomium subverted by the poet's following his own advice? Accuracy can be a double-edged weapon.

'You alone are you.' The phrase resonates, a bare truth, at the heart of the extravaganza.

My tongue-tied Muse in manners holds her still,
While comments of your praise, richly compiled,
Reserve their character with golden quill   3
And precious phrase by all the Muses filed.
I think good thoughts, whilst other write good words,
And like unlettered clerk still cry Amen   6
To every hymn that able spirit affords
In polished form of well-refinèd pen.
Hearing you praised, I say, ''Tis so, 'tis true,'   9
And to the most of praise add something more;
But that is in my thought, whose love to you,
Though words come hindmost, holds his rank before.   12
    Then others for the breath of words respect,
    Me for my dumb thoughts, speaking in effect.

Outwardly admiring of his rivals' art, with a deftly visual comparison he puts them in their place. While his muse stays in the background like a modest and demure girl, others' verses announce themselves vaingloriously. An exquisite sense of their self-consciousness (line 3) and grandiloquence (4) undercuts the speaker's deferential pose. And yet his apparent courtesy is not all a fraud. In part a cover from which to conduct a subtle attack, the pose also mirrors the self-effacing nature of the man. If his friend likes his rivals' poems, who is he to say he should not?

So the poem presents the divided personality of its writer. The same opposition is manifest throughout: we know our poet as we read. Self-doubt and self-belief hang together in a precarious unity. Unusually explicit in his case, it is a mark of the artist.

'Reserve' (3) amounts to 'preserve'; 'character' is the written letters. 'Filed' (4) is 'polished', also 'sharpened' with the back-suggestion of the quill pen. Line 5 is lovely, the good girl in her simplicity keeping to the background, while under her prim demeanour another gender has another agenda. ('Other' is 'others'; there is the usual sense of a number of rivals and one in particular.) The clerk is a parish clerk who loudly leads the congregation in its responses and amens; hence the hymn; but 'that able spirit' does not quite seem to find its ease in the line in which it appears, 7. It may be the 'better spirit' of 80 (from which 'tongue-tied' is repeated), the rival poet; or any talented writer, 'that' as 'which'. 'Spirit' may look forward to the next sonnet, where suddenly it is very much more tangible; or it may be an attempt to continue the metaphor of church and congregation. 'Able' may be a misprint for 'abler', with reference to one rival in particular. Or perhaps there is a meaning we miss now that was more available then. In any case it presents only the tiniest hitch.

The poem nicely deflates the self-regarding poetry of the rival or rivals, while appearing to defer to it; and finds good reason for the writer's dry patch. The paradox of the tongue-tied muse who seems to be able to deliver a sonnet at will, as sharp-tongued as you like, is so familiar, in one guise or another, that it needs no comment. But it seems to me the last four lines come to a deeper point. Thought and silence are at a premium. The final phrase seems to say more than is on the page. 'In effect' is 'in reality': silence is the true speaking. There is no reason to suppose Shakespeare knew of the silence of the Buddha as such. But many have had the same insight. It is only a hint here, riding under the canopy of a love poem, so to speak. Yet if one is inclined to take the Sonnets, however loosely, as a single poem, it can be seen as about more than love. It carries about it the elastic, changing personality of the individual, made visible by a defining commitment. It is of the betrayal of words and of words in their truth. It is a journey of self-knowledge, *Hamlet* from the inside.

Was it the proud full sail of his great verse,
Bound for the prize of all too precious you,
That did my ripe thoughts in my brain inhearse,   3
Making their tomb the womb wherein they grew?
Was it his spirit, by spirits taught to write
Above a mortal pitch, that struck me dead?   6
No, neither he, nor his compeers by night
Giving him aid, my verse astonishèd.
He, nor that affable familiar ghost   9
Which nightly gulls him with intelligence,
As victors of my silence cannot boast;
I was not sick of any fear from thence.   12
    But when your countenance filled up his line
    Then lacked I matter; that enfeebled mine.

Returning to the ship 'of tall building and of goodly pride' of 80, Shakespeare is finally unambiguous as to its worth. 'The button is off the foil,' remarks Dover Wilson. It is possible the rival was George Chapman, who announced in verse a visitation from the spirit of Homer that led to his translation of the *Iliad* and the *Odyssey* (that Keats so much admired). Lines 3–4 aptly describe a kind of creative death at the moment of taking wing in words. 'Spirit' (5) may mean energy or imaginative power, but I think it is at this point that the gloves are off (to be less Shakespearian than Dover Wilson), and at last our man can let fly. (It is the final sonnet to refer to a rival poet in the sequence as it stands.) The spirit, then, is a supernatural being within the rival that the spirits of those long dead tutor in his amazing poetic craft.

Shakespeare's scorn comes out beautifully in a single word. The 'affable familiar ghost', presumably some kind of ethereal composite of the rival's support team, visits him (in dream?)

with tips ('intelligence'), and *gulls* him, night after night. Finally in exasperation the truer poet has broken free from cover. It is hardly the other's verse that that has cowed him into laying down his pen. But the friend's interest in it has dealt a body-blow. 'Countenance' (line 13) is both face and favour. I see 'filled up his line' as suggesting a physical unity as the poems are brought near the face to be read; and also a swelling of the sail of the first line, an ennobling or enrichment, as if imparted by the nod of approval. And so we have another reason for the prolific author's silence.

He clearly views the 'supernatural soliciting' the other appears to be known for as crackpot. But many in the pre-modern audiences of *Macbeth* would have half-believed in the witches. The idea of a heavenly familiar to lend counsel and aid was widespread (as it still is in diluted form). Gerolamo Cardano, a widely-read thinker of the 16th century, is described in Robert Burton's *Anatomy of Melancholy* (1621) thus: 'Cardan . . . out of the doctrine of Stoics, will have some of these genii (for so he calls them) to be desirous of men's company, very affable and familiar with them.' Perhaps both Burton and Shakespeare were using a version of Cardano's words (his most popular work was translated into English in the 1570s). Otherwise Burton was using Shakespeare's; or there is an unlikely coincidence. At any rate the poet's phrase, though he may have scorned the idea behind it, is a rather splendid one.

A number of sonnets follow on loss and separation. If one takes the order of the poems as the author's there is a clear impli-cation of his (his persona's) being edged out by another. But the ordering may be Thorpe's. In any case the "why" of separation does not matter. The Sonnets are what they are, a rhapsodic sequence of the near and far, in terms of a force that is all about us (see note to sonnet 12, end).

Farewell, thou art too dear for my possessing,
And like enough thou know'st thy estimate;
The charter of thy worth gives thee releasing;   3
My bonds in thee are all determinate.
For how do I hold thee but by thy granting,
And for that riches where is my deserving?   6
The cause of this fair gift in me is wanting,
And so my patent back again is swerving.
Thyself thou gav'st, thy own worth then not knowing,   9
Or me, to whom thou gav'st it, else mistaking;
So thy great gift, upon misprision growing,
Comes home again, on better judgement making.   12
    Thus have I had thee, as a dream doth flatter,
    In sleep a king, but waking no such matter.

I remember listening to W.H.Auden on the radio quoting line 1 for the double meaning of 'dear'. I think he may have appreciated the sequence in part and whole as much as anyone has or will. Beneath a financial/legal estimate of worth and its consequence, the poem's suggestion is that what is dear to one, one does not own. The acceptance by the speaker of his separation from the beloved is at the full. Now and then a sonnet comes up that commits the whole man. When this happens the rhetoric is there to make a statement, the song is there to enrich the truth it carries, the poetry is at its finest.

Such is the conviction here that two potentially clumsy lines are absorbed into the whole with barely a flicker. Lines 9–10 recall sonnet 11.1–4 in a slight awkwardness (syntactic and rhythmic) of the verbal construction; but here it is as nothing. The feminine rhymes add a plaintiveness to the questions of 5–6 that is deepened by a steady increase in understanding of the terms of the situation. 5–6 bear witness to the withholding of the claims of the self. Still we are at an early stage of a process of awareness carried out in the first twelve lines of every sonnet, an internalisation of the fact. The acceptance is near the surface; by the end of the dodeka it is entire. The hurt that lingers seeks no way out.

The couplet confirms the realisation. The contract was based on a misjudgement of the speaker's value by the friend, or an undervaluation of his own worth. It is torn up and an altogether new settlement (so to speak) concluded. So much of the sequence to the man is to do with the disappearance of the ego, a wavering state, approached, attained, lost, re-found. The shifting base of the personality is forever key to the whole. No truth is a settled one apart from the unfaltering fact of love.

Line 5 simply and memorably dismisses the enforcement of any claim; while on a narrower reading of 'granting' it contributes to the elaborate metaphor. Couched in a financier's legalese the extended image of bestowal and withdrawal, the rights and wrongs of ownership, sets up a cynical interplay with its subject-matter; the calculating mind as against the uncalculating heart. The tension that arises is part of the point: the speaker works through one as he comes to the other. The poet is playfully agile with the image even as the man behind the words is close to tears. The feminine rhymes add to the lightness. So one can discern a rueful shake of the head, if one wishes not only to hear but to see the speaker; or even a half-laugh in the face of loss.

The song is like a spell. At the end the speaker is woken, as if from a false reign. All that went before is telescoped in the couplet. The touch in the repeated '-king' is revelatory, as the eyes blink open.

When thou shalt be disposed to set me light,
And place my merit in the eye of scorn,
Upon thy side against myself I'll fight   3
And prove thee virtuous, though thou art forsworn.
With mine own weakness being best acquainted,
Upon thy part I can set down a story   6
Of faults concealed, wherein I am attainted,
That thou in losing me shall win much glory.
And I by this will be a gainer too,   9
For bending all my loving thoughts on thee,
The injuries that to myself I do,
Doing thee vantage, double-vantage me.   12
    Such is my love, to thee I so belong,
    That for thy right myself will bear all wrong.

The farewell of 87 is either not yet or back in the past; in either case the juxtaposition of that and this is faintly surprising. Again there is the sense of a roughly-assembled thematic group that may not be chronological. Here the tone is light, almost dainty; the sentiments are more or less those of 49 but without the focused inner character of that piece. The couplets are very different. The tendency of the whole here is to a calm end, a breath of the pure air of self-abnegation; while the last line of 49 is a lightning-stroke. A different order of poetry speaks in the earlier-placed poem. But there are many quieter numbers dotted about the collection, perhaps a majority. And as with the first seventeen, that "tilt at windmills" to manufacture an argument for the young man to 'get a son', these too have a lustre of their own. Under cover of the theme of severance the sonnet-form is itself wooed, the poet's ardour here seeming to lie chiefly in the gentle reiteration of a point already made, to provide a light song. If one can set aside the knowledge of what he is capable of with all guns firing, so to speak, such a piece as this renders its own salute.

The point is a good one and the poet goes at it single-minded. Never in haste, always in tenderness, he traces a path whereby the friend can be at ease with himself, in the event of their separation. It is not as if the song had nothing to say. The details of the agreement he sets out, to accord blame only to himself, are hardly to be taken literally. The speaker is scarcely going to "bad-mouth" himself to all and sundry and if he did, so far from winning glory in losing him, the young man would probably be ribbed for ever having taken an interest. The over-statement is never more than a means. But it is vital, leading to a truth the reader instinctively divines as he follows it through. Beyond the hyperbole is an ideal of love. The reader also knows that over-statement is part of the nature of one person's unqualified bond with another. Without breaking new ground, the poem tells a tale that needs to be told.

A couple of half-buried asides add a tang of the here-and-now. 'Forsworn' in line 4 may refer to the friend's being economical with the truth in allowing the speaker to 'bear all wrong' (14), or it may hint at a more active betrayal. And the final phrase (as so often) has more in it. It is what it says, he will take all the responsibility; it is what it is also heard to say, he will lie about everything, voicing what should be the other's true words; and hard on the heels of the latter realisation, the 'wrong' has something unspeakable in it. Yet all holds together. Despite a certain intricacy of texture the clarity is overriding, the lark sings. It may not be a hymn at heaven's gate (29), but on sullen earth too, the muse has her delight.

Say that thou didst forsake me for some fault,
And I will comment upon that offence.
Speak of my lameness, and I straight will halt,   3
Against thy reasons making no defence.
Thou canst not, love, disgrace me half so ill,
To set a form upon desirèd change,   6
As I'll myself disgrace, knowing thy will:
I will acquaintance strangle and look strange,
Be absent from thy walks, and in my tongue   9
Thy sweet belovèd name no more shall dwell,
Lest I, too much profane, should do it wrong,
And haply of our old acquaintance tell.   12
> For thee, against myself I'll vow debate;
> For I must ne'er love him whom thou dost hate.

In the same vein as the last, but with more regard to the daily detail of being apart, the speaker lightly affirms his support for his abandonment. There is a grim enough time ahead (lines 8–10) and yet the verse proceeds trippingly along. A light chord is struck: but it is in other poems that the raw nerve is exposed. It may be that the writer often approached the same area of internal difficulty, without making headway past a certain point. Yet such was his skill with the sonnet (and delight in its making) that in several cases of an incomplete expression of a certain hurt, a complete and vital poem is produced.

This assumes a significant autobiographical element in the writing. It is simply a hypothesis; but (unfashionably) I find line 3 telling in this respect. The suggestion of a physical infirmity is repeated from 37.3, a detail that if taken as such adds particularity throughout. It may be that the speaker refers to his lame verses as an outstanding 'fault'; the adjective (punning with defective metric 'feet') was in use as such, and metrically unsound verse might 'halt'. Similarly in 37 'lame' may simply mean 'decrepit'. But there why should it be due to 'Fortune's dearest spite'? And here 'my' and 'I' in line 3 are very direct. In 37 he may be referring to a deep-seated wish to have been able to take on star parts as an actor; and here (to make the point a vivid one) he may be saying he will exaggerate his limp, if the other cares to mention it as one of his faults. So he will 'comment' by drawing extra attention to it.

One would like to know, though the detail is unimportant. But not everything that matters is important. Unfortunately the detail of Shakespeare's life has become a battleground for the Big-Endians and Little-Endians of Swift's satire, who go to war over an egg. I break it in one way but am content if people choose the other.

Line 6 is perhaps an indication that the youth has found another bosom companion, and by accepting and expanding on every criticism the speaker will make it seem right for him to have done so. 'Profane' (line 11) may carry something of the original meaning from the Latin more consciously than now, 'outside a holy place'. The picture of the speaker avoiding the places where the other walks, pretending not to recognise him ('look strange', as a stranger), making a taboo of his very name, appeals in its easy visibility. We see the imagined figure with the inner eye even as the mind fails to identify fully with its purist approach. Two final remarks: 'acquaintance' is hardly a word the poet would use, as we shall see, to describe his closeness to the woman. And the final word can be taken lightly, summing up a rueful response to being "dropped" or ignored. Or it is an outburst in a syllable. In which case, concluding with an unusual emphasis, the speaker does indeed for an instant show his hand. Yet a suggestion of hyperbole allows the compliment of the whole to hold.

Then hate me when thou wilt: if ever, now,
Now while the world is bent my deeds to cross;
Join with the spite of fortune, make me bow,   3
And do not drop in for an after-loss.
Ah do not, when my heart hath 'scaped this sorrow,
Come in the rearward of a conquered woe;   6
Give not a windy night a rainy morrow,
To linger out a purposed overthrow.
If thou wilt leave me, do not leave me last,   9
When other petty griefs have done their spite,
But in the onset come; so shall I taste
At first the very worst of fortune's might,   12
    And other strains of woe, which now seem woe,
    Compared with loss of thee will not seem so.

It is as if the last word of 89, gaining in presence, removes a rock from a cave's mouth and the poet can be open about his deepest fear. After the knowledge revealed by 87 of an inescapable rift, 88–89 appear now to be moments-in-waiting, attendant on an entrance that is itself something like a storm. Here is no dallying with the situation, no purist stance that makes little sense in everyday terms. The reader can wholly understand the speaker's need to have it over and done with. The familiar wish to withdraw from his friend's ambit, allowing him all the licence in the world, is suddenly more urgent and real. There is a vehemence, a quickened beat. Here is the force of the man.

As opposed to a casual interest as to whether the writer really was lame or not (89), I am almost glad not to know what (beside the situation with the friend) was plaguing him here (line 2). The poetry is too strong for such specifics. What it did not need, neither does the reader. 'Do not leave me last' (9) may also suggest his abandonment by others; but in the main it refers to a later time, when other 'petty griefs' have played themselves out. A military image (mainly in lines 6 and 8) mingles in a decisive intent with the rough-and-tumble of lashing weather. The latter metaphor that gives line 7 is probably foreshadowed in 4: 'drop in' did not mean 'pay a casual visit' at that time and it seems likely to suggest the 'rainy morrow'. Perhaps with 'after-loss' it had a farming reference as to loss of crops. However, the casual visit does work very well, 'drop in' almost spat out, for a sarcastic interjection, so to speak, as within the heavier tone of the whole. One would like to think Shakespeare meant it as such; it does not seem impossible that he anticipated the later common usage. Otherwise it provides an interesting example of an accidental refreshment of poetic meaning over time.

'This sorrow' (line 5) I take as the comparatively 'petty griefs' rather than the main one. I do not think he foresees a recovery from a penultimate stage of separation, as it were. It is remarkable how beleaguered he perceives himself to be. 110–111 mirror a fierce gloom and outright anger, respectively, at his general situation, and there are a number of other references. 121 is close to fury at being gossiped about. It does not matter: he is more ruthless with himself than the outside world can be. And whatever one may feel as to his general tendency to seek out a lonely space when not in favour with his friend, that owes much to an instinctive and admirable generosity, and a little to a masochistic streak perhaps – one cannot but admire his resolve, as clear here as anywhere. It is driven, with a gale behind it.

After which the beautiful restraint of the ending brings a notable moment to its close.

Some glory in their birth, some in their skill,
Some in their wealth, some in their body's force,
Some in their garments, though new-fangled ill,   3
Some in their hawks and hounds, some in their horse;
And every humour hath his adjunct pleasure,
Wherein it finds a joy above the rest,   6
But these particulars are not my measure;
All these I better in one general best.
Thy love is better than high birth to me,   9
Richer than wealth, prouder than garments' cost,
Of more delight than hawks or horses be,
And, having thee, of all men's pride I boast;   12
    Wretched in this alone, that thou mayst take
    All this away, and me most wretched make.

There is a delightful plainness about this. The full gust of
feeling again is held back; the point is a philosophical one – till
at the end a threat is apprehended and a chill enters proceed-
ings. By then the danger appears a mortal one. A simple device
cleverly used, the reversal points up the speaker's abandonment,
once 'all this' is taken away. 'Thy love' (9) comes to include the
happiness of all men, in its enjoyment the speaker is at one with
all the world; so that the final phrase is sharp with loneliness.
The dodeka is a fanciful expression of joy, the couplet real.

His abhorrence of cosmetics evidently extended to new fash-
ions in clothes (3). One warms to the old grump, while
wondering what the first reader, or supposed reader, may have
made of it. No doubt a good deal in the first four lines might
have applied to the youth. But here we have a puzzle of the
sonnets in miniature: the presence of the addressee, so to speak,
varies. Much of the time he (and later, if to a lesser extent, she)
is nominally in attendance, summoned up by 'thy' and 'thee'

(here), and not really listening. By which I mean the author is speaking to himself as much as to the other; with the more direct outward address reserved for the couplet. Once the presentation is made the inference is drawn. All poems are more telling at or towards the end; but Shakespeare's chop-logic style is apt to underline a conclusion rather more than in many other writers. The rhymed couplet he adopted is perfect to close out an argument of the heart; and in a piece such as this one may almost sense him lift his head and look at the subject – the person addressed – as the last words are spoken. Whereas in the poems where he is able to declare the full force of his feelings from the start, as 87 and 90 of the recent ones, the couplet has its salient effect, but after the silent interlocutor's presence in full. A voice of more poetic power is to hand, if a subject is met head-on.

'Humour' (5) is 'temperament'; 'cost' (10) is 'pomp'. For some reason I cherish line 9 a little. The light signal of its alliteration touches on a truth. 'These particulars are not my measure' (7) may be heard as said both by the persona ('An incidental pleasure is not what I rate happiness by') and in the far background, by the poet ('I am not occupied by personal details but a 'general best' ', line 8). An essence that is attached to the friend, exists between them, and defines the speaker, is the subject of all his lines. 'These particulars' (beyond a few references to character, most forcefully perhaps in the first sonnet of all) are not his 'measure', which can mean air, tune, melody. I am not saying the poet intended this further meaning, and yet he may have without knowing; and even if he did not, still it may be there.

A final thought: I wonder if the first 'wretched' (line 13) is correct. A word or two meaning something like 'Brought low' may have been supplanted by printer's error. Yet it serves.

But do thy worst to steal thyself away,
For term of life thou art assurèd mine;
And life no longer than thy love will stay, 3
For it depends upon that love of thine.
Then need I not to fear the worst of wrongs,
When in the least of them my life hath end; 6
I see a better state to me belongs
Than that which on thy humour doth depend.
Thou canst not vex me with inconstant mind, 9
Since that my life on thy revolt doth lie.
O what a happy title do I find,
Happy to have thy love, happy to die! 12
But what's so blessèd-fair that fears no blot?
Thou mayst be false, and yet I know it not.

Following on from the last this again dallies with the spectre of
sadness, and in the playful elaboration of an idea, allows some-
thing light and true and serious to be said. 'Steal thyself away'
(line 1) nicely picks up on the sense of ownership (91.12),
reminding us in passing of an instability at the heart of the
friend's commitment. The conceit of the dodeka, absurd in itself
– the least rejection and my life is over – rests on a valid search:
to find something durable to say on the nature of possession.
What does one own in love? Lines 7–8 provide the answer. Even
though the couplet leaves them adrift at the end, in the wake of
a renewed awareness of the here-and-now, they are said; and as
other lines here and there in the series, cast a momentary light
across the centre of the stage. By which I mean they add to a
scattered description of love; and the further object of the writer,
to say the unsayable, and of the reader, to grasp it, is touched
upon, as if with a transient clarity.
'Revolt' (line 10) is a switch to another point of view, or

perhaps of sides (hinting at a third-party presence the last line comes out with). 'Title' (line 11), 'right of possession', carries on the underlying theme, which (having made its point) founders in a bathos of overstatement, if such a thing is possible. I find it almost impossible that the spare, clipped mind that turns out hundreds of lines (including some in this piece) that exemplify an exactness of poetic thought, can wallow in the emotional bath of line 12. It is as if the same composer were to exhibit Bach's precision, Beethoven's passion, and a failed entry in the Eurovision Song Contest. It has its reasons of course: as a bridge to the cold shudder of suspected fact, via the ornate line 13, line 12 lays it on thick with a sense of blinded joy, a self that is lost in fancy. But the absurdity of the conceit turns in on itself and the line is not the poet's happiest one.

The last line speaks for both present and future. The betrayal is more than an interest in another's poems, one feels: we remember the offence of 41. Is this the 'worst of wrongs' (5), the 'least of them' (6) a cold-shouldering by the friend? Or perhaps lines 5–6 are to be left unspecific, with the sense that any loss of his friend's love will kill him, and all imaginable wrongs of the kind are the same. Or (as always) both. A little mystery stays over from 3–4: 'thy love' and 'that love of thine'. I expect they mean the same thing, and that in the repetition the author was merely indulging in a slightly otiose emphasis. The poem may well have been one of those he did not get around to revising. Or does line 4 refer to a third party? As such it takes a kind of buried added point, as does 'the worst of wrongs' in turn. It is a part of the Sonnets' identity to hint, imply and leave the reader guessing, if not the first reader (or readers, as we may see when we come to those to the woman).

So shall I live, supposing thou art true,
Like a deceivèd husband; so love's face
May still seem love to me, though altered new,   3
Thy looks with me, thy heart in other place.
For there can live no hatred in thine eye;
Therefore in that I cannot know thy change.   6
In many's looks, the false heart's history
Is writ in moods and frowns and wrinkles strange;
But heaven in thy creation did decree   9
That in thy face sweet love should ever dwell;
Whate'er thy thoughts or thy heart's workings be,
Thy looks should nothing thence but sweetness tell. 12
    How like Eve's apple doth thy beauty grow,
    If thy sweet virtue answer not thy show!

The dramatist in the poet continues to propel his character on and off stage, a rhymed soliloquy for each new appearance, to keep his audience up-to-date. It is a one-man play of many moods. I am reminded of a toy theatre I played with as a child: one would slide a two- or-three-inch character onstage at the end of a rod and speak for it. At the same time, the poet to the fore, we live and relive directly with the speaker the record of a kind of odyssey. In a piece such as this – the considerable majority – I suggest the dramatist has the upper hand. In the more powerful pieces the poet takes over more or less entirely. It is a subtle amalgam of means used to a relatively minor extent by all writers of personal poems. But whichever aspect is the more visible, neither is the more important: means to an end.

    The first word leads on from 92.14. As Duncan-Jones notes, he will be as Othello would like to have been. 'I had been happy if the general camp, / Pioners and all, had tasted her sweet body, / So I had nothing known.' The reminder of the actual stage's 'deceivèd husband' is startling in its difference; but considering the phrase 'thy heart's workings' the same editor also recalls the Moor's comment on Iago's words: 'They are close denotements, working from the heart'. Why I mention it will become clear in the note to the next sonnet. The Garden of Eden seems to lie at the back of proceedings ('deceivèd husband' and 'heaven in thy creation' deepening the apple's shine); there is a murmur of original sin behind the façade of the friend's sweetness. But what is of more than passing interest is the gender play.

'The master-mistress of my passion' (20) is cast in a less equivocally female part, an Eve to an Adam. It would be easy to comment in broad terms on the likelihood of roles adopted within a homoerotic and perhaps homosexual relationship; but I tend to take the unabashed name-costume, so to speak, more as an indication of the writer's penchant for the donning of the other gender's trappings, as often in the plays. Naturally the younger man, still with something feminine to him, can be lent a woman's persona at times by the artist; an element of sexual attraction is acknowledged, a sheen, a loveliness in the youth's appearance, in this poem all too lovely. But just as the dramatist loves to throw gender around, so the habit can crop up in the poems to dramatic effect. It is a means of presentation, it takes the attention; it has its own truth, but need be no more than what it is, a reference to a physical aspect that we know already. Whether it also carries a reference to the female character in general as being duplicitous is another matter: with the poems to the woman in mind I think it does.

This is not one of the great poems. Still it has a trustful ease, an intimate tone of its own. So the character pops back off-stage.

They that have power to hurt and will do none,
That do not do the thing they most do show,
Who, moving others, are themselves as stone,   3
Unmovèd, cold, and to temptation slow;
They rightly do inherit heaven's graces,
And husband Nature's riches from expense;   6
They are the lords and owners of their faces,
Others but stewards of their excellence.
The summer's flower is to the summer sweet   9
Though to itself it only live and die;
But if that flower with base infection meet,
The basest weed outbraves his dignity.   12
    For sweetest things turn sourest by their deeds;
    Lilies that fester smell far worse than weeds.

This is a quite fascinating development. I am of the opinion that Shakespeare was involved with the writing of *Othello* at the time and drew on the "sonnet-situation" to explore and define the main part. As before (notably 69.11–14) the lover sends out a warning to his friend; meanwhile the dramatist ponders an extraordinary creation of the stage.

'Keep up your bright swords, for the dew will rust them.' Othello has a natural authority to begin with: he can prevent an ugly brawl in the streets of Venice as effortlessly as he can defend himself against a charge of witchcraft. The public and private sides of the man are under his perfect control. The first quatrain captures the man of authority who knows how to exhibit power and not to use it in the wrong way. I take 'cold' (and 'as stone') as defined by the rest of line 4, not pejoratively in this context. The second quatrain portrays, quite simply, the mien of the great. Shakespeare again and again in the plays returns to the question of what is greatness, in what different guises does it appear. It is intimately bound up for him with the expression of a personal authority; and always self-restraint is a part of the answer. Some of his most memorable creations come about by virtue of the lifting of that restraint. True greatness does not waste nature's riches, nor is it in the slightest concerned with its own excellence; it is the business of others to keep an eye on it if they so wish, to treasure it (the 'stewards', the summer and the flower). The final four lines show what happens to Othello as a result of Iago's machinations, and compare him to his nemesis, who comes off better. 'From this time forth I never will speak word,' declares the villain after his arrest; nor does he (as we suppose, despite tortures to come), exiting the play with more dignity than the Moor. The comparison is unavoidable; and here the author has it in brief.

He wrote one of his outstanding poems to do so. The drama of the sonnets takes second place, in this one instance, to that of the stage. The poet's visionary power exceeds the confining circumstance of the series, as a number of times elsewhere (66 most notably of all). The steady, quiet confidence of the octave's statement, a sonorous thud in the background almost suggesting such a person walking about, is replaced by an unassuming tone, delicious by contrast, in lines 9–10: and then the warning. Shakespeare does not forget the required surface: the final line, a reprise of 69's ending but with a stinging lash to it, would surely burn at the boy's mind. One wonders if he read it: in its lack of direct reference to the friend this is one of the most impersonal of the poems (another is 116). One wonders many things to do with this infuriating collection of Olympian verses. It is rare that we can see the playwright and the sonneteer as one, and their convergence here seems so pronounced as to perhaps suggest a mental illusion. Or there may be mileage in it.

How sweet and lovely dost thou make the shame,
Which like a canker in the fragrant rose
Doth spot the beauty of thy budding name: 3
O, in what sweets dost thou thy sins enclose!
That tongue that tells the story of thy days,
Making lascivious comments on thy sport,   6
Cannot dispraise but in a kind of praise;
Naming thy name blesses an ill report.
O what a mansion have those vices got   9
Which for their habitation chose out thee,
Where beauty's veil doth cover every blot,
And all things turns to fair that eyes can see!   12
    Take heed, dear heart, of this large privilege:
    The hardest knife ill-used doth lose his edge.

A gentle word of advice, wreathed in smiles, abruptly changes
delivery. The last line is as blunt as can be. The contrast between
that and the previous thirteen itself reveals an attitude on the
author's part to the rich language of love he loves to use: to an
extent it is decorative material. With a point to be made the
filmy-eyed cover, though never disowned, is snatched away. A
beady-eyed onlooker has the last word.

The youth's reputation – his 'budding name' (3) – has taken
a hit. The plant imagery is continued and a caterpillar ('canker',
2) rampant. It may be for a particular offence, perhaps with the
poet's mistress, or getting some young woman "into trouble",
or for a growing name as a ladies' man; in any case the warning
is a familiar one. But one cannot doubt a deliberate intent in the
final line. I take it as a kind of phallic proverb to do with vene-
real disease. The contrast with the foregoing wafting cloud of
hyperbole could not be more telling.

A tendency to the sexual *double entendre* is a part of the character of the sonnets to the young man, an in-joke between the two of them as I see it; and part of the joke is that one cannot be sure when the hidden meaning is in fact intended. I have no idea when it is or not and so have made little of the possibility; but here it does seem worth noting. On the face of it 'the hardest knife' here is 'the most powerful quality'. The secondary metaphor, if it is there, is an apt reminder from the older man.

Yet one cannot dismiss the warmth and indeed the sincerity that is threaded through the "filmy cover", just as one cannot deny the loving affection of 'dear heart' (13). If much of the vocabulary of the language of love is an overstatement, that is of its nature; and a poetic conceit has the virtue of admitting to its own extravagance. We pick up something of the boy's personality here: there are people, not yet quite launched on the world, whom one 'cannot dispraise but in a kind of praise' (7). 'O what a goodly outside falsehood hath,' remarks Antonio, the Merchant of Venice, after comparing an evil soul, a villain, to 'a goodly apple rotten at the heart'. One senses that the "warning" poems are concerned not only with the present situation but with who the youth may grow up to be. There is an almost parental tenderness at the same time as a need to "tell it as it is", a not uncommon state of affairs, and one not unlikely to deliver a mixed message.

'Lascivious' in line 6 is in part a transferred epithet and in part a jab at the gossip-mongers. When similar stories are spread about the writer himself (121) the jab has a great deal more punch behind it. 'Turns' in line 12 is the Q (original edition) reading and works with 'veil' as subject and 'all things' as object. I fancy the author wrote 'turn', for a more decisive end-line before the second *volta*, but one cannot be sure.

Some say thy fault is youth, some wantonness,
Some say thy grace is youth and gentle sport;
Both grace and faults are loved of more and less;   3
Thou mak'st faults graces that to thee resort.
As on the finger of a thronèd queen
The basest jewel will be well esteemed,   6
So are those errors that in thee are seen
To truths translated, and for true things deemed.
How many lambs might the stern wolf betray   9
If like a lamb he could his looks translate;
How many gazers mightst thou lead away
If thou wouldst use the strength of all thy state!   12
    But do not so; I love thee in such sort,
    As thou being mine, mine is thy good report.

The poem opens with a light abandon, by its easy turns of meaning conveying the youth's licence, within a supple rhythm. A dolphin plays in the lines. 'More and less' (3) is 'high and low'. 'Resort' (4) suggests the faults queueing up, cap in hand, to be turned to graces; an odd caprice, but part of the aristocratic air of the main section. 'The strength of all thy state' (12) completes the picture of an absolute power. Shakespeare loves to play with opposites and this is full of them. But the couplet is of a different nature.

It repeats that of 36 exactly and I think by printer's accident. The idea of the reputation's transference feels imposed. The text works, but not as well as in 36, where the introduction of the first person is not at all abrupt and the couplet seems a natural development. Perhaps the first four words of line 13 were the same and whoever set the print picked up an old tray for the two lines. While a poet may well begin two poems with the same line it is very unlikely to happen with the ending, unless that is a refrain and not, as in the sonnets, the revelation of an inner discovery. The whole makes sense, but it is an unsatisfactory situation, and I propose to make it more so.

'But do not so; for with them into danger
Thou too art drawn, my heart, and I thy stranger.'

As an amendment it is "wrong" in a number of ways; but the exercise has been useful for me in highlighting a certain strength of Shakespeare's writing. Whatever subtleties a couplet may half-conceal it is always also direct. The personality of the speaker is unmistakeable, if (as anybody's) undefinable; or to put it another way, a charismatic persona is always on hand. As in any true poem the speaker is *there*. That he is at the same time self-effacing is no contradiction: we are aware of him, and sense who he is as much as if he were a real person. After which to look back at my effort does me no good at all. But I have learnt something from it.

It may be a moment to list the poems since 62 that stand out for me (see 63 note). 64 for a moment of vision and its darkening; 65 for a passionate encounter with Time; 66 for a blazing condemnation of the unjust; 73 for a *pianissimo* expression of frailty and love; 87 for the poignancy of a claim's withdrawal; 90 for a head-on collision with the worst; 94 for an account of the tragic flaw.

Behind these great passages of poetry is an ordinary person speaking, an uninhibited background presence. Someone who knows who he is and who can be known.

How like a winter hath my absence been
From thee, the pleasure of the fleeting year!
What freezings have I felt, what dark days seen,   3
What old December's bareness everywhere!
And yet this time removed was summer's time,
The teeming autumn, big with rich increase,   6
Bearing the wanton burden of the prime
Like widowed wombs after their lords' decease.
Yet this abundant issue seemed to me   9
But hope of orphans and unfathered fruit;
For summer and his pleasures wait on thee,
And thou away, the very birds are mute.   12
 Or if they sing, 'tis with so dull a cheer
 That leaves look pale, dreading the winter's near.

This and the next play with the seasons to touch on a chill at
the heart of separation. 'Pleasure' (2) is the year's delight and its
delighting, at once its rich part and a richness for it to rejoice
in, as a prince or jewel. An ambivalence lingers throughout; the
piece is suspended in a kind of uncertainty. 'This time removed'
(5) is the period of being apart, not yet over. It began in the
summer: and then what happened? The summer's promise was
not delivered. Or was it, but in disappointing fashion? The
'abundant issue' (9) is either still in the womb or borne forth.
The three lines (6–8) that lead to this almost celebratory phrase
are loaded with life and munificence, 'teeming', 'big', 'rich',
'increase', 'wanton', 'prime'; and a line charged with a grandiose
heaviness, that both bears out the hope of 6–7, and negates it,
'widowed', 'decease' (8). 'Bearing' itself is left in no-man's-land,
neither before nor after birth. 'Hope' (10) seems to turn the after
into before, 'fruit' again to after, with the glory taken away. It
is a poem not of actuality but of anticipation. A scenario that

would fit is the friend's imminent return from a long journey and the speaker half-hoping for a joyful reunion but expecting the worst.

He describes his December of separation with a dramatic openness, 'What freezings have I felt, what dark days seen . . . ', that does not quite convince. The phrases move too quickly, the exclamations are too abrupt. 'Old' (4) as 'late-year' or 'late-month' (not 'familiar') introduces a thumping scene that is felt and not felt, all round one and distant. Only Shakespeare can be at once lacerating and playful. Is he looking back at an extreme state no longer felt, almost jovially? Hardly. Then why the light structural support, that leaves it in the shallows? Again the sense is of a less than absolute reality. To an extent lines 3–4 partake of the Baron Munchausen effect (68 note) where the poet half-makes it up. But in the light of other pieces one cannot doubt an inner sincerity; the suffering has been real. And the ending beautifully shows it still is.

'Wait on' (11) is 'await' and 'attend on', the year's prime acknowledging its prince, no pleasure of the seasons admitted in his absence. And the couplet brings us a new December, very different from the earlier one, whisperingly quiet, foretelling a bareness that can only be hinted at. In literary terms it would be a sin to say what it may be. After the rhetorical flourishes a muted metaphor; after the known past an unknown future. It is the most delicate ending of a sonnet I know. The foregoing uncertainty is the louder and lesser part of a held breath. So a piece of sonnet-music is brought to its close.

Line 8 recalls 3.5–6. The poet is casual with the female form. It appears to me insensitive; after all, he is writing for posterity. Women will read his lines. But he is who he is.

From you have I been absent in the spring,
When proud-pied April, dressed in all his trim,
Hath put a spirit of youth in everything,   3
That heavy Saturn laughed and leaped with him.
Yet not the lays of birds, nor the sweet smell
Of different flowers in odour and in hue,   6
Could make me any summer's story tell,
Or from their proud lap pluck them where they grew.
Nor did I wonder at the lily's white,   9
Nor praise the deep vermilion in the rose;
They were but sweet, but figures of delight,
Drawn after you, you pattern of all those.   12
    Yet seemed it winter still, and you away,
    As with your shadow I with these did play.

A different chill awaits, one that does not penetrate to the bone, but enfolds the mind in a kind of absence. A mist of idle doubt is all the speaker is left with at the end. Or rather, all the speaker *is*. Again a diminuendo returns the voice to its solitary owner, from speaking out to speaking in. Everything is so much there: April in its magnificence, the figure of the old god of gloom stomping the ground in joy, birdsong, floral scents and shades, the white and the red in a surreal dreamlike intensity, suddenly insubstantial, a fragile thought alone lingering. The speaker is all but one with the 'pattern' he perceives (12) in mind only. A different way into the seasons brings into being another tribute, another self-portrait with it.

The personification in 2–4 is unusual and splendid. Chaucer would have loved it. Line 4 is a tour de force, the spare clarity of the dancing words leaving behind an unforgettable picture. (And behind that, one of the wan unresponsive poet.) 'A sad tale's best for winter' says the young prince of *The Winter's Tale*, but line 7 has a glimpse of the opposite in a rich phrase in passing. Line 8 contrasts with it a little too sharply, perhaps, both in idea and the sudden quick plucked words. By now an unreality is settling in: a world of Platonic forms, or of one such form, is superimposed upon the all-around; and a whisper remains, still dancing to April's lost tune. It has been said the last phrase is a contradiction: that having nothing to do with the flowers and so on, 'I with these did play'. But he has much to do with them and they with him, in the state of mind that comes into its own, almost not there, a wistful half-being holding the stage, replacing all material fact, at the poem's end.

The winter is over; it is spring. Summer's pleasures are strongly hinted at. 'Yet seemed it winter still . . . ' The sonnet may imply two kinds of absence for the friend, away on a journey, and back but finding no time to see the speaker. It is a wondering poem, a step further on in the episode from the last one. The poet does not want to be too explicit. Meanwhile in his interplay with the figure of Time, again he has sung a song of the seasons, and added to the chain.

'And every stone I wind off like a reel,' said Dylan Thomas at the end of *Once it was the Colour of Saying*, a poem I am not sure I understand; or rather, I am sure I do not understand. The line is preceded by 'Now my saying shall be my undoing,' and the gist of it all may be the transference into poetry of the acts and words of ordinary life. The last line sometimes comes back at me in relation to a poem's completion: the task is done, the experience unhooked from the passing moment. Another way of being has taken it on. A series of poems will have such an element more to the fore. Each new stone is wound off from the past, onto a visible chain. All are different and all will have their place.

The forward violet thus did I chide:
'Sweet thief, whence didst thou steal thy sweet that smells
If not from my love's breath? The purple pride   3
Which on thy soft cheek for complexion dwells
In my love's veins thou hast too grossly dyed.'
The lily I condemnèd for thy hand,   6
And buds of marjoram had stol'n thy hair;
The roses fearfully on thorns did stand,
One blushing shame, another white despair;   9
A third, nor red nor white, had stol'n of both,
And to his robb'ry had annexed thy breath;
But for his theft, in pride of all his growth,   12
A vengeful canker eat him up to death.
    More flowers I noted, yet I none could see
    But sweet or colour it had stol'n from thee.   15

While this carries on the idea of the youth's beauty lying behind
that of all flowers, in terms of poetic quality it is altogether out
of place. In fact it is one of a half-dozen sonnets that were either
not by Shakespeare or by him in frivolous or otherwise detached
mood. This one could even be a collaboration between the poet
and the youth, poring over a sonnet of Henry Constable's and
"sending it up". For some time I have wondered about the young
man's part – if he read them, if he existed, et cetera – as the silent
side of this poetic conversation. Who is to say he was not in part
an ally of his friend's intention, to frame an undying description
of love? There is a strained exaggeration about the whole of this
poem, something ridiculous. I sense laughter behind it. The fact
that it has an extra line (uniquely in the collection) may or may
not be a hint to look at it differently.

    The Constable poem includes the lines:

'The violet of purple colour came,
Dyed with the blood she made my heart to shed.
In brief, all flowers from her their virtue take;
From her sweet breath their sweet smells do proceed . . . '

There are many other echoes of contemporary sonnets in Shakespeare's but this may be there for a reason: as in 130 he is guying the absurdities of conventional love hyperbole. And as such, instead of an unaccountable "lame duck", the poem is in its way rather splendid.

There are a number of intricacies of meaning within the lines that it seems unnecessary to explore: to do so is to become hostage to the sly intent; and in any case, the minor twists and turns of the maze amount to nothing. 'On thorns' (8) could mean 'on tenterhooks'. 'Sweet' in line 15 is presumably 'scent' as in line 2. 'Eat' (13) is 'ate'. Otherwise it's too much of a game. The meditative ending stays with one a touch; the little it says is said well. But it does not seem enough. Looking at line 2 again, one is struck by the unShakespearian quality of expression and metre both. The former is forced in one way, the latter in another (compare the tighter monosyllabic line 98.8). The whole thing screams caricature. Or another hand: and who knows how it came to be in the bundle of manuscripts that Thorpe set in print? It seems incidentally another argument that Shakespeare did not oversee the edition.

In *Hamlet* there is a 'violet in the youth of primy nature, / Forward, not permanent, sweet, not lasting . . . ' Laertes is advising his sister not to take the prince's interest in her too seriously. In *King Lear* 'Sweet marjoram' is a nonsensical password. One may speculate; but merely conclude the poet was bound to no single recipe, in his use of flowers and herbs.

Where art thou, Muse, that thou forget'st so long
To speak of that which gives thee all thy might?
Spend'st thou thy fury on some worthless song, 3
Dark'ning thy power to lend base subjects light?
Return, forgetful Muse, and straight redeem
In gentle numbers time so idly spent; 6
Sing to the ear that doth thy lays esteem,
And gives thy pen both skill and argument.
Rise, resty Muse, my love's sweet face survey, 9
If Time hath any wrinkle graven there;
If any, be a satire to decay,
And make Time's spoils despisèd everywhere. 12
    Give my love fame faster than Time wastes life;
    So thou prevent'st his scythe and crooked knife.

A run of four poems from 100–103, on the theme of the silent Muse, seems to leave 99 high and dry, stranded in its superficiality. Conceivably it may stand for 'some worthless song' (3), a 'base' subject without 'light' of its own (4). Still I find the juxtaposition strange. In any case it seems now the poet is genuinely anxious to continue in his quest, not to waste time or to misdirect the *furor poeticus*, the poetic passion. There is an urgency the reader does not doubt, though it is scarcely a need to say again what he has already said so well. Rather, it may be, there is an underlying need to complete a journey. Back, then, to the pilgrimage.

'Forgetful' (5), 'resty' (here 'sluggish', 9), 'truant' (101.1), the Muse – his inspiration – is berated. 'Make answer!' (101.5). One feels he is near to cursing himself; and then one remembers the artful side of his art's despair. Out of the expostulation more poems are born; the war with Time, the nearness to an ideal, all that possesses the poetic persona is revisited; and in the new formulation a step or two is taken along the way. As each of Rembrandt's self-portraits is an attempt to "make it new" so is almost every last one of Shakespeare's sonnets. There is an artfulness, a self-serving element, in all art; it is part of how it is made. Here one feels the author is very much back on track.

'Gentle' (6), as an opposite of 'base' (4), as well as a refined ease, may suggest a touch of nobility; as in 81.9 where in part it seems to serve the same purpose, to take note of the friend's high station. The implicit hint of a class system in verse suits Shakespeare's age better than our own. A sonnet-sequence probably had something of an aristocratic air to it by its very nature; while dramatic dialogue featuring "low-life" was often in prose. On another point, I wonder if the poet took the verbal idea of time's redemption (5–6) from Paul's Epistle to the Ephesians ('See then that ye walk . . . as wise, redeeming the time, because the days are evil'). T.S.Eliot in *Ash Wednesday* certainly did ('Redeem / The time. Redeem / The unread vision in the higher dream . . . '). What a world of difference there is between the two poets. Here we are aware of another besides the speaker, which can happen in Eliot's verse, but rarely. And (for what it is worth) we are told something more of him: he esteems the speaker's verses (line 7). One only hopes it is for their innate quality, and not the mere fact of their subject-matter. But his interest in the rival poet's offerings may give one pause.

For the first time (as far as I remember) the youth's beauty is presented as perhaps already prey to Time. The answer is a race with decay that love's "fame", its enduring expression, must win (13). But the final phrase is ominous, strangely powerful. The scythe is suddenly no cliché, but a 'crooked knife' of hostile intent. The battle with the enemy is rejoined, more quietly than of old, and a little more grimly.

O truant Muse, what shall be thy amends
For thy neglect of truth in beauty dyed?
Both truth and beauty on my love depends;   3
So dost thou too, and therein dignified.
Make answer, Muse! Wilt thou not haply say,
'Truth needs no colour with his colour fixed,   6
Beauty no pencil, beauty's truth to lay;
But best is best if never intermixed'?
Because he needs no praise, wilt thou be dumb?   9
Excuse not silence so, for't lies in thee
To make him much outlive a gilded tomb,
And to be praised of ages yet to be.   12
    Then do thy office, Muse; I teach thee how,
    To make him seem long hence as he shows now.

The conversation with the Muse is continued, a dramatic device
to add edge to the conversation with himself. 'Amends' (1)
amounts to 'excuse'. Again the Muse (or her product) is 'digni-
fied' (4) by the subject-matter. It is difficult to escape the
inference of the friend's high status. In the supposed answer
'pencil' is 'paintbrush' and 'lay' is 'apply' (7). The terms of the
argument are exceptionally clear. Perfection needs no 'colour' or
'pencil'. No image can ever do it justice. Line 8 suggests the risk
or inevitability of adulteration. One thinks of the Islamic stric-
ture against representations of the Prophet. Shakespeare finds a
robust answer though; or rather, his would-be active side coun-
ters the passive (itself active in the poem's writing, in the poet's
paradoxical way). Line 9 is splendidly direct; and the exposition
in 11–12 of what art can do, simple as it is, is perfectly to the
point. In the couplet the original has the comma after 'how'(13);
I retain it, with the idea of 'I' standing for 'I'll'. Line 14 seems
to stretch on and on, yet not to be too long (unlike 99.2, also

monosyllables). Some have seen an indication of falsity in 'seem' but I take it in good faith. For me the undertow of the last line is a fine drawing-out of the 'ages yet to be'.

'I teach thee how': something about the phrase lingers. It has a touch of schizophrenic drollery – one recalls Launcelot Gobbo's inner debate as to whether to quit Shylock's service in *The Merchant of Venice* – but that is not, I think, what delays my moving on to the next point or poem. I suppose it is the confidence he has in his ability, once the spark is struck: it is an inverse way, perhaps the only way, of showing the importance of true inspiration. And with that thought one can say a little more on the "second-class" sonnets, so termed only by comparison to the truly great poems. Each can make their own list but none will deny, I imagine, a telling gap in poetic power between the latter and the bulk of the series.

'Rise, resty Muse . . . ' (100.9). Perhaps Shakespeare is searching for the spark but has to be content with what he can do. In the personal poems it is less ubiquitous than in the great plays, perhaps because of the limited cast of characters. Yet what I call the journeyman sonnets, such as the above, make progress each in its way, and he knows this. To wait for the tinder to present itself and the spark to catch is the passive part of the artist's being. And something meanwhile can take place on a lower level, which may discover a richness of its own, and come to be an integral part of the *oeuvre* or within it, the series.

W.H.Auden in the preface to his Collected Shorter Poems speaks of the small minority of them 'for which [the author] is honestly grateful, [but limited to which] his volume would be too depressingly slim.' But with his own sonnet-series, *In Time of War*, the lesser and the greater go hand-in-hand. And so it is with Shakespeare.

My love is strengthened, though more weak in seeming;
I love not less, though less the show appear;
That love is merchandised whose rich esteeming   3
The owner's tongue doth publish everywhere.
Our love was new, and then but in the spring,
When I was wont to greet it with my lays;   6
As Philomel in summer's front doth sing,
And stops his pipe in growth of riper days.
Not that the summer is less pleasant now   9
Thank when her mournful hymns did hush the night,
But that wild music burthens every bough,
And sweets grown common lose their dear delight.   12
    Therefore, like her, I sometime hold my tongue,
    Because I would not dull you with my song.

We may have an example of mid-poem inspiration here. Lines 1–4 set up a familiar expectation: a governing trope from the world of barter, on the lines of 'I will not praise that purpose not to sell' (21.14). But line 4 sets off a new train of thought, and the remainder has a rhapsodic element to it in background and foreground, a rare delight. Dispensing with regret, more lenient with himself for his silence, the writer finds himself propelled into a celebration.

It is of the past; and yet the lightness of the lines has the richness of the present too. The busy tongue of line 4 brings the nightingale to mind (Philomel), that stops singing in early summer: and there it is, a perfect metaphor for the exuberance of early love, that knows when to quieten down. 'Mournful' (10) I find fascinating. Except for its slower repeated notes (at a stretch), the nightingale's song can hardly be described so; and yet it seems able to touch off such a mood in the listening human on a summer eve (as notably in Keats' ode). Line 8's exuberant echo turns to 10's tender melancholy; and both are passionately recollected in 11. Somewhere Ezra Pound, speaking of Yeats' line 'The fire that stirs about her, when she stirs', says it has occupied his mind for many a year, 'and I am not done with it yet'. So line 11 for me. Some take 'that' in it as 'because', following line 9; but I hear it as the demonstrative pronoun, referring back to the hymns and the piping. The line settles on a branch of the mind; and for a second I am almost dizzy with the suggestion of the early days of love.

'But that wild music burthens every bough.' I cannot bring myself to turn the verb to its modern spelling, as I have done elsewhere. The fancy that the nightingale stops its song for the same reason the poet has done is no impediment to the pictorial understanding. In any case one can take 'in growth of riper days' as one likes. One wonders if the poet was at all concerned with the contrast in tone between 11 and 12. The latter line is adequate but no more (as a number of line twelves); a touch sententious in its good sense, possibly echoing a proverb. But I cannot imagine another way to close out the dodeka and turn to the last stage, so to complete the outward shape of the poem and the argument. Sometimes, in the reader's own journey, there is a pause, a coasting, rather than the steady controlled acceleration of an underlying intent or suggestion, that the greatest poems seem effortlessly to manage. Here a matter-of-fact tone in line 12 enables an undisturbed "change down" into the quiet voice of the couplet, stating a preference at this time in the friendship for a comparative silence.

'His' (line 8) is general: its, his or hers. 'Dull you' (14) is both 'weary you' and (referring to a previous argument) 'show you in a less than perfect light'. Within the theme of a loss of creativity, the sonnet is something of a happy diversion. If it is to be seen as all a contrivance, an excuse for not writing, it is surely as beautiful an excuse as has been penned.

Alack, what poverty my Muse brings forth,
That having such a scope to show her pride,
The argument all bare is of more worth   3
Than when it hath my added praise beside.
O blame me not if I no more can write!
Look in your glass, and there appears a face   6
That overgoes my blunt intention quite,
Dulling my lines and doing me disgrace.
Were it not sinful then, striving to mend,   9
To mar the subject that before was well?
For to no other pass my verses tend
Than of your graces and your gifts to tell;   12
    And more, much more than in my verse can sit,
    Your own glass shows you when you look in it.

Back to the pure form of beauty: and what remains, over and above the music of a charmingly contrived sonnet? Line 5 leaps out at one, a frustrated outburst; while lines 11–12 quietly carry the conviction of a deep intent. The many different approaches the poet takes to rationalise a proposition – which may be that of procreation, rejection, unsatisfactory output as a writer, there are others – suggest not that the proposition is invalid but that he is a poet at play. Applying a Kantian precision of argument to the presentation of his terms, he is able to work the changes on a theme, and so gradually to allow his deepest feelings to find a voice. That he is concerned more with the ideal than the particular, with an undying expression of love more than the immediate object of his affections, seems by now to lie within the accepted intent of the first series (1–126). Wherever one looks more evidence comes to light; witness the official flattery, nicely put, in 13–14 as compared with the *sotto voce* certainty at the back of 11–12. He has chosen the young man mind and heart to carry his dream to reality: he loves him, and as surely he is committed above all to the quest of the Renaissance sonneteer. The end and purpose, barely statable in words, is by the reach of the imagination to catch and give a shape to a concept that civilisation cannot do without. Donne's "holy sonnets" touch on it in a different way. At the back of it all is the Arthurian adventure to find something of inestimable value. The knight is the sonneteer and the grail is love.

Since already I may have ventured too near the ideal, I will take the opportunity to explore what may be said of the particular, the feelings for the young man that burn their way through the poems. A homoerotic strain appears in both classical Arabic and classical Greek literature, no doubt others. The suggestion of pederasty is not absent, at least in the Greek; but the dominant aspect is the passionate admiration by a male of male beauty. It is comparatively rare in Elizabethan writing – Richard Barnfield wrote of a shepherd's love for a young man – but seems a natural enough product of a male-dominated society, which Shakespeare's certainly was. Since we have a poem (20) that disavows the pederastic intent and another (151) that unashamedly uses the heterosexual act to explore a matter of conscience, we may as well take the writer as heterosexual in his physical life. But he loved a man; he shared sexual puns with him; as a poet he employed the beauty he saw in him, and the need he constantly felt to be near him, to guide a great work; and ultimately it is the nature of this work that we seek to define, when discussing the writer's sexuality. It seems clear enough to me that the ideal of pure love, to which the series may be said to be directed towards, is one that lies beyond the body's urges, whatever they may be. I would imagine that in the mind of the writer it is one that any physicality beyond an embrace would sully.

To me, fair friend, you never can be old,
For as you were when first your eye I eyed,
Such seems your beauty still. Three winters cold   3
Have from the forest shook three summers' pride,
Three beauteous springs to yellow autumn turned
In process of the seasons have I seen,   6
Three April perfumes in three hot Junes burned,
Since first I saw you fresh, which yet are green.
Ah yet doth beauty, like a dial hand   9
Steal from his figure, and no pace perceived;
So your sweet hue, which methinks still doth stand,
Hath motion, and mine eye may be deceived;   12
     For fear of which, hear this, thou age unbred:
     Ere you were born was beauty's summer dead.

Perhaps the 'fair friend' has looked in the mirror (103.14) and spotted a wrinkle. Somehow I hope not. While one is aware of his vanity throughout, it is tolerable in the background. Perhaps Shakespeare is wise in not letting us know too much about him.

Whether or not it comes from a need to reassure (and the inference need not be drawn), the octave carries a touch of true sincerity. A three-year time period was not uncommon in love poetry; yet something in these lines carries conviction. They seem to have the gladness of an anniversary about them. The poet likes to touch on the seasons in their 'process' ('procession', 6); and the final line brings back the summer, in an underplayed emphasis, to fine effect. It is the seasons' last mention, though the poet is by no means done with Time. (The sonnets to the woman have other concerns.) Time is the enemy; the battle with it is the entire means of securing the end and purpose of the first series; still there is a beauty to be had in its lesser engagements, so to speak, and this is a skirmish that is won. The poem seems to be in about the right place for a minor victory, towards the end of the epic account. Again one feels the author had a hand in the ordering but not perhaps the final say.

As in 100 it is accepted the youth may be ageing. Indeed now he is so. The dial (9) is a clock-face (or sun-dial, as in 77); the 'figure' (10) at once the youth's body and a number on the dial's face. In the latter view the beauty of the day unconscionably fades. Beneath the fixity is a sense of change. In the octave 'pride', 'beauteous', 'hot', burned', 'fresh', 'green' are all set against 'cold'; while in 9–12 'steal from' and 'no pace perceived' define an imperceptible motion. In the couplet the letter b has a ringing finality. The age 'unbred' (13) is a future generation, perhaps with a hint of its being low-born or boorish. Such a hint is an optional addition; one excludes, and includes, to suit oneself – as I have done with the looking-glass and the 'fair friend'. Like the refined screens of a futuristic electronic world, the Sonnets extend an invitation to an audience for their further involvement. And always, if one so wishes, one can ditch the special glasses and take what is offered merely as it comes.

I realise it is not so easy: the sense of a double meaning and how far to take it can plague one. But I have found that what is directly on offer can carry one along; and the rest tends to find an accommodation with the mind, if one does not probe and pester it too much. For the reader for whom such an approach is unsatisfactory, perhaps this reading will be of some use overall. If so it will be in part by offering suggestions at once to be cast aside. A poem can be a cunning beast, when the creative power behind it is of such a quality, and the depth of feeling to hand has not been such as to exhaust its mental energy. Yet its art, once and always, is to reach a familiar understanding with the reader, in terms of beauty.

Let not my love be called idolatry,
Nor my beloved as an idol show,
Since all alike my songs and praises be   3
To one, of one, still such, and ever so.
Kind is my love today, tomorrow kind,
Still constant in a wondrous excellence;   6
Therefore my verse, to constancy confined,
One thing expressing, leaves out difference.
Fair, kind and true, is all my argument,   9
Fair, kind and true, varying to other words;
And in this change is my invention spent,
Three themes in one, which wondrous scope affords.   12
    Fair, kind and true have often lived alone,
    Which three, till now, never kept seat in one.

A sally from an unexpected angle pays a compliment, reiterates a loyal devotion, and more interestingly to the reader, and I fancy to the writer, examines the Trinitarian doctrine of three Persons in one God. The compliment is a gloss, a kind of wishful thinking, at least that part of it that venerates the character ('constant', 'kind and true'). The loyalty that bespeaks it is no gloss; rather, Shakespeare is kind and true to his friend. 'To constancy confined'(7) is an apt description of his love for the youth, at least in its poetic portrayal. The compliment bears out and adds to the image of perfection the friend embodies. The series is continued and the pilgrim is a step nearer journey's end. But without intruding upon its surface, the poem also carries a resolution of a kind of the theological issue. The exact meaning of Trinitarianism, and non-Trinitarianism, is at the root of Christian thinking. The writer takes an opportunity to make his own sense of the three-in-one paradox, under cover of the conventional love poem and using its language.

In Shakespeare's time the illicit Roman Catholic religion was accused of idolatry; the Puritan argument saw the worship of Mary and of saints and relics as a form of polytheism. Non-Christian religions also were considered idolatrous. True belief could not deviate from a single narrow focus, with a tripartite splintering of the light at the centre. Whether Shakespeare cherished a religious belief as such, beyond any outward form of observance he may or may not have followed, is a moot question. A later sonnet is relevant as we shall see. But he will naturally have been very aware of a debate at the heart of the Church; and here, safely, and as a poet, he takes part in it.

One illuminates the other: the glimmer of the Christian insight the unique status of the beloved; and the human fondness the austere ideal of divinely inspired love. Without going into either side in detail (the one wearing its heart on its sleeve, the other intricate and self-contained), I would draw attention to the focus on an individual unity, followed by the 'three themes' (12); and to the final hint of the uniqueness of the godhead, different from all other. In its way the piece is a tour de force.

It includes a comment on the writer's art. 'Varying to other words' (line 10) speaks volumes, especially when lines 11 and the second half of 12 are added. There is a phrase in Anglo-Saxon, *wordum wrixlan*, which can simply mean to exchange words, as in dialogue; or it can be applied to the re-telling of a story. The latter is what the poet does, instinctively developing and re-working a theme, whether his own or another's. In the Sonnets there is a single main theme, woven of a number of strands, 'which wondrous scope affords' (12). With no disturbance to the particular context, we have a sense of the wide-ranging artist.

When in the chronicle of wasted time
I see descriptions of the fairest wights,
And beauty making beautiful old rhyme   3
In praise of ladies dead and lovely knights;
Then in the blazon of sweet beauty's best,
Of hand, of foot, of lip, of eye, of brow,   6
I see their antique pen would have expressed
Even such a beauty as you master now.
So all their praises are but prophecies   9
Of this our time, all you prefiguring,
And for they looked but with divining eyes,
They had not skill enough your worth to sing;   12
 For we, which now behold these present days,
 Have eyes to wonder, but lack tongues to praise.

Past and future generations are called on from time to time to point up the shining star of the present. 104.13–14 addresses a future generation; here there is no direct address but the summoning-up of a golden age of literature. One wonders what Shakespeare had been reading, and in what style and language. 'Chronicle (1) is 'record'; 'wasted time' is simply 'the past', with a hint of Time's ruinous power turned on itself. 'Wights' (2) is an archaism for 'people'; 'blazon' (5), 'list' or 'declaration', with an heraldic association adding to an olde-worlde setting. In line 3 the beauty of the subjects of the old poems lends itself to the art of the 'antique pen' (7), which may as well have ('would have', 7) been taking on the youth himself as subject, such is its power. Following this up, the writer suggests the old poets saw through to the present time: for how else can their poems have captured what can only be his beauty? This fancy turns out to be a way of casting an aspersion on modern-day poets, including himself, and perhaps referring in his case to his 'silence'. ('For' in 11 is 'since'; in 13 it is 'while'.)

It is a simple enough path the poet treads and there is little to say on the content that has not been said before. Some hear in 'all you prefiguring' (10) an echo of the Christian story's supposed prefigurement in the Old Testament. The poet may be continuing the daring adaptation in 105 with the hint of a Christ-like uniqueness; but it would be difficult then not to hear an aspersion cast too on modern religious practice in the last line, which somehow one doubts. In any case it is a hint at most, hardly worth spending time on.

What is worth returning to is that path and how the poet goes down it. In the course of writing this I have read a fair number of sonnets of the time, and earlier times, and while some poets match Shakespeare's lucidity and ease (Petrarch and Michelangelo), no other poet-persona is as *present* to the reader. No-one else argues with as much commitment: though half the time (and more) the argument is specious, one sees a stabbing finger as one reads, and sometimes it is turned, like an accusation, on the speaker himself. No-one else has remotely such a range of tone. There is a sonnet by Michael Drayton (see note to 48) that begins, 'Since there's no help, come, let us kiss and part. / – Nay, I have done, you'll get no more of me . . . ' A magically arresting opening, with an octave that does not let it down, is followed up by a finely-written sestet looking to a last-chance reprieve for Love. (Lines 11–12: 'When Faith is kneeling by his bed of death,/ And Innocence is closing up his eyes . . . ') Outside the Shakespearian canon it is unique, as far as I know, for its dramatic quality. But the two halves of the poem are too different in tone for it to discover a Shakespearian unity. Even so it stands alone as a worthy rival.

Not mine own fears nor the prophetic soul
Of the wide world dreaming on things to come
Can yet the lease of my true love control,   3
Supposed as forfeit to a confinèd doom.
The mortal moon hath her eclipse endured,
And the sad augurs mock their own presage;   6
Incertainties now crown themselves assured,
And peace proclaims olives of endless age.
Now with the drops of this most balmy time   9
My love looks fresh, and death to me subscribes,
Since spite of him I'll live in this poor rhyme,
While he insults o'er dull and speechless tribes.   12
    And thou in this shalt find thy monument,
      When tyrants' crests and tombs of brass are spent.

Something has happened. Not only the apparent references to outside events, but even more, the extraordinary mood that hangs over the poem, as of a lifting miasma, gives us a speaker coming to terms with a new situation. As for the events, by far the likeliest are the death of Queen Elizabeth (line 5) and the accession of James, that settled an alarmed country down wonderfully well (6–8). The Earl of Southampton, a leading candidate for the young man, was released from prison. I am bound to say that this sonnet sways me back to voting for him, so to speak, after having been half-persuaded by Dover Wilson (47 note) to change my allegiance to William Herbert, later Earl of Pembroke. It's the first phrase that does it, 'Not mine own fears', with lines 3–4 all too suggestive of incarceration. But who it is matters a good deal less than who he was to the speaker.

In Shakespeare's way other meanings offer themselves. 'My true love' (3) may be the mental abstract, its 'doom' (4) the friendship's end, a presentiment marvellously reversed; while one is at liberty to take the idea of someone or something now freed from imprisonment together with that, or separately, or not at all. With a few remarkable metaphors the poem outlines a time of unexpected and widespread stability, a sense of a new confidence, and indeed a feeling of triumph. But the deeper mood is the miracle of the piece. The slowed processional pace, the quiet glamour of the images, the sense of wonder crowned with a certain knowledge . . . the sonnet is a coronation in small.

I have taken a certain licence with 'confinèd' (4). The original has 'confin'd', and editors keep the disyllable (as, 'cónfin'd'). But the shift in stress to the syllable on the right in so many words since Shakespeare's time persuades me to modernise. In any case the poet uses it elsewhere with the modern stress. It is a trivial point to make in the context of the poetic richness on offer; but again I am unwilling to take up the critic's dabbling yardstick. I would like to move on and leave behind a magnificence untouched. Still I am unable to do so without a tribute to the opening two lines, that take the reader's mind out of itself, to set it on the adventurous path of a poem, with an alchemy for which there are no words.

I note that the poet speaks of his own survival with that of his verse. It is the first and last time he does so explicitly. 'I'll live in this poor rhyme' (11) is unambiguous. His poetic legacy finally is extended to himself as well as the other, and is not mentioned again. 'Subscribes' (10) is 'submits'; and death is the lesser writer. A final statement of the primary purpose takes over (13); and a splendid last line seems to consign the past age to outer darkness. Suspicion, wrongful imprisonment, the police state, all are gone. At the same time the line seems to mock the transitory world of politics and power for ever.

What's in the brain that ink may character
Which hath not figured to thee my true spirit?
What's new to speak, what new to register,   3
That may express my love, or thy dear merit?
Nothing, sweet boy; but yet, like prayers divine,
I must each day say o'er the very same,   6
Counting no old thing old, thou mine, I thine,
Even as when first I hallowed thy fair name.
So that eternal love in love's fresh case   9
Weighs not the dust and injury of age,
Nor gives to necessary wrinkles place,
But makes antiquity for aye his page,   12
    Finding the first conceit of love there bred
    Where time and outward form would show it dead.

This is the last time the poet dwells on his writing (115 and 116 include a reference). As in 76 he defends the repetitiveness of the 'outward form' (14) of what he writes, but in a most interesting way. The octave is natural-sounding, the sestet impersonal and less spontaneous; yet the latter takes up and expands the concern of the former with a fine sweep. The poems he writes now, he says, say the same as the first ones. (Line 8, with 'hallowed thy . . . name', continuues the poet's trespass in the garden of sacred terms, that might have been offensive to some.) 'Love's fresh case' (9) is a beautiful expression for the Sonnets themselves. The latest of them have no objection to the 'dust and injury' (10) of the earliest (of at least three years' vintage, it would appear from 104). Their pages will take those for an example. The 'first conceit of love' (13), despite the lapse of time and what one would naturally assume, the look of the situation (line 14), still applies. What drew the speaker and his friend together is as strong as ever. 'Eternal love' (9) has its freshness still and that is why he sees no reason to change what he says or (less explicitly here) how he says it.

Of course there is more going on. Lines 9–11 tell us that love, always renewed ('in love's fresh case'), takes no account of the other's ageing. (Perhaps – God save the mark – the friend needed to hear this.) And 'antiquity' (12), with an immediate reference to the earlier sonnets, has a stronger lodging in a Golden Age of poetry as in 106. This latter suggestion takes over the poetic current, so that while the surface still holds of the 'first conceit of love' in the poet's manuscript, beneath there is a powerful pull to the unknowing prefigurement of the present, in the portayal of beauty by writers of the past. The compliment to the youth is the more telling for its unexpect- edness. As so often in these poems, the two meanings do not seem to jar, but Peitho and Euterpe, the Greek goddesses of rhetoric and music, join in their powers to allay the reader's mind. For good measure the 'outward form' of line 14 has three shapes to it: the surface appearance of the early manuscripts (and maybe of their content), the 'dead' look of things of the far past, and the unvarying form of the Shakespearian sonnet, the 'noted weed' of 76.6. (Others take all this somewhat differently, which is understandable.)

A secondary meaning of 'page' (12) is 'servant', which fits. 'Bred' (13) can have a present sense, 'being bred' as one reads the old pages. I imagine (whether Shakespeare's or of further antiq- uity) they are to be seen as wrinkled somewhat. Incidentally, 'necessary' is a glorious word for 'wrinkles', is it not? Sometimes the shape, the feel of a word allows the mind to home in on the target, here almost to trace it out. Finally, the last line does seem to hint at an apparent loss of 'the first fine careless rapture' (Browning); and it may be no coincidence that the next two poems tell us of the speaker's own absence.

O never say that I was false of heart,
Though absence seemed my flame to qualify;
As easy might I from myself depart 3
As from my soul, which in thy breast doth lie.
That is my home of love; if I have ranged,
Like him that travels I return again, 6
Just to the time, not with the time exchanged,
So that myself bring water for my stain.
Never believe, though in my nature reigned 9
All frailties that besiege all kinds of blood,
That it could so preposterously be stained
To leave for nothing all thy sum of good: 12
    For nothing this wide universe I call,
    Save thou, my rose; in it thou art my all.

It is the speaker's turn to wander, and to face a charge of deser-
tion; the boot is on the other foot. At once the love affair (for
such, as pictured, it is) is a more equal matter, the speaker no
more in sole possession of the moral high ground. Several of the
remaining poems of the first series present a decidedly less
passive persona than that we are used to: the injured party,
forced to cry out at times, suffering in silence. While the
nobility of such a position can scarcely fail to leave an impres-
sion, the more rounded picture adds a touch of colour overall;
everything becomes more real. At the same time a new
poignancy enters the situation.

    As to what form the wandering takes, there seems to me to
be (as so often) a suggestion that is there to titillate rather than
inform. I imagine a promiscuity more likely social than sexual:
but since there is no fact to the matter, it matters not. The
speaker's re-announcement of loyalty, as though the blip has
never happened (line 7), even so amounts to a re-discovery; and

refreshed with a new event as much as a new argument, the series finds its way forward.

'Qualify' (2) is 'modify'. 'Just to the time' (7) I take as returning to the time he set out, as if there had been no interim ('not with the time exchanged'). Tears may lurk below the surface of line 8. The language of line 10 is taken up with a vengeance in 121. 'Preposterously' (11), Booth tells us, 'still carried the precision of its Latin root, *praepostere*, 'in a reversed order' '. The rose at the end reminds of 'beauty's rose' at the start of it all (1.2). Across a shadow-play of stance and voice from 1 to 126, an underlying devotion does not alter.

Over the series the simplicity of the narrative is part of the appeal. It is so too in the individual poems, whether relatively straightforward, as the above, or dallying with double suggestion in the couplet. Shakespeare's artifice is like no other. In the plays the sheer intellectual energy that ferments within the lines, quick-moving in argument and at times feverishly quick in imagination, image giving way to image, is always at the service of the plot. The story-line is accessible, and made more so, not less, by the author's mental ingenuity; though quite how he manages this at times is a mystery. In the Sonnets the writing formula is the same. We know where we are, despite the cunning underlay. In each poem (bar a frivolous half-dozen) a dramatic directness is not in doubt: the character of the speaker is all too present. The voice itself is a forthright one, even though it can be prone to extra effects in the margin of meaning. Where there is a direct address to the friend it is anything but orotund, as so often in the other sonneteers, but sharp. 'O never say . . . That is my home of love . . . Never believe . . . ' – the above poem has an urgency, an edge; and so it is too when the speaker is more alone, the debate or discussion more of an internal one (as for instance 121).

Shakespeare is nothing if not spontaneous. He has the gift of speech; the reader is alert.

Alas, 'tis true I have gone here and there,
And made myself a motley to the view,
Gored mine own thoughts, sold cheap what is most dear,   3
Made old offences of affections new.
Most true it is that I have looked on truth
Askance and strangely – but by all above,   6
These blenches gave my heart another youth,
And worse essays proved thee my best of love.
Now all is done, save what shall have no end;   9
Mine appetite I never more will grind
On newer proof, to try an older friend,
A god in love, to whom I am confined.   12
    Then give me welcome, next my heaven the best,
    Even to thy pure and most loving breast.

The speaker is in a mood where he cannot bear himself. A motley is someone in a jester's outfit, here it seems someone who has made a fool of himself, laughed at not with. The verbal phrases of 3–4 with a measured emphasis spell out the perverse element in one that makes the same damn mistake time after time, with oneself, with other people. (The first quatrain has had a resonance in my life.) A minor meaning of 'gored' was 'furnished with different-coloured pieces of cloth (gores)', as was a jester's costume. But the goring as by a bull's horns of his own thoughts, the values he stands by, gives a vicious hook to the sorry figure he has cut. This is a man who is angry with himself. He has 'looked on truth' (5) as others have looked on him. 'Blenches' (7) are glances off, a turning-aside of the eyes (with a hint of 'flinches' but more doubtfully at that time of 'blanches'). 'Grind' (10) is 'sharpen'. The final line has another 'most' in Q, the original text so far as we have it, 'most most loving'. It makes the line both metrically and semantically clumsy; I am inclined to see it as a printer's error. The single superlative is more emphatic and the revised rhythm (with a slight accent on 'thy') somehow welcoming, an alleviation of the earlier harshness.

The poem is a blend, it would seem, of self-lacerating home truth and a kind of apology. As an escape from the former, the latter is not entirely convincing, lines 8–12 carrying the effect of a lucid wishful thinking; but there is no mistaking the sincerity of the ending. The speaker offers comfort to the other and finally to himself. There is a novel by Wilfrid Sheed in which a motorist, travelling alone, pulls over and for a few minutes reviews his general situation with a kind of brutal lashing of the mind; after which, exhausted, he drives on. This sonnet can be seen as a reminder of the subtly evolving temper (or emotional colour) in a poem. Here its path is plain. Anger, and a sense of helplessness, give way to a moment of splendid defiance (line 7), after which the honesty is of a different kind. Relief is sought in vows of devotion, no doubt from the heart; and the exhausted figure at last finds a sanctuary from his enemy, himself.

The poem may have been written in the aftermath of a quarrel. There are other such moments (for instance 90, 'Then hate me when thou wilt . . . '). With the speaker's admission (line 1) of gadding about (to be repeated more strongly in 117), there is the sense, a little more, of things coming to a head. Like charges repel: one wonders at the change in the electrical field and what it may betoken. Yet re-reading the poem, one wonders more at the moment in the lay-by, so to speak, the excoriating first six lines.

O for my sake do you with Fortune chide,
The guilty goddess of my harmful deeds,
That did not better for my life provide   3
Than public means which public manners breeds.
Thence comes it that my name receives a brand,
And almost thence my nature is subdued   6
To what it works in, like the dyer's hand.
Pity me then, and wish I were renewed;
Whilst, like a willing patient, I will drink   9
Potions of eisel 'gainst my strong infection,
No bitterness that I will bitter think,
Nor double penance to correct correction.   12
 Pity me then, dear friend, and I assure ye,
 Even that your pity is enough to cure me.

The anger is turned outwards. A startling, almost dumb-founding energy has hold of the opening lines. A fury at the situation he has got himself into is answered by an almost raving promise to remedy it by extreme measures; and finally allayed by his turning to the one true remedy, a loving understanding. The poem stands out as a savage moment of self-knowledge, but more as a tribute to friendship

The goddess Fortune is to blame for his sullying himself with the ways of (a section of) the public, the common herd. 'Public means', with the example of the dyer, must surely refer to his profession, the theatre, writing for it, acting in it. Whether it is for a particular action or merely a blemish by association there is a slur on his name; and he is in danger not only of behaving no better than the world he works in, but of becoming an irre-deemable part of it. It comes over as a class "shudder", unexpected in the playwright of so many riotous inn scenes and banter of soldiery and nobility of soul in the low-born. The revulsion at seeing his own behaviour mirror that of the crowd is not merely there to play to an aristocratic disdain on the part of his friend; it is deep in him. Of course he is to blame not Fortune, as recognised in 'penance' (12). Whatever the background it has sparked a rare poem of the heart's affection.

I take 'manners' as the object of 'breeds' (4). W.H. Auden called a book of his essays *The Dyer's Hand*; did he see a great ink-stain born of writing? 'Eisel' (10) is vinegar. In line 12 'correction' may be 'punishment' that a double penance will correct, make the more apt, with a grim word-play as the point is made. Or it may be 'improvement', on the lines of making 'assurance double sure', ramming the point home. I prefer the former but both are there.

We have journeyed some way in three years (104, and seeing the sequence as in more or less chronological order). Despite a series of absences of heart (or at least of physical presence) on both sides, there is a tried and tested closeness without which this appeal would not have been made. The way line 14 undercuts the frenetic hyperbole of 9–12 suggests the speaker finds a sanity, or calmness, with his friend he can scarcely come to on his own. It is not a settled relationship but it is one of deep knowledge and need, one senses on both sides.

The first two lines of the next sonnet lead one to hazard at a particular act that has brought shame on the speaker, rather than a general kind of low behaviour in low company, as it may be, or a taint by association. We cannot know and it does not matter. Certainly with the two poems together he appears to be in a crisis of some sort. The 'brand' sears (5 above): it is more than the 'blots' and 'bewailèd guilt' of 36. Yet in keeping with the concertina of mood-offerings to be heard throughout the first series, its remaining pieces vary considerably in tone. One can do no more than take each outburst, each quiet reflection, as it comes.

Your love and pity doth th' impression fill
Which vulgar scandal stamped upon my brow;
For what care I who calls me well or ill,   3
So you o'er-green my bad, my good allow?
You are my all the world, and I must strive
To know my shames and praises from your tongue;   6
None else to me, nor I to none alive,
That my steeled sense or changes right or wrong.
In so profound abysm I throw all care   9
Of others' voices, that my adder's sense
To critic and to flatterer stoppèd are.
Mark how with my neglect I do dispense: 12
    You are so strongly in my purpose bred,
    That all the world besides methinks y'are dead.

A rush of gratitude for the loving reassurance offered by the other brings on a strange sense of severance from the rest of the world. The dent of public infamy is for a time filled in, the stigma removed; to retain the effect, the speaker enters a state of near-solipsism. If the sonnet is read in this way the difficulties that many editors have found seem to fall away. George Steevens in his edition of 1780 called lines 7–8 'purblind' and 'obscure'; and most since have tended to concur, also shaking their heads at line 14. But all would agree, I suppose, the piece attests to a tendency of the persona of the poems to take cover in an isolated and extreme position; even if now it is not the friend he is distanced from.

The speaker will not accept a word of praise or criticism from anyone else. He is hardened against the faintest possibility of their value judgements affecting his: any who begin to try to judge him, or anything of his, are dead to him and vice versa. 'Sense' (10) can be plural, hence 'are' (11). The adder is proverbially deaf but I think another and very different sense may lurk. It is interesting that the poet brings in well with ill (3), praises with shames (6), right with wrong (8), and then flatterer with critic (11). He may (also) have responses to his poetry, his dramas, in mind. Does not an adder's readiness to strike out at anyone, whatever the approach they may have made, suggest a writer all too ready to react to comment on his work? It does to me; and I can accept the deaf reading alongside the hyper-sharp. He is dull now even to what he used most to be on the lookout for, poised to respond to.

Line 12 is a touch self-contradictory in paving the way for the *coup de grâce*, so far as the outside world is concerned. Whether 'my neglect' is my inattention to others or theirs to me, and of course (as in 7) it is either or both, how I deal with it ('dispense'), with a strong overtone of how I ignore it, would not naturally require another to take note. Yet the shrug leads on to the final conceit: the idea is gestural, he seems to say, not to be taken literally. It is still a marvellous dismissal.

The friend is so present in him, so much of his inner being, that the rest of the world can go hang. It does not exist. Not only those offering unwanted opinions, the whole lot of you, he says, are nothing. 'Y'are' (14) is 'ye are', a plural form after the singular of the line before; the speaker scornfully addresses the extinct mass in the final phrase. The rest of the world is set beside his friend, as different as death from life.

The couplet rhyme is the same as in 104 and 108. 'Unbred' 'dead', 'bred' 'dead', 'bred' 'dead'; something is stirring in the poet's mind to do with life and its conclusion. Who knows what planning, conscious or not so conscious, went into the series? The repetition may or may not say something.

Since I left you mine eye is in my mind,
And that which governs me to go about
Doth part his function, and is partly blind,   3
Seems seeing, but effectually is out:
For it no form delivers to the heart
Of bird, of flower, or shape, which it doth latch;   6
Of his quick objects hath the mind no part,
Nor his own vision holds what it doth catch.
For if it see the rud'st or gentlest sight,   9
The most sweet-favour or deformèd'st creature,
The mountain or the sea, the day or night,
The crow or dove, it shapes them to your feature.   12
    Incapable of more, replete with you,
    My most true mind thus maketh mine untrue.

Still in a daze, the poet ponders a paradox of loving. The eye has been paired with the heart before (24, 46, 47) as separate components – or opponents – within the possessed anatomy, so to speak: the object has been both to compliment the friend by way of a pretty conceit, and to finesse a new refinement in the portrait of love and the lover. Here the mind has been taken over. Throughout the dodeka it is passive, as the eye plays merry havoc with everything that comes into its range. The eye (or 'his own vision', 8) is the subject of all the verbs except 'left' (1), 'hath' (7) and 'maketh' (14). The effect is of a continual transformation: a lover's paradisal state of reflection, while apart from the beloved, everything turning to the fair one's form. In passing, I would note a (possible) borrowing by W.H.Auden in his first sonnet of *In Time of War*, 'Till finally there came a childish creature, / On whom the years could model any feature, / And fake with ease a leopard or a dove . . . ' But he is on a different tack.

Through the eye the mind seems to subjugate Nature. One thinks of a later philosophical doctrine, Berkeley's *esse est percipi*, 'to be is to be perceived', that takes the governing power of the mind to its logical end. It is that power that Shakespeare glimpses at, behind the infatuated play. It is wonderful how aspects of Nature appear and disappear, with a kind of transitory being, in lines 9–12. Finally the mind takes the responsible part, grammatically; and a question is opened, to be explored in the next piece, as to its role in love. What indisputably is, has changed; then is the mind a falsifier?

The final two words have prompted a deal of discussion. Some see a dropped 'eye', or an elided 'my eyes' as in 'm'eyne' (the text is 'mine'). Some see 'untrue' as a noun. I take the words as they are and seem to be. The loyal love of the 'most true' mind, under the eye's controlling power, makes what is to all intents and purposes a new mind, one that no longer has regard for what is in front of it, but only what it has left behind. A second 'mind' is to be understood at the end, 'mine' standing for 'my mind', and so 'my mind untrue', one that distorts the shapes of nature. But there is a typically Shakespearean piece of prestidigitation going on. Within the apparently definite statement of the last line an unanswerable question is posed. The first 'true' may be what truly is in an altered world where love reigns supreme. In this reading the second mind (after 'mine') is the old one. Here loyalty to one's love has changed the actuality before it. Love's form is the stronger reality. It is as if a vision is unveiled and as quickly veiled again. The speaker has it both ways: at once admitting the norm and rising above it, he allows the mind its adventures. After all, it is delivered into endless error by the eye's bewildering and beautiful shenanigans.

Or is it on the right track at last?

Or whether doth my mind, being crowned with you,
Drink up the monarch's plague, this flattery?
Or whether shall I say mine eye saith true,　　　　　　　3
And that your love taught it this alchemy,
To make of monsters and things indigest
Such cherubins as your sweet self resemble,　　　　　　6
Creating every bad a perfect best,
As fast as objects to his beams assemble?
O 'tis the first, 'tis flattery in my seeing,　　　　　　　9
And my great mind most kingly drinks it up.
Mine eye well knows what with his gust is 'greeing,
And to his palate doth prepare the cup.　　　　　　　12
　　If it be poisoned, 'tis the lesser sin
　　That mine eye loves it and doth first begin.

I have the sense with a few of the sonnets of a private agenda,
something shared between the two men that the outsider can
only guess at. It may be a joke, as perhaps in 99, or differently
in 135 and 136; or as here, as it seems, the intricacies of a meta-
physical conceit, in this and the last piece turning in part upon
an extra-poetical exchange. At a guess then: the speaker, over-
come by the fervour apparent in their latest reconciliation,
cannot stop thinking about his friend. 113 illustrates this in the
form of an obsessive delusion which may not be a delusion, since
love is all-powerful. 114 investigates further: where does it
come from, the torrent of images of the other, sweeping away
the frame of things, making a new reality? While the answer
that the poem finds says something about their friendship that
may need saying, and continues the grand series of courtly
compliments, there is an arcane feel to it all: one could be poring
over an elaborate response to an objection from the friend
perhaps. Did he accuse the speaker of going too far? If it is some-

thing of an overworked exercise, however, the poem has its memorable moments (lines 2 and 10 to my mind); and once understood is rather charming. If the energy driving the poet on at this point is still a little wild, it is (as always) tempered in the task of composition; and a touch of elusive humour gleams out, as here and there in the double series, beneath the inherited solemnity of the sonnet-convention.

Is the mind responsible for the transformed appearance of everything? No, it is absolved: it is the eye, that flatters the mind, knows what it likes ('gust' is 'taste', 11); that prepares the drink, and enjoys it no end himself. He is the official taster (final phrase) and rightly will be the first to suffer if the drink is bad (as the conceit has it). If it had been otherwise and the eye 'saith true' (3), then 'your love' (4) would have been to blame – unthinkable. The writer's mind is party to the transformation (that now is all from bad to good) but passively so. It has been instigated entirely by that rascal the eye. It is accepted that the effusive speaker has been "over the top", perhaps; but it is a mere peccadillo on the part of a junior member of the household, the eye, rather than a diktat from the head, the mind, led on by the youth himself. Beneath what may be an apology for getting things wrong is the light brush of a deeper truth. Love gets things wrong. It is not all-powerful. Far from uttered, the thought lies there, like a seed. It may be the quietest hint that we are entering the final stage of a journey.

'Poisoned' (13) is strong. It may contain a passing allusion to the friend's betrayal of the speaker, who finds a new way to appear to take some of the guilt onto himself. If so it is the final reference (in this series) to the affair; as if to say it is all but forgotten. I sense in the intimate tone of the piece a shared enjoyment of the argument. It may be going too far, but I can see the two men reading the poem together, appreciating the way it has all worked out.

Those lines that I before have writ do lie,
Even those that said I could not love you dearer;
Yet then my judgement knew no reason why   3
My most full flame should afterwards burn clearer.
But reckoning Time, whose millioned accidents
Creep in 'twixt vows, and change decrees of kings,   6
Tan sacred beauty, blunt the sharp'st intents,
Divert strong minds to th' course of altering things –
Alas, why, fearing of Time's tyranny,   9
Might I not then say, now I love you best,
When I was certain o'er incertainty,
Crowning the present, doubting of the rest?   12
     Love is a babe; then might I not say so,
     To give full growth to that which still doth grow?

The surface question is conducted with spirit, but it is not diffi-
cult to see where the heart of the writer, and the heart of the
poem, lies. The battle with Time moves on. The so-called lie (1)
of previous poems is excused and the enemy is defied, the poet's
love burns ever brighter – but the enemy is feared, and more
than feared. Its immensity, its power to intervene, form an insu-
perable barrier. The sentence that brings them into being
cannot finish. The mournful 'Alas' (9) is hardly to regret a forced
inaccuracy, as the surface would have it, but more a crying-out
at an overwhelming blank wall, a destiny of change. Against
which Love as the boy Cupid puts up a plucky fight.

     The listing of Time's powers (5–8) recalls Macbeth's paean
to sleep, that he knows is denied him after the murder. There
too the sentence does not – cannot – finish, but is interrupted
by the unforgettable 'What do you mean?' of his wife. So the
lover interrupts his perilous meditation here. 'Tan' (7) suggests
both 'darken and 'toughen' (as in turning skin to leather);

'sacred' is 'inviolable', the three-word phrase like a compressed explosive; while line 8 seems to outrun the pentameter yet to be perfectly contained by it. 'The course of altering things' reminds of the chief effect of Time, as it stretches out, never to have a stop.

Line 5 presents a grammatical ambiguity that makes little difference in the end. Is Time the reckoner or is it the speaker (as in 'fearing', 9)? If the speaker, now taking account of Time's might, the sentence does work as a whole, though the list still comes to an unexpected end. If the ominous powers of Time start with an inclusive one, as in bringing to a reckoning, the reading emphasis follows more naturally, and it is certainly the alternative I favour. But they come to the same thing: if the speaker is "reckoning", thinking about Time, it is deprived of its first descriptor, which nevertheless is understood both by what follows and in the underlying ambiguity the mind may pick up at some level. If Time is doing the reckoning the speaker is still obviously thinking about it. I imagine it was not an intended ambiguity but it scarcely matters. The more powerful poetry I hold in this case lies in the more abrupt.

The couplet is deft. The speaker excuses the 'lie' on the grounds of 'crowning the present' (12) while looking to the future at exactly the same time. 'To give' (14) is both to endow and to encourage; and the last line as a whole encapsulates another of love's paradoxes. Not only is it at once all-powerful and illusive (113), here it is at its full and never at its full ('still doth grow'), just as mighty Cupid is never more than a babe or boy. Yet the line is satisfying in itself and as an end to the poem. Can love ever be complete? The question is raised, it is seen as unanswerable, yet in such a way as not to disturb the mind as it takes in the words. The poet performs his magic turn again.

Let me not to the marriage of true minds
Admit impediments. Love is not love
Which alters when it alteration finds,   3
Or bends with the remover to remove.
O no, it is an ever-fixèd mark
That looks on tempests and is never shaken;   6
It is the star to every wandering bark
Whose worth's unknown, although his height be taken.
Love's not Time's fool, though rosy lips and cheeks   9
Within his bending sickle's compass come;
Love alters not with his brief hours and weeks,
But bears it out even to the edge of doom.   12
    If this be error and upon me proved,
    I never writ, nor no man ever loved.

There are four sonnets that do not directly refer to the beloved or at once summon his or her presence to the fore. The others are 121, 129 and 146, all to do with the speaker's faults. This stands alone as celebratory in a universal sense. It is an easy step to assume the said presence and the reader takes it as a matter of course. Nonetheless there would seem to be an urgency about these four, a need for the general statement to take at least a surface precedence. This is not to say that others are less urgent as to the particular situation.

Shakespeare makes love's case once and for all. The first sentence echoes the marriage service and defines the terms: it is a wedlock of minds, as it has been all along. 'The remover' (4) may be one of the parties who is absent for a while; or it may be transitive, a person or situation that disrupts or puts a strain on things. 'Mark' (5) is a beacon or lighthouse ('seamark'), that cedes poetic place to a guiding star to the steersman in a boat ('bark') lost in a storm. The star's altitude can be known but not how precious it is, an enduring aside on the nature of love. At the risk of over-exposing a metaphor's mystery, I take 'height' to suggest the facts that can be known, the things that can be said, when we met etc. . . . one need not go on. 'Love's not Time's fool' (9) splendidly non-personifies: throughout the dodeka it is all but a person, and here anything but an inferior to the familiar old man with the scythe. The 'bending sickle' (10) underlines the difference (see line 4). 'Doom' (12) is Doomsday as much as death. It is a series of statements in 1–12, rather than a developing argument, that lends credence to the idea of a true union, and makes us believe in its certainty.

The couplet is no less straightforward: Shakespeare foregoes all complexity save a gentle irony. A reference to his past writing (14) as in 115.1 indicates, perhaps, a gathering-up of ideas, or loose ends, as an end to the series approaches. Here he may also have in mind his plays and other poems, to contemplate which is to lead one to wonder, yet again, about the private side of an individual so in touch with the public.

If ever a writer was created by his nation's language and the ways of the world it is he. In the Sonnets surely is a clue of some sort to his ability to touch a nerve, in the minds of those who hear his words, in the awareness of those who witness his dramas. A private intensity, almost manic at times, we might have guessed at; but there is something else that chimes with the effort and intelligence involved. There is a danger of arguing backwards here, and it is true that the burning preoccupation of the first series could hardly be foretold. But through the shabbiness of human error and limitation, never to lose sight of a pure ideal – a gigantic effort of holding focus, of formulation of the invisible – seems on a par, as a more private experience, with the spectacular commitment to the more public issues of the plays.

Accuse me thus: that I have scanted all
Wherein I should your great deserts repay,
Forgot upon your dearest love to call,   3
Whereto all bonds do tie me day by day;
That I have frequent been with unknown minds,
And given to time your own dear-purchased right;   6
That I have hoisted sail to all the winds
Which should transport me farthest from your sight.
Book both my wilfulness and errors down,   9
And on just proof surmise accumulate;
Bring me within the level of your frown,
But shoot not at me in your wakened hate;   12
    Since my appeal says I did strive to prove
    The constancy and virtue of your love.

A step away from the ideal, we are back in the world of human
error, appealingly admitted to, if with a final appeal that may
have been turned down. Again a more independent-minded
persona is before us: it is as if the force of the poet has at last
entered the lover's sphere of action. A certain unity can be felt
to operate behind the final paragraphs of the long soliloquy of
the first series, the voice and the life together. This does not
necessarily make for better poems; but it may add a sense of
further commitment to the outcome.

    Line 3 seems to refer to actual visits, given the next few lines;
but it can also suggest a (lack of) summoning-up of the friend's
love, or of his for the friend, in a more general way. 'Frequent'
(5) as well as 'often' carries a sense of the verb, 'to frequent'.
'Level' (11) is 'aim', an archery term. Lines 7–8 are delightfully
dogged, wilful as he admits; and the ticking-off that is lying in
wait has an amusing touch of the judicial manner and mien
(9–11). The ending is pure sophistry and somehow quite

beautiful. Perhaps it is the unusual and seamless transition from dodeka to couplet, with the change in tone compelling us, with the imagined recipient of the plea, to listen; perhaps it is a disarming note of sincerity – he may mean it at the time – that stems from the emotive 'wakened hate' followed by 'constancy and virtue'. These and more: and an underhand sting in 'virtue' may be part of it too. How constant is the youth? It could be that this sonnet has an intended link with the last, as a test of love not bending with 'the remover'; though the difference in tone between the two gives the possibility little weight. Yet the last line does put it in touch.

One cannot help but imagine the playwright going here and there among people, known and unknown, and indeed spreading his wings ever outward (lines 5–8), simply to be a part of the dynamic rattling world. It is inconceivable that the thunderstorms of speech on stage did not have something of a gadabout behind them, however silent and still a figure he may also have been. Of course there is no absolute proof the author of the sonnets is the author of the plays. There is the name attached to the publication, as to *The Passionate Pilgrim*, 1599, that included two of the second series, 138 and 144; and there is Meres' comment (see note to 76). The few links that may be discerned in the text (for an example see note to sonnet 8) or content (note to 94) are not conclusive. Yet the quality of the poetry in plays and poems puts the matter beyond doubt, I should think. In this poem I fancy I can see or hear the playwright: there is a freshness, an energy, a defiance, a personality at work, all subsumed in the end in a gesture of open surrender. And a gesture it may be, but it mirrors something more serious, an appeal to be accepted, even forgiven, an honest errant man, giving himself up to the service of something greater. This is the indelible figure of the Sonnets.

Like as, to make our appetites more keen,
With eager compounds we our palate urge;
As, to prevent our maladies unseen,   3
We sicken to shun sickness when we purge;
Even so, being full of your ne'er-cloying sweetness,
To bitter sauces did I frame my feeding;   6
And sick of welfare, found a kind of meetness
To be diseased ere that there was true needing.
Thus policy in love, to anticipate   9
The ills that were not, grew to faults assured,
And brought to medicine a healthful state
Which, rank of goodness, would by ill be cured.   12
But thence I learn and find the lesson true,
Drugs poison him that so fell sick of you.

It is as though, the excuse for his absence provided by the last
sonnet having been rejected, the poet comes clean. There is a
devastating honesty in this. Beneath the sonneteer's skin a
different animal moves: all at once we see the force of the man
turn on the relationship itself. His "discovery" in the next piece
that 'ruined love . . . grows fairer than at first, more strong, far
greater' is likely to be of little comfort to the friend, whom for
the first time we may sense as in Shakespeare's shoes, in thrall
to the dominant character. The very clarity of the argument here
tells a story; one can almost feel the pain being inflicted by the
lines. It has been a time in coming, but a crisis now finally vali-
dates the love affair. (For so we may term it, a literary fact.
Whatever the historical origin it exists forever on the page.)

The speaker is in overdrive; he instigates everything, and
describes what he has done with an angry nonchalance. Love as
an illness is in the courtly tradition. Spenser has, 'Long
languishing in double malady / Of my heart's wound and of my

body's grief . . . ', and Sidney, 'Sick to the death, still loving my disease . . . ' Even to quote such occasional lines of his predecessors indicates a difference in Shakespeare: he does not wallow. 'Eager compounds' (2) are 'bitter concoctions'. 'Policy in love', it is implied, is an error (see 124.9). 'Rank' (12) is 'rich', 'overflowing', but carried a negative association as now, 'gross', 'rotten'; similarly 'sick of' (7, 14) could mean 'weary of'. The implication is inescapable: the speaker says 'ne'er-cloying' (5) but means 'cloying'. The 'bitter sauces' are outside friendships he now regrets: as 'medicine' (11) and 'drugs' (14) they are harmful, even fatal. Of course the intent, at least so far as the sonnet is concerned, is to re-establish his standing with his one true friend. But the subliminal content speaks louder. It shouts between the lines, steals the air-waves. There is a split: the outer man wishes to explain away his behaviour, to return to the 'pure and most loving breast' (110). The inner man cries freedom.

In context this is heady stuff. In my view we have the stages of an argument, in the sense of an almighty row, laid out before us. When Shakespeare lets his anger show, whether it is with the world (as in 66), Time (*passim*), his public image (111, 121), or here with his private situation, the poetic harvest is rich. From first to last of the first series (with the sole exception of 99) an urgent quality of speech is present, whatever the mood, subdued to tempestuous. It is like an indrawn breath. It is this that the plays naturally offer, with the words spoken on stage; and here too is the immediacy of the Sonnets. In a sense every poet is a dramatist, every dramatist a poet. A personal poem is a stage event, the narrator his own protagonist. The resolution can be a temporary one, as here (with more poems to come), yet still have its own finality. From first breath to last a drama is acted out. Urgency is all.

What potions have I drunk of siren tears,
Distilled from limbecks foul as hell within,
Applying fears to hopes and hopes to fears,   3
Still losing when I saw myself to win!
What wretched errors hath my heart committed,
Whilst it hath thought itself so blessèd never!   6
How have mine eyes out of their spheres been fitted
In the distraction of this madding fever!
O benefit of ill! Now I find true   9
That better is by evil still made better;
And ruined love, when it is built anew,
Grows fairer than at first, more strong, far greater.   12
    So I return rebuked to my content,
    And gain by ills thrice more than I have spent.

The 'poison' of 118.14 is held up to the light. 'Siren tears / Distilled from limbecks foul as hell within', to describe false overtures of friendship from others, is almost frightening. 'Limbecks' are alembics, stills; the 'tears' they manufacture are perhaps of apparent sympathy for the speaker's woes, his sense of stigma. 'Applying' seems a little clumsy, 'administering' as in medical treatment; but the oppositions of 3–4 quickly take over, with a searching *double entendre*. Are the hopes and fears, the losing and winning to do with the recovery of "health"; or are they of the thrill of wooing new friendships, of making new conquests? Line 6 gives force to the latter idea, and 7–8 still more. 'Been fitted' (7), which I take as 'set firmly' outside their sockets, or(/and) propelled as by fits, is 'bene fitted' in the original Q text; with a clear pun in line 9. A dizzying sense of freedom spins about the octave, as he pursues a course of social vagabondage, and possibly more.

A sexual aura can be felt to float about the lines. Stephen

Booth's commentary traces every conceivable such allusion throughout the sequence, and concludes: 'William Shakespeare was almost certainly homosexual, bisexual, or heterosexual. The sonnets provide no evidence on the matter.' Yet he produces a host of readings in which more or less hidden sexual terms can be overheard. With the majority of the poems to or about the man one is led to wonder what may be going on. There is however a similar play on female-related terms over the sequence as a whole. I think that in many cases Booth's ears are pinned too far back; but there is enough to suggest a tendency to a certain kind of word-play. It is likely to be an in-joke between the two men (that may have included a sharing of the second series to the woman). It is probably best to stay with Booth's conclusion.

The sonnets to the man are deeply informed by the idea of the lover's quest, that includes a religious dimension. The soul of the knight is at stake, whether his object is a beautiful lady or the holy grail. To have so many sexual allusions (of whichever orientation) as a reflection of an actual state of affairs seems doubtful, even in a literary form at some remove from the mediaeval land of legend and faerie. At any event the aura adds a zest to this piece; and the sestet, as in 110, has a fetching simplicity. As in 110, too, it fails to persuade; and one can only imagine the dissatisfaction of the other at a further false apology, as he may well have seen it. Despite their pious avowal of having learnt a lesson for good and all, this and the last two poems carry an increasing note of revelling in revelry, so to speak; in the light of which nothing is worse than an apology not meant. The wanderer is still glad of his straying. His friend has shown his displeasure, he has been 'rebuked' (13) as he sees it; and he seems to feel the worst is over.

That you were once unkind befriends me now,
And for that sorrow which I then did feel
Needs must I under my transgression bow,   3
Unless my nerves were brass or hammered steel.
For if you were by my unkindness shaken,
As I by yours, y'have passed a hell of time,   6
And I, a tyrant, have no leisure taken
To weigh how once I suffered in your crime.
O that our night of woe might have remembered   9
My deepest sense, how hard true sorrow hits,
And soon to you, as you to me, then tendered
The humble salve which wounded bosoms fits.   12
    But that your trespass now becomes a fee;
    Mine ransoms yours, and yours must ransom me.

Not only as a description of a crisis of love, but as a defining
moment of love's bond, this poem to my mind stands apart from
the rest (though it seems perfectly placed in the series). With
its troubling admission of blame and exploration of where it
leads, and the far-reaching completeness of the final statement,
it informs me more deeply than any other short poem I know of
the nature of love's shared experience.

The speaker refers to a time when the friend cruelly wronged
him. It may be reflected in 34. On the present occasion he has
wronged his friend and can only gain an idea of the other's hurt
by thinking of his own, back then. By this he sees the awfulness
of what he has done. At the centre of the poem lies the unde-
fined, perhaps undefinable 'night of woe' (9), which may be the
dark time of a terrible argument, or one that took place in the
night. He wishes that at that time he had 'remembered / My
deepest sense'. This is defined in the next phrase; the Q text has
the commas as shown above. I take it naturally as stated. Is not

the playwright's deepest sense 'how hard true sorrow hits'? His deepest preoccupation is to do with the nature of authority and power, in the state and in the individual. But the great tragedies tell unerringly of what he is most keenly attuned to. The five words say it perfectly. Had he remembered it that 'night', instead of being carried away by the passion of the moment, he would have 'tendered / The humble salve which wounded bosoms fits' (12), a beautiful line for an apology where there is need of one.

The friend managed it (11). Perhaps the couplet of 34 shows us how; 'ransom' comes up there too, the only other time in the collection. Now the speaker's apology is the poem itself. The couplet of a Shakespearian sonnet often carries the burden of the overall statement's resolution at once lightly and as it were significantly, as if conscious of its onus. The final import is such as to deflect any trivialisation of the issue: it is a conscious mind, that lets us in on a final thought, rather than a self-conscious air. Here the last word says everything. It is not only the speaker's offence that is to be discharged in the light of the friend's (as is the friend's by his). His very person is to be set free, his life. This is his apology, and his request for forgiveness: the recognition that his life is indeed nothing, after what he has done. His only hope is for the other's understanding.

Early in my notes I ventured to lay the groundwork for a discussion of some kind related to what I called 'pronoun play', as a way into exploring how Shakespeare presents love's central aspect. The containment of the other's self, its "housing", that amounts in some respect to an exchange of identity, is I think undemonstrable. It is too deep and intimate a thing. Yet it is a theme; and its most tangible expression is here.

'Tis better to be vile than vile esteemed,
When not to be receives reproach of being,
And the just pleasure lost, which is so deemed   3
Not by our feeling, but by others' seeing.
For why should others' false adulterate eyes
Give salutation to my sportive blood?   6
Or on my frailties why are frailer spies,
Which in their wills count bad what I think good?
No, I am that I am, and they that level   9
At my abuses reckon up their own.
I may be straight, though they themselves be bevel;
By their rank thoughts my deeds must not be shown.   12
    Unless this general evil they maintain
    All men are bad, and in their badness reign.

Still overcharged, the poet turns with a vengeance on those in the outside world who criticise his behaviour. While in 111 he is acutely aware of a stigma to do with his profession, and specifically the 'public manners' it has infected him with, here he seems to refer to a reputation gained for sexual conduct. If the 'brand' his name receives (111.5) at the present time is of a slightly different stamp, so is his indignation; here he stands alone. Splendidly he denies not the charges but people's right to make them. I imagine his 'sportive blood' (6) has led to a number of encounters: but interestingly, he does not quite admit to the charges either (see line 11, where 'bevel' means 'zigzag', 'crooked'). The sonnet implies that a certain level of promiscuity on his part may (or may not) have taken place; but what matters is people's readiness to admit to their own faults, not what they have to say of the faults of others. In its way it is a philosophical poem on the theme of respect for the individual, if with a highly personalised slant.

As to which, the conduct he hints at may as well be with women as with men. As with a few other sonnets there is no more than an implied awareness of the youth or "dark lady", and precious little of that. The poem seems to fit into the sequence where it is, as a final expression of present anger, and as a fore-runner to 129 that is all to do with lust. And yet it should be remembered that the 'frailties' (7) may be, or include, failings of another kind.

The ending in my view is generally misread. I see a lost full stop after 'shown' (12) – the 'n' in Q appears to be smudged – and a far stronger statement in the couplet than if line 13 is subordinate to 11–12, and 14 merely descriptive of 13. If people do not accept that we are all frail, fallible beings (13), all such deniers are not only bad – but 'in their badness reign' (14). If you like, they are filthily bad. The commonly accepted reading, by which there is no pause more than a comma's worth after 'shown' (12), makes a kind of sense, but a comparatively feeble one, with a weakening of the couplet that is anti-Shakespearian, and no acceleration of meaning in the final phrase. It can be argued both ways, but this way should be indicated too; *et nunc manet in te*, I am tempted to say with André Gide, and now it rests with you.

In line 3 'just' is 'valid'; 'so' is 'vile'. 'Wills' in line 8 can have the sense of 'sexual organs' (male or female), as well as of 'wishes'. Does he have the Puritans in his sights? 'No, I am that I am' (9) echoes God's words to Moses (*Exodus*, 3.14). Booth says this makes the speaker sound 'smug, presumptuous, and stupid'. Again it is for the reader to judge. I hear a personal statement, no matter where the poet found it, ideally suited to the theme of an unusual and magnificent poem.

Thy gift, thy tables, are within my brain
Full charactered with lasting memory,
Which shall above that idle rank remain   3
Beyond all date, even to eternity;
Or at the least, so long as brain and heart
Have faculty by nature to subsist;   6
Till each to razed oblivion yield his part
Of thee, thy record never can be missed.
That poor retention could not so much hold,   9
Nor need I tallies thy dear love to score;
Therefore to give them from me was I bold,
To trust those tables that receive thee more.   12
    To keep an adjunct to remember thee
    Were to import forgetfulness in me.

Sonnet 77 appears to accompany the gift of a notebook of 'vacant leaves' to the friend. Here the friend has given the speaker a notebook ('tables' is 'table-book', as in *Hamlet*, 'My tables, – meet it is I set it down') which instead of keeping he has given away. It seems to have stored within it a testament of the friend's love; the poem is an apology (infinitely lighter in kind than that of 120) that takes as its excuse the imprint of that love on the speaker's mind and heart. It may be a literal recording of the notebook's words in the memory or a full and true knowledge of a love that goes beyond words. There is no reason why the book of 77 should not be that of 122; there is something about the poet's offhandedness, in belittling the offence, that suggests it may be so. The underlying point of the poem is the speaker's absolute love for the other, that includes the knowledge of the other's love for him, such that no written record is needed of it. At the same time the tone is a touch dismissive of the friend's efforts and care. To cast a somewhat beady eye on the situation:

it seems the speaker at this time is a little in the ascendant, and (despite the apparent recent levelling-ground of 120) cannot resist what a strategist might term a marginal power-play. Giving away the notebook (whether or not it is the same one) might be a part of that. These days one's sympathies are with the friend. At all events the poem is in remarkable contrast to the last few, in its light-handed particularity; a reminder that the vision behind it all is a dramatist's, for whom passions come and go – perhaps even his own – on an ever-changing stage.

'Charactered' (2) suggests the letters of the words, the characters, set down in the brain in their rank (3), or rows, from the original. 'Razed oblivion' (7) may consciously echo *tabula rasa*, then in use, for the obliterated 'table' of the brain in death. Line 4 seems effusive, with the second quatrain quickly bringing the sentiment to order, yet permitting it to remain – possibly a clue to a somewhat hasty composition. 'Idle rank' (3), 'poor retention' (9) and 'tallies' (10, notched sticks to keep score) are all faintly scornful of the words in their written state in the book. The 'tables' of 12 are of course the stored pages of his brain, that can only die with him. 'Adjunct' (13) is something additional, an "extra". The final line, light as it is, has a Shakespearian cunning. On the one hand a touch of humour enables the writer, as one fancies, to get away with the loss. He has, after all, been forgetful in that; and so to end with a mock shaking of the head, at the thought that he need keep the book as a reminder of anything, makes the moment at once a solemn and a light-hearted one. And it is more. 'Forgetfulness' can also carry a sense of death's oblivion (as in *Richard III*, 'The swallowing gulf / Of dark forgetfulness and deep oblivion'). A hint of what is to come finely ends, on a typically complex note, a poetic occasion of untypical – and delightful – ordinariness.

No, Time, thou shalt not boast that I do change.
Thy pyramids built up with newer might
To me are nothing novel, nothing strange;   3
They are but dressings of a former sight.
Our dates are brief, and therefore we admire
What thou dost foist upon us that is old,   6
And rather make them born to our desire
Than think that we before have heard them told.
Thy registers and thee I both defy,   9
Not wondering at the present nor the past;
For thy records, and what we see, doth lie,
Made more or less by thy continual haste.   12
    This I do vow, and this shall ever be:
    I will be true, despite thy scythe and thee.

'There is no new thing under the sun,' says the Preacher in *Ecclesiastes*, a proverbial idea behind 59, where it is overturned by the 'composèd wonder of your frame'. Here it runs deeper, and is used in support of the ideal of love itself. It is allowed to stand, as it tells of a truth behind Time's rollercoaster of assumed power. Beyond Time is Love where nothing changes.

One may ask what the fact that the speaker stays true in his affections (lines 1 and 13–14) has to do with the waxing and waning of the things of Time (2–12). After all the argument could be an admission of such waning to come, since like it or not we are among those things. In what respect is it that 'thy records, and what we see, doth lie' (11)? The clue is in the 'I'/'we' opposition: that 'we' are in Time's power does not mean that 'I' am. The 'I' is in part the voice of Love as it were in human guise. Just as Time is both staged and named as a person ('thy registers and thee' 9, 'thy scythe and thee' 14), so Love's presence is felt, even in the absence of any naming term. To put it differently, the 'I' of lines 1, 9 and 13 becomes an 'I' in perfect balance and opposition to the figure of Time in the final line and word.

'The obelisks which adorned the triumphal arches built to greet James I in the City of London . . . were described as pyramids,' Katherine Duncan-Jones tells us; and reflecting on the re-emergence (however minor) of a theme from ancient Egypt may have led Shakespeare into the train of thought of the poem. 'Dressings' (4) is 'reworkings'; 'foist' (6) is 'palm off', used in cheating with dice. Time toys with our minds (lines 7–8), deceives us for ever; again and again we are gulled by apparent novelties. But there is another way to take, of the heart's constancy, less external and more true. There is the touch of a more than usual finality in the tone of the poem. One could almost feel the speaker is close to a sense of completed outcome, where the ideal that (in spite of all) he is entirely committed to, is not so very far from its realisation. The adjective of the final line gathers in significance.

To complete the list, if merely for the pleasure of referring back to them, of the sonnets to the youth that for me be-pinnacle the series (see notes to 63 and 96): for the dawning ray of a new realisation, 107; for a marriage of impure and pure, 110; for an outburst of self-anger, 111; for a clear sighting of the ideal, 116; for a double-edged self-accusation, 117; for its searching and beautiful apology, its grief, its wisdom, 120; for a searing confirmation of the unassailable fact of individuality, 121. The poem that all the series dovetails into, 126, not a sonnet in the modern sense, holds worthy place at the foot of the swarming constellation, one of its brightest stars.

If my dear love were but the child of state,
It might for Fortune's bastard be unfathered,
As subject to Time's love. or to Time's hate,   3
Weeds among weeds, or flowers with flowers gathered.
No, it was builded far from accident;
It suffers not in smiling pomp, nor falls   6
Under the blow of thrallèd discontent,
Whereto th'inviting time our fashion calls.
It fears not policy, that heretic,   9
Which works on leases of short-numbered hours,
But all alone stands hugely politic,
That it nor grows with heat, nor drowns with showers.   12
   To this I witness call the fools of Time,
    Which die for goodness, who have lived for crime.

In the final three sonnets to the man (123–5), before the *envoi*, there is a touch of quiet certainty, as if at journey's end. The persona of the poems has arrived at a knowledge that is to be had of love. Whether or not the order is entirely Shakespeare's own, whether or not there are sonnets missing or inserted, the series as we have it, as well as being something of great beauty, is the authentic account of an exploration. It has been a search blindly driven by a yearning than which there is no greater human need. From its anodyne – yet charming – beginning to the present point, where in a sense life has found its true end, there is the air of an ongoing purpose. Something has been tugging at my mind, on and off, as I have followed the long excursion: at last, with the writing of this note, it has come free; I can see what it is. When I was fourteen my imagination was taken by the account in the news of the Commonwealth Trans-Antarctic Expedition, led by Vivian Fuchs: a hundred-day trip that I followed at the time as I could, but did not know I remembered. I hope the personal association, which is only of the distant background, does not obtrude on the journey anyone else may make to come to terms with whatever it is that holds the sequence together.

'Love is a babe' (115.13); here a different child: but not of circumstance or chance ('state', line 1, perhaps also 'dependent on the state'). The poem describes its life as it were from conception (line 5) to maturity (11). 'Gathered' (4) is both 'in among' and 'swept away by Time': the enemy cannot enslave it to apparent good fortune or bad. Fortune is as we would say an absent father (2); life as subject to time is either falsely privileged (6) or discontented, perhaps cynically so (7–8). But love's provenance is elsewhere and its flourishing has nothing to do with where it may appear to be implanted. It is not the outward situation that nurtures it. Nor is there 'policy in love' (118.9): that is another enemy, in league with Time (9–10). Love takes the power of the foe to itself (line 11). Once 'builded' (5), it is.

The poet continues to draw on religious language with 'that heretic' (9). In general I think he does this momentarily to tap into the power of such a field, without advancing further, and by no means to take up a set stance in it. There are two sonnets to come that may have a direct bearing on his spiritual life, the next and 146. Here an adventurist vocabulary, if one may call it that, appears to set up what may be a current example for the couplet. Wrongdoers are duped by Time, in the form of some dogmatic argument, into seeking martyrdom. He may have the Catholic conspirators of the Gunpowder Plot in mind; or perhaps an earlier event. Line 13 echoes 116.9 ('Love's not Time's fool'); the sublime generality of that poem finds a more particular colouring here. He can tell of Love's vital quality, so different from that of the witless moral fools who dance to Time's commands, children of state all.

Were't aught to me I bore the canopy,
With my extern the outward honouring,
Or laid great bases for eternity,   3
Which proves more short than waste or ruining?
Have I not seen dwellers on form and favour
Lose all, and more, by paying too much rent,   6
For compound sweet forgoing simple savour,
Pitiful thrivers, in their gazing spent?
No, let me be obsequious in thy heart,   9
And take thou my oblation, poor but free,
Which is not mixed with seconds, knows no art
But mutual render, only me for thee.   12
     Hence, thou suborned informer! A true soul
     When most impeached stands least in thy control.

The debate is concluded. A line of strong denial beginning 'No,
. . . ' marks sonnets 123–5 (and 121 but scarcely before). Here
the speaker makes his position unmistakably clear in terms that
leave nothing to be said. Life is reduced to the essential. The
third quatrain answers the first two and the couplet, quite
simply, sends Time packing.

The start may well be another reference to the new monarch's
august procession through London. It would mean nothing to
the speaker to have been one of the select aristocratic few who
'bore the canopy'; nor to have laid the foundations of magnifi-
cent buildings, perhaps a ritual of the same occasion. (I like to
think of line 3 as a description of Shakespeare's achievement as
a dramatist, ironically enough.) He dismisses temporal values
and the 'pitiful thrivers', 'spent' in their envious longing (line
8). 'Obsequious' (9) is 'dutiful', perhaps with 'till death'
implied. The sense of a religious service is stronger in 'oblation'
(10), an (unadulterated, 'not mixed with seconds') offering to

the deity; and the couplet suddenly dramatises what, I suppose, is behind all religious services, an escape from the clutches of the power of darkness. If Time is the informer, whom does he inform? Is there a suborner in Shakespeare's inner world? I think this is as near as he gets to a personification of evil; and it must always be remembered that the "I" is not necessarily him; though in 146, that deals more directly with the matter of the soul, it is hard to imagine a persona behind the words other than the poet's own. (There may be a further allusion to a public event in the couplet, a 'suborned informer' on the political stage.) While the imperative of line 13 is a splendid rejection of the enemy for good and all, it creates a dramatic encounter out of nowhere, and the reader is momentarily taken aback. But what a way to conclude a life-and-death tussle.

The "pronoun play" that I have remarked on in earlier sonnets, and that reaches its apogee in 120, has its inner point confirmed here at the end of the final dodeka or exposition of the first series. The exchange of love, the loss and gain of identity that the series is dedicated to, is summed up in six words. Behind the love stories of the plays, behind the wedding service, behind any betrothal at any time in any tongue, there is one deed, one intent, one principle of love. The chronicle of 1–126 is ended, and the search of the knight errant at last rewarded, by the all but holy arrival, in poetic terms, at a state of 'mutual render, only me for thee'.

As so often, but now with the air of a completed step, the ending says much in a little. The soul's impeachment, its charge of sin, seems to come from all sides, a result of the betrayals of Time. Every accusation – of the outside world, of the speaker's against himself, or his doubt as to what amounts to the maturity of his friend – all are refuted by the true knowledge of love's exchange. The step is taken to freedom.

O thou, my lovely boy, who in thy power
Dost hold Time's fickle glass, his sickle hour;
Who hast by waning grown, and therein show'st   3
Thy lovers withering as thy sweet self grow'st;
If Nature, sovereign mistress over wrack,
As thou goest onwards, still will pluck thee back,   6
She keeps thee to this purpose, that her skill
May Time disgrace and wretched minutes kill.
Yet fear her, O thou minion of her pleasure!   9
She may detain, but not still keep, her treasure.
Her audit, though delayed, answered must be;
And her quietus is to render thee.   12

The finality of the couplet rhyme tolls throughout an elegiac adieu. Time traditionally holds an hourglass or a scythe; until this moment, the boy has magically withheld them. Now death trumps beauty. It may be merely a coming-of-age that the speaker foresees, the passing of a fleeting triumph, an adolescent beauty; but behind the scenes there is more at work. The last two lines tell of a final surrender. Under the mantle of his persona, and yet beyond it, the poet at last discovers his true aim, and embraces the object of his quest, by letting go.

There is some discussion as to whether a modern apostrophe, singular or plural, is to be found for 'lovers' (4). I doubt it: the non-possessive word balances 'sweet self'; and so far as the singular is concerned, it seems to be a moment for the speaker not to intrude. Typically self-effacing, one of a number of admirers, he observes and comments from afar on an act that is to come, an epic surrender. Beauty will go, but stays in the song; love goes, but the breath of it stays for ever in beauty's inspiration. The series finds its only end, a ceding to Time of the living fact, yet not the laurels.

The shortened and decisively altered poetic form draws its own line under proceedings. The rhetorical verve is as present as ever, the reduction in terms of length of delivery coming with dramatic effect after the *volta* at line 9. The recognition that Nature shall at the last lay down her resistance, and pay her dues to Time, inspires as fine and complete a poetic effect as we have seen. One wonders how the author came to it. He may have sensed the need for a new ending: a usurpation of the couplet by couplets, so to speak; and of its space (lines 13–14) by silence. The financial metaphor that appropriately brings matters to a close, allowing Time's material and decisive effect upon the pristine, is itself weighted to perfection. Nature's final invoice ('audit', 11) is paid by her relinquishing her favourite ('minion', 9) to the enemy. An account paid in full had 'quietus est' written on it, 'it is settled'; and 'quietus' could carry an overtone of death (as in *Hamlet*, 'When he himself might his quietus make / With a bare bodkin'). 'Render' (14) seems to take on the exchange of love and love's being in 125.12, there conveyed by the only other use of the word in the Sonnets, now to deliver the all and sum into the hands of Death. And yet with all this there is no more than the ceding of a point: the youth's beauty is to fade. Both the outward and inward intent are present to the reader, the end of a temporary perfection and the end of life, a divided concept of undivided outcome, such is the poem's unity. In some way, too, the same may be said of the rhapsody of poems before it, as the first series comes to an end.

There is no victor. Different works and workings of existence, different powers clash and are at one. The sequence is shot through with a titanic battle even as a blessed harmony plays within. It is a journey like no other.

In the old age black was not counted fair,
Or if it were it bore not beauty's name;
But now is black beauty's successive heir, 3
And beauty slandered with a bastard shame;
For since each hand hath put on Nature's power,
Fairing the foul with art's false borrowed face, 6
Sweet beauty hath no name, no holy bower,
But is profaned, if not lives in disgrace.
Therefore my mistress' eyes are raven black, 9
Her brows so suited, and they mourners seem
At such who, not born fair, no beauty lack,
Sland'ring creation with a false esteem. 12
    Yet so they mourn, becoming of their woe,
    That every tongue says beauty should look so.

15

A number of sonnet-sequences were split into contrasting parts. 127–154 is very different from 1–126: there is no sense of devotedness to an ideal (rather the reverse). The idea of beauty is engaged with, and with it the idea of loving; but the deference of the first series is no more. 'Fair, kind and true is all my argument' (105) sums up the speaker's worshipful attitude to the young man. Now the argument is precisely the opposite: which makes for an interesting handful of sonnets to the woman.

The first introduces the motif of the shock of her looks. She has black eyes and perhaps a darker than usual complexion; for this, says the poet, she would have been counted unbeautiful in the past; and in later sonnets "black" can have an ugly force to it. Here the negative connotation is slight and overturned. Because of the ghastly modern habit of cosmetic applications ('a bastard shame', 4) beauty is no more, its place has been vacated. Line 6's alliteration nicely illustrates the overlay of a cosmetic prettiness. Black is beauty's 'heir' (3), stepping into the vacuum.

A thrill in line 9 is not accounted for by the conceit of the eyes mourning on account of those who (sarcastically) 'no beauty lack' (11), but with 'art's false borrowed face' (6) slander creation (12). It is the gleam in the speaker's own eye, so to speak, at the downright attractiveness of his lover, that alerts the reader for the first time to the magic of sexual closeness. Puns are one thing: this is real. The couplet continues the conceit to decide the matter of the new beauty enchantingly in black's favour. The poem tells a story of physical attraction, almost of falling in love. The sheen of the fair youth's beauty, that the speaker was conventionally so enamoured of, never had this directness; nor did the love that he was so consumed by present any problem relating to his inner involvement (except the 'eye-heart', 'eye-mind' discussions for the sake of further compliment). In this series the speaker is to grapple with a compulsion. At the same time, as in the first series, he is to show love's ease, the even keel. I cannot help but think the 'fair/black' opposition as mirrored in the man and the woman is intended (see 144.3–4 for the direct suggestion, with 'fair' also as 'light of hue'). 'From fairest creatures we desire increase' goes the first line of the whole collection, re-starting now with line 1 above. The two portraits are independent despite the tangling of the two stories; yet in the contrast a larger theme is at work.

In line 10 the Q text has 'Her eyes so suited': some editors keep it but the repetition from 9 jars. Is this Shakespeare? 'Brows' (meaning eyebrows) is the usual emendation and I follow it in part for the seemingly effortless alliterative pattern the verse so typically creates. The letters m and s cast an unobtrusive charm over the sestet and b lends a shade more emphasis. In fact it is the significant opening letter of the sonnet. It is hardly conclusive – just a thought.

How oft when thou, my music, music play'st
Upon that blessèd wood whose motion sounds
With thy sweet fingers, when thou gently sway'st,   3
The wiry concord that mine ear confounds,
Do I envy those jacks that nimble leap
To kiss the tender inward of thy hand,   6
Whilst my poor lips, which should that harvest reap,
At the wood's boldness by thee blushing stand.
To be so tickled they would change their state   9
And situation with those dancing chips,
O'er whom thy fingers walk with gentle gait,
Making dead wood more blest than living lips.   12
    Since saucy jacks so happy are in this,
    Give them thy fingers, me thy lips to kiss.

Here and there in the second series an unobtrusive phrase gives a world away. A simple affectionate touch says more than the elaborate language all round it. Such is 'my music' (1). The whole piece makes a telling contrast wth sonnet 8 ('Music to hear . . . '); this is light-hearted, intimate. We see him standing by her as she plays the virginals, bowing her body a little, as some do at the keyboard. (I take 'sway'st' (3) as intransitive and 'sounds' (2) as in sole control of 'the wiry concord' (4). Q has a comma after 'sway'st' but tends to end its lines with a comma and so is inconclusive.) The conceit itself is absurd but does not pretend to be otherwise, part of a courtly convention that lingers, to hand if needed, its main work done. The jacks pluck the strings when the keys are pressed; Shakespeare may have used the term to indicate the keys themselves, to which they are attached; or perhaps, as Katharine Wilson tells us, the player held a hand over them to stop them jumping out of place, playing with the other. The latter scenario seems likely, with a flurry of quick kisses on the palm ('the tender inward of thy hand', 6); but it scarcely matters. 'Jacks' are also common fellows; but within the poem as it stands I do not see a hint of a woman who is too free with her favours. In the context of the series as a whole it can be seen a little differently. In either case the mood is not accusatory but flirtatious, daring; the poet is making a pass; 'living lips' (12) is almost a darting-forward, the move sealed by the firmer phrase at the poem's end. As a compliment it rivals any in the first series; but of course it is of a wholly different nature.

The flow of verse and argument is untroubled and finely-spaced: the three quatrains unfold symmetrically, ending with a fine emphasis (line 12); after which the shy bystander is as bold as the dancing chips (indeed bolder). The poem is a pleasantry but a perfectly-executed one; and pleasantries are part of love. I fancy I can hear the light tinny notes, the 'wiry concord' as my mind sight-reads the poem. It makes a strange contrast with the next one.

There is altogether less of a sense of order in the second series than in the first. There are more poems of a dubious authorship also, at least to my mind (135, 136, 145, 153, 154, with only 99 earlier). I see the poems to the man more as a conscious project, those to the woman more as occasional pieces. But an occasional piece can be as stormy as any other. Shakespeare has something to say in the next poem that does not mention the woman, except by implication, and could not have been said in those to the man. A very few times in my reading I have beem almost frightened to read on. Once was in 1959, studying Sophocles' *Oedipus Tyrannus* for A level Greek. Another was a few years later when I first read the following poem.

Th'expense of spirit in a waste of shame
Is lust in action, and till action lust
Is perjured, murd'rous, bloody, full of blame,   3
Savage, extreme, rude, cruel, not to trust,
Enjoyed no sooner but despisèd straight,
Past reason hunted, and no sooner had,   6
Past reason hated, as a swallowed bait
On purpose laid to make the taker mad,
Mad in pursuit, and in possession so,   9
Had, having, and in quest to have, extreme,
A bliss in proof, and proved, a very woe,
Before, a joy proposed, behind, a dream.   12
    All this the world well knows, yet none knows well
    To shun the heaven that leads men to this hell.

'Spirit' (1) can be sexual energy or semen. 'Waste' has its homophone 'waist' in tow. At the end 'hell' can be 'vagina'. They are the secondary meanings behind the screen of a thunderous cataract, a lurking edge. Much is made of a misogynistic impulse behind the "dark lady" sonnets, but in truth a self-hatred, to be sensed here, is the deeper current. Yet the observer within the writer stands outside the torrent, describing, detailing, capturing the phenomenon. 'Heaven' (14) is strong: he sees both sides.

    The poem itself is a taking-by-force, a ruthless charge down the page. As the reflection of a blind urge the succession of adjectives and adjectival phrases (lines 3–12) drives home, like a rush of blood, what it has to say. The helplessness at the end, and the bitter self-knowledge, complete the vestigial picture of sex without love, that seems almost to take place as we read. Often a poem carries an internal sketch of its subject, so to speak, as a stylistic aspect that goes some way to validate the intent.

In 66 the delivery is of a similar resistless power. There it is the uncountable instances of the world's injustice that the form adapts itself to. Here it is the mating adventure.

'Batter my heart, three-person'd God; for you / As yet but knock, breathe, shine, and seek to mend,' exclaims John Donne in one of his "holy sonnets" not so many years later, that seeks its end (which happens to be a devastating sexual metaphor) in a fierce litany of verbs. Sonnets of Gerard Manley Hopkins, too, can burn at the mind in a kaleidoscopic descriptive fury. Both poets have Shakespeare's ability to let the mind dwell on the detail, to pause in full flow. Here it is remarkable how slowly the single words and phrases can be taken, as if there were a cold eye lingering on the horror, even as it flashes by. The poem can perhaps be taken with 146 as two moments in the whole collection where the person behind the lines most takes himself to task.

It is a part of the reality of the second series. Shakespeare is doing something different from the first; even if, as is likely, their composition overlapped. A need for honesty pulsates through the poems, while before it was a need for commitment. What is splendid is the way the poet, in both series, takes the convention by the scruff of the neck and does something different with it. His couplets too in the poems to (or about) the woman are less tricky. But (typically) he is in a knot of mixed feelings he cannot prise apart. Perhaps the proximity of the last sonnet to this is not as strange as may at first appear. The hint of self-loathing we sense here may go some way to explain a later dismissiveness towards the woman, including moments of outright insult; he is as childish as the rest of us in coping with his own failings, however searingly he may picture them when he has a mind to. The negative charge of this piece is fearsome. One might wonder if his, or her, finer feelings could survive such a compulsive outspokenness. Nevertheless there are sonnets to come of a different kind.

My mistress' eyes are nothing like the sun;
Coral is far more red than her lips' red;
If snow be white, why then her breasts are dun;   3
If hairs be wires, black wires grow on her head.
I have seen roses damasked, red and white,
But no such roses see I in her cheeks;   6
And in some perfumes is there more delight
Than in the breath that from my mistress reeks.
I love to hear her speak, yet well I know   9
That music hath a far more pleasing sound;
I grant I never saw a goddess go –
My mistress, when she walks, treads on the ground.   12
    And yet, by heaven, I think my love as rare
    As any she belied with false compare.

Perhaps the most anthologised of the Sonnets, this is usually taken in too much of a negative light. A mood of merciless honesty is tempered by a deep affection, and not a little humour. He is tired of bad writing, the never-ending flow of hackneyed images in the sonnets and no doubt other poems of his contemporaries; and in a realistic – and not harsh – description of his mistress's attributes when up close, contrives a delightful lampoonery. Sonnet 21 showed a similar exasperation with the 'painted beauty' of the rival poet's verse to the young man; but here it is more important to speak the truth. A literal appraisal of her qualities in the light of common overstatement is somehow wonderfully refreshing. Closeness is all: her eyes, lips, breasts, hair, cheeks . . . one can sense the speaker's embracing the actuality, not a picture in his head. As for her breath, it must be remembered that 'reeks' (8) was much less of a put-down than now, here meaning something like 'seethes', and continuing the moment of nearness. Similar references to her speaking and walking allow a little distance into the event behind the scenes, so to speak; and the couplet reflects a love founded on true knowledge.

Many hear a sneer in 'dun' (3); but most white women I imagine would find being told their breasts were white as snow a little wearying, preferring to be taken as they are. That is the spirit of the poem. I admit to not being sure of a poetic animus in 'reeks' – the word could be used a little negatively – but am inclined to doubt it, for what comes immediately after it. 'I love to hear her speak' (9) is one of those throwaway remarks that speak volumes.

The 'sweet ornament which truth doth give' (54.2) in the first series is less to do with the world as it is. The adornment of an ideal reality – no doubt nurtured by a true and deep love – is more to do with the human spirit, that stands out against the depredations of Time. The cheeks the first series shares with the second are more than a gender apart; the roses of one are the antithesis of the other. The dark lady is set against the fair man in every way possible: the poet is exploring the worlds of the perfect and the real, both employing the imperfect speaker as narrator; both rooted in the heart. The overall collection itself is far from perfect, the second series in particular a little dubious in overall consistency (even with allowance made for an unexpected range); but it is complete enough for the sequence to be seen as one, and the two parts as complementary.

Every great poet must invest in these two worlds. To do so they will re-charge the means of saying. Shakespeare's weariness with what I have called the disease of 'goldengate' (51, 83 notes), when a mere prettiness gives the lie to beauty, is revealed here: he is merciless with false poets. But not with the person in front of him, whom three times he is proud to call 'my mistress'. Booth calls this piece a 'winsome trifle'. I call it a love-poem.

Thou art as tyrannous, so as thou art,
As those whose beauties proudly make them cruel;
For well thou know'st to my dear doting heart   3
Thou art the fairest and most precious jewel.
Yet in good faith some say that thee behold
Thy face hath not the power to make love groan;   6
To say they err I dare not be so bold,
Although I swear it to myself alone.
And to be sure that is not false I swear,   9
A thousand groans, but thinking on thy face,
One on another's neck, do witness bear
Thy black is fairest in my judgement's place.   12
    In nothing art thou black save in thy deeds,
    And thence this slander, as I think, proceeds.

A complication has entered the story. Sonnets 40–42 cry out against the young man's taking up with the speaker's lady-love; this and a number of the ensuing poems may have been written round about the same time, a harsher outcry directed to the woman. One cannot but imagine it was the same affair, and one that hurt the speaker immeasurably. From now on "black", the new beautiful, is a heinous shade too; the speaker is shocked, trying unsucccessfully to come to terms with the collision of his two worlds. (One may imagine he introduced the two characters.) Anger, love, longing and lust all follow, with "black" a dancing term meaning now one thing, now the other. At each occurrence one can almost hear the poet beating his head against a wall. In the vivid immediacy of the second series the sense of an aggressive bewilderment, of a problem too deep to be resolved, makes an aching contrast with the devotedly loyal adventure of the first. The lovers' triangle is doubtless the same. But the different poetic treatment it receives is telling.

The new addressee, in this first shock, could be the old one in the first four lines. Then a sharp shift (I would say clumsy lurch) into the domain of female hegemony over the male, in which the speaker appears to lose his composure entirely, leads to a deft and scything put-down. (Booth memorably calls it 'a single graceful razor stroke'.) With the stabbing accusation of line 13 the speaker is "on his toes", his poise recovered: and line 14 is as neat a line as is in the Sonnets. A measured 'as I think' leaves the opinion of some, that her hue makes her unbeautiful, the only issue worth a momemt's debate, the only possible slander. Their wrong idea stems from the blackness of her deeds – an immutable fact.

It is a delightful demonstration of the power of an unobtrusive phrase. The speaker's mock gravity, the more evident by the contrast with the desperate groans, confirms the issue. But certainly he is torn between love and hate; and one may reflect on this aspect of the persona of the latter series. Does it not in its very limitedness add something in retrospect to the figure of the first? A bloody-minded element that with a reflected backward energy, so to speak, may even set the knight-errant more squarely on his steed? There is no denying a compelling presence behind the poems from the very start – again and again the speaker emerges, almost visibly before us. The hellish frustration of a problem that will not go away adds itself to the picture. In the same way a passionate undying loyalty from the first series enters the second.

One may speculate, too, as to a background narrative: the poet makes it almost unavoidable. The woman would have been (probably several years) older than the youth. He may have talked of him to her. Or (/and) he may have alerted the youth's interest with tales of a dark beauty, perhaps showing him the first one or two poems. Who knows?

Thine eyes I love, and they, as pitying me,
Knowing thy heart torment me with disdain,
Have put on black, and loving mourners be,   3
Looking with pretty ruth upon my pain.
And truly not the morning sun of heaven
Better becomes the gray cheeks of the east,   6
Nor that full star that ushers in the even
Doth half that glory to the sober west,
As those two mourning eyes become thy face.   9
O let it then as well beseem thy heart
To mourn for me, since mourning doth thee grace,
And suit thy pity like in every part.   12
    Then will I swear beauty herself is black,
    And all they foul that thy complexion lack.

He has been shut out (unsurprisingly, if his mistress saw the last poem). Returning to the magical black eyes he constructs a plea for forgiveness, or at the least understanding. The tentative tone here is that of 128; but the light tune the lines play lacks the sparkle of that sonnet. It is a less hopeful dalliance, that ends with a vow of an unexpected vehemence, with the clipped rhyme of the couplet. The last line raises more than one question.

The first lays the groundwork for his case. 'Thine eyes I love' is another of his passing admissions of fondness, so easy to miss (see 130.9). 'Torment' (2) is probably an infinitive with 'to' before it understood; to edit to 'torments' may be too direct. The 'morning'/'mourning' homophone nicely catches a hope at once lit by expectation and clouded by disappointment. His 'pain' (4) is unspecified: whether merely of rebuke, or of sexual rejection, or the latter in favour of another (the other), we do not know. But he finds in her "blackness" a circuitous approach to take that is becoming familiar. The second quatrain interestingly would seem to focus on her skin colour. The 'grey cheeks of the east' and the 'sober west' (6, 8) seem to reflect the facial complexion, perfectly set off by the eyes. One recalls 'Why then, her breasts are dun' and 'If hairs be wires, black wires grow on her head' (130), and wonders if she may not have been partly of African heritage. I do not see why such a lady might not have found herself in such a position as to be playing the virginals some-where on a regular basis, and our man to have seen her, to have gone to see her again and again, and to have fallen for her like a ton of bricks (128).

It might explain the emphasis of the final line, that other-wise is a little puzzling. It may be a mere repeat of the oath in line 13, in which case it has an unexplained forcefulness about it: suddenly he is hammering the table. It may include a cunning opposite of what it says: if line 13 is to be taken as a contradiction in terms and so a lie, then the lie continues with 'foul' and the true foul are those like you. But he has established both in this poem and before that he means what he says about finding her attractive. He may be wrestling with his predilec-tion, and using it to hurt both her and himself, by implying it is altogether wrong; but still (in this case at least) it seems too much a departure from what has gone before. But what if she is of mixed race? It would explain why 'some say that thee behold / Thy face hath not the power to make love groan' (131.5–6), and also something of his self-horror at being so attracted. Despite his universal sympathies he was also a man of his time. I am not at all sure how far I adhere to it, but there is a case for the suggestion, for what it is worth. In some part, in the play with "black" in the second series, he may be both in thrall to a prejudice, and able to forget it entirely. And it makes sense of the blanket dismissiveness of the last line.

Beshrew that heart that makes my heart to groan
For that deep wound it gives my friend and me.
Is't not enough to torture me alone,   3
But slave to slavery my sweet'st friend must be?
Me from myself thy cruel eye hath taken,
And my next self thou harder hast engrossed;   6
Of him, myself and thee I am forsaken –
A torment thrice threefold thus to be crossed.
Prison my heart in thy steel bosom's ward,   9
But then my friend's heart let my poor heart bail.
Whoe'er keeps me, let my heart be his guard;
Thou canst not then use rigour in my jail.   12
    And yet thou wilt: for I, being pent in thee,
    Perforce am thine, and all that is in me.

If there is a key theme to the second series it is possession in
love. Whether it is by the black eyes, or in the heart's owner-
ship, or of the sexual act; or whether it is the tyrant sin of vanity,
or a crazed longing for the loved one, that racks the speaker on
the stage; whatever the plague in the air, these sonnets bear
witness to a brute fact. In this one the language of an uncaring
domination is everywhere, until the couplet, that surrenders to
the new enemy. Time has made its exit (amazingly the word
itself does not appear in 127–154). We are close up to an aspect
of love that is rarely discussed as openly as in this shorter,
slightly chaotic sequence. Quite simply, it is the madness of the
irrational.

    I do not imagine Shakespeare formulated it as a distinct
object but rather went by instinct, mining the vein. The detail
of servitude in this sonnet is overpowering: every line of 1–12
is a dramatic expression of conquest or its consequence.
'Beshrew' (1) is 'A curse on' or 'Devil take'; the speaker is far

from ready to haul up the white flag at this stage. 'Engrossed' (6) is a business term meaning 'monopolised' as of a commodity. 'Crossed' (8) is 'thwarted'; one is to understand 'It is' at the line's beginning. 'Bail' (10) is not the financial term one assumes at first sight; the following line indicates a rarer use, 'confine', 'have in charge'. The reasoning behind the sentiment of line 12 is interesting in that it doesn't matter. Is it that to hurt the youth's heart is inconceivable (Booth), or that the speaker's heart is so happy to "bail" the youth's that it cannot itself be hurt, and 'rigour' – at this moment in the argument – cannot operate (Duncan-Jones)? Since the conceit of the hearts occupying each other's space like electrons shot by Cupid is intrinsically quite ridiculous (even if a recognised trope in the courtly love convention), the uncertainty of a minor point within it is of academic interest only. The conceit is a time-server, occupying the page and providing an argument, both as it were for form's sake, until something more meaningful can be said.

Before the couplet, however, an aura of violence has its own story to tell. Deeply hurt himself, the speaker is outraged, as he intimates, that his friend has fallen by the same hand. And one senses he is shocked to the core at the double betrayal. Line 9 magnificently restates what in sonnet 22 is given comparatively vapid expression, and I am tempted to refer to as the heart-quark interaction; except that by sheer poetic force it is made to stand for something real. Possession happens. Cruelty is a part of love, a necessary part, exercised as much by the situation as by any separate person. It is actual in this poem; it breathes.

The couplet harks back to the self-effacement of the first series, echoing it too with a typical "pronoun play". But there is an extra sting. He fears for his friend, who may have to suffer all he already has, if not more (line 6). But the dominion of love is absolute.

So now I have confessed that he is thine,
And I myself am mortgaged to thy will,
Myself I'll forfeit, so that other mine   3
Thou wilt restore to be my comfort still.
But thou wilt not, nor he will not be free,
Fot thou art covetous, and he is kind;   6
He learned but surety-like to write for me
Under that bond that him as fast doth bind.
The statute of thy beauty thou wilt take,   9
Thou usurer that put'st forth all to use,
And sue a friend came debtor for my sake;
So him I lose through my unkind abuse.   12
    Him have I lost, thou hast both him and me;
    He pays the whole, and yet am I not free.

This follows on from 133.14, 'so now' (1) meaning 'now that'.
The financial metaphor, a favourite recourse of Shakespeare's in
these poems, takes over the whole piece. One cannot help but
speculate upon his affinity for the jargon – a stint in the office
of a firm of solicitors? – even if one knows one will get nowhere.
There appears to be a file in his mind more ready of access than
the odd buying and selling of a property might create. Yet it
was clearly a deliberate move, to offset the sphere of love's
belonging against the tacky world of legal ownership and debt.
But one can do too much reading between the lines.

By 'forfeit' (3) he may mean both 'deliver myself up as your
(sexual) property' and an abandonment more absolute and inde-
finable. The severity of possession, that leaves its mark on the
verse as a whole, is like that of the iron hand of the law. The
woman is seen as merely acquisitive. 'Surety-like' (7) – an inter-
esting word, that needs a poet's touch to stop it falling over itself
– is 'as a guarantor'. The idea of the friend falling into the preda-

tory clutches of a vamp through an act of misguided altruism is not one we are realistically expected to agree with; rather the opposite, one imagines, with the friend being covetous and the speaker kind (*pace* line 6). But as before in the poetic account the speaker will do anything to protect the friend's virtue, or rather his vision of it, which is essential to the place the youth occupies in the overall setting. It is partly as a result of the intrusion of the woman into the sacred territory of the ideal that her persona receives the treatment it does. More directly, however, one senses anger on the part of someone who is normally long-suffering in his private life.

'The statute of thy beauty thou wilt take' (9) is one those lines it is a pleasure to write out. The t sound makes it wonderfully precise. We have seen 'usurer' (10) before with a sexual connotation (4.7), there 'profitless', here anything but. Line 11 has an unaccountable appeal. Perhaps it is the speaker's complete acceptance of the artificial excuse he has created for his friend; he wants to believe it so much that momentarily he does. What might have been blame is turned to an admission of his own debt, with an undertone of gratitude, for an attempt to help that misfired. I suppose it is the speaker's love for the youth, as revealed by the line, that is appealing. Or it may be more the effect of a compact and well-turned phase. Again, one can fossick about between the lines too much, in this case for a metal that is assuredly there, and as assuredly not to be given up to the prospector. More simply, 'my abuse' (12) is on the surface the injury done to the speaker by his offer of forfeiture being rejected, with a reminder of the real hurt beneath. He assesses his position. The friend appears to have cut him out (the deeper import of 'he pays the whole', 14). The last phrase leaves us with the familiar figure behind both series, forever at the service, and in the power, of love.

Whoever hath her wish, thou hast thy will,
And will to boot, and will in overplus;
More than enough am I that vex thee still,   3
To thy sweet will making addition thus.
Wilt thou, whose will is large and spacious,
Not once vouchsafe to hide my will in thine?   6
Shall will in others seem right gracious,
And in my will no fair acceptance shine?
The sea, all water, yet receives rain still   9
And in abundance addeth to his store;
So thou, being rich in will, add to thy will
One will of mine, to make thy large will more.   12
    Let "no", unkind, no fair beseechers kill;
    Think all but one, and me in that one will.

Strewth. This and the next sonnet are piffling nonsense. No more than jejune *jeux d'esprit*, they have no place in a serious poetry collection and I very much doubt if Shakespeare sanctioned their inclusion. I am inclined to doubt he wrote them at all. While a case can be made for his roaring with laughter as he and his friend send up the bizarre situation, which if they are both named Will does have its ridiculous side (given a common meaning of "will"), the grimly low poetic level indicates the absence of the master and perhaps the apprentice taking up the quill. The master might have kept the results in the collection as a memento, later taken as authentic by Thorpe. Of course there is nothing to suggest such an apprenticeship (though 77 and 122 may make us wonder). I suggested a collaboration for 99, where a case can be made for a soulless parody of a writing style that is not without its own impressive artifice. But here the artifice is merely juvenile. Another alternative, no doubt acceptable to unorthodox (non-Stratfordian) participants in the authorship debate, is an intention on the poet's part to leave unmistakable evidence that his name was Will – when it wasn't. In a way this theory is more appealing than the collaborative-joke idea; but there is comparatively sober evidence elsewhere in the Sonnets for Will as the author. 57.13 and 89.7 carry a possible pun on the name; while 143.13 has a stronger air of the same, in a context unlikely to admit of deception or ruse.

I suppose I had better come to the central point. "Will" was a term for both the female and the male sexual organ. If William Shakespeare and (say) William Herbert as the poet and the youth were present or past sexual partners of the lady of these verses . . . need I go on? The reader can work out the puns for him or herself. The rudeness of the two poems is entirely juvenile, in a way I find difficult to associate with the poet of the other sonnets about the woman, disdainful of her appearance though some of them are. There are reasons for his ambivalence as to her hue: "the world's" view, his anger at her behaviour with the youth, perhaps a latent prejudice within himself. But the sniggering caricature of a nymphomaniac is of a different nature. He is insulting to her elsewhere – but this puerility is merely ridiculous.

Booth has an interesting suggestion as to 'beseechers' (13), citing evidence of a possible homophone with 'besiegers' elsewhere in Shakespeare. The idea helps the weak ending of the line ('kill'). Duncan-Jones has a fine interpretation of the difficult first three words of that line. The Q text has 'Let no unkinde, no faire beseechers kill, . . . ' If 'let' is 'stop saying', then we have a plea that fits well with the whole. 'Stop saying "no", unkind one . . . ' Both editors accept 135–6 as genuine. Perhaps they are, an untypical afterthought on 'thy will' of 134.2. But such an afterthought is more likely to be someone else's.

If thy soul check thee that I come so near,
Swear to thy blind soul that I was thy will,
And will, thy soul knows, is admitted there;   3
Thus far for love my love-suit, sweet, fulfil.
Will will fulfil the treasure of thy love,
Ay, fill it full with wills, and my will one.   6
In things of great receipt with ease we prove
Among a number one is reckoned none.
Then in the number let me pass untold,   9
Though in thy store's account I one must be;
For nothing hold me, so it please thee hold
That nothing me, a something, sweet, to thee.   12
    Make but my name thy love, and love that still;
    And then thou lov'st me, for my name is Will.

The raucous tone of 135 is softened by a kind of conciliatory address throughout, though the insult is no less. In fact the apparently affectionate overtures make the sneer in 'things of great receipt' (7) and other phrases the louder. On the tenderer side of the supplicant's "pitch" the use of 'sweet' (4, 12) stands out, if it is accepted as a term for the addressee rather than an adjective in an uncharacterstic inversion for the preceding noun. (The Q text does not have the surrounding commas some editors, with whom I concur, supply.) The blend of scorn and fondness is curiously well managed; following a finely telling poetic venture in line 1, it gives me pause. Perhaps the obvious answer, that Thorpe knew what he was doing, is the right one after all, and Shakespeare is the author of these two and all the rest. But identity of authorship easily ran astray: the majority of the twenty poems in *The Passionate Pilgrim* (1599), on the title-page all Shakespearean, are probably by another hand or hands. Taking the two sonnets together as one, I can envisage the two men crowing over a frivolity of the apprentice, perhaps set on his way in 136 by the master. But it is a far-fetched scenario; and now I come to think of it, one with plenty of drink on hand.

I cannot imagine the "dark lady" was presented with these two sonnets. It is of course unclear which if any poems may have been read by the addressee of either series, assuming such characters existed in real life. The direct pronouns 'you'and 'thou' of so many tell us nothing. But while I cannot see her reading these two, I find I can imagine the drinking session more and more. These two attacks – for such they are – seem to belong to an undertone of sexual punnery often to be sensed in the first series at least. The excessive nature of the love-conceit may well stem from the shock both men have received at the lady's treatment of them and their friendship (with a diminished sense of their own responsibility in the matter). Booth's edition of the Sonnets, a seminal work on bawdy puns if ever there was one, makes a scenario of the two friends sharing an in-joke not unlikely. One may be sceptical, as I am, of the vast majority of the possible double meanings his assiduity leads him to discover; but a significant few very probably are intended.

A later poem (151), entirely free of sniggering, has the writer engaged in a frank presentation of the act of sex that appears to give the lie to the gross puerility of these two verses (hardly poems). Yet again and again Shakespeare takes us by surprise in the plays with a quicksilver ability to change stance and authorial standing, so to speak, letting the work itself, as it reaches completion, reveal his deepest intention. So too in the Sonnets he can take a new view, a new tone (especially in the latter series), that we had not expected but that plays a part in the whole. His consistency is not our consistency.

Thou blind fool, Love, what dost thou to mine eyes,
That they behold and see not what they see?
They know what beauty is, see where it lies,   3
Yet what the best is take the worst to be.
If eyes, corrupt by over-partial looks,
Be anchored in the bay where all men ride,   6
Why of eyes' falsehood hast thou forgèd hooks
Whereto the judgement of my heart is tied?
Why should my heart think that a several plot,   9
Which my heart knows the wide world's common place?
Or mine eyes, seeing this, say this is not,
To put fair truth upon so foul a face?   12
   In things right true my heart and eyes have erred,
   And to this false plague are they now transferred.

The convention the writer has established of the lady's appearance as unfavourable to the world at large, but not to him, and yet to him, is taken up again: it is a means of expressing a complex and profound dissatisfaction within himself. It is at once a convention that can be shelved – as in the next sonnet – and, when in operation, a bitter fact. It is as if the dramatist within the poet can switch on a character within a character. No doubt the black eyes/dark looks were there in the woman he knew (or conceived of); the variable lies in his response to the situation. His is the character the dramatist is playing with. The speaker is the protagonist of the Sonnets, a unique and altogether remarkable figure on their stage.

   The second quatrain is enthralling. The interplay of heart and eyes, entertainingly presented in 46–47, is recaptured with a pictorial exactness. Commentators invariably take 'the bay where all men ride' (6) as a devastating sneer at the woman's promiscuity. Lines 9–10 certainly back that up ('several' in 9 is 'separate', 'reserved'). Yet it is less than that, and more. It is not as pointed as the physical references of 135–136, suggesting more a tendency to be available than the act itself: the accusation would seem to be an angry reaction to her association with the speaker's friend. The eyes are anchored in the bay. I do not think he means they are fixated on one area of the body. Rather, they have succumbed to what all men succumb to: female witchery. 'The bay where all men ride' is a splendid term for that place that men are caught in as they bob about in life, forever and forever tied to the sexual allure of a pretty woman. The speaker is furious that the heart follows the eyes' judgment and he finds himself inescapably in love with her.

He rails against his infatuation. Lines 11–12 are additional pointers, if very far from conclusive, to the idea I have tentatively proposed that she may have been of mixed race (132, note). An absolute difference between what he sees and what he wishes to see is unlikely to herald an everyday unattractiveness, especially considering that the youth appears to have fallen for her as well. The opposition of 'fair truth' and 'so foul a face' (12) is illuminating. Could not it reflect, quite simply, a longing for a markedly different facial hue from that which he sees in front of him?

It also reflects a longing for the purity – as he sees it – of the fair youth. She is in every way the antithesis. ('Fair' is used to an extent ambivalently: 'beautiful', 'fair-skinned'.) The speaker is almost crushed between the collision of his two worlds.

He resists by railing at her. His heart and eyes are under new ownership ('transferred' 14). It is nothing less than a plague that possesses them. (There may be a hint here of a sexual disease, as we shall see later.) And again he captures the other side of love.

When my love swears that she is made of truth
I do believe her, though I know she lies,
That she might think me some untutored youth,   3
Unlearnèd in the world's false subtleties.
Thus vainly thinking that she thinks me young,
Although she knows my days are past the best,   6
Simply I credit her false-speaking tongue;
On both sides thus is simple truth suppressed.
But wherefore says she not she is unjust?   9
And wherefore say not I that I am old?
O, love's best habit is in seeming trust,
And age in love loves not to have years told.   12
    Therefore I lie with her, and she with me,
    And in our fault by lies we flattered be.

The writer's *angst* as to the lady's hue of eye or skin is discarded as if it had never been. He has something to say about love that works, not Cupid's dart that brings distress. Entirely out of the courtly convention, and his own savage twist on it, he turns to an aspect a good deal ignored in literature, the reciprocal forbearance of love in the world as it is. I love this sonnet for its insouciant humour and sense of the everyday; for its clarity and (apparent) honesty; and above all, in the context of all the rest, for the equal footing of the two characters.

It is possible to take 'lie' in its double sense at beginning as well as end, with the thought that the main problem has not gone away; but it seems more natural to be straightforward at that point. 'Flattered' at the end I find a little weak. The line reads well with the alliterated f and l but one senses a sonnet-ending that did not quite materialise. It so happens that this is the one poem we have an earlier version for, in *The Passionate Pilgrim* of 1599 (see 117 note), that is significantly different. It is likely to be an imperfectly recalled transcript from a reading of this text, or something more like it, a good few years before the 1609 publication. Its ending, 'Therefore I'le lye with Love, and love with me, / Since that our faultes in love thus smother'd be', is uncomfortably worse to my mind. I have played with it myself – my excuse is that composition within a poem teaches the critic in a way nothing else can. What I have learnt here is that the author is not the sort to moralise for the sake of it. With the rest as above, 'And so, 'gainst truth a-lying, love lies free' is wrong on other counts too (as well as simply being irrelevant). Too much word-play, of a sort that in any case belongs more to the first series, makes it a fairly ghastly effort. But I can recommend the exercise nonetheless.

'O, love's best habit is in seeming trust' (11), also a far cry from the first publication, has the essence, and says much in little. ('Habit' is 'custom' and 'costume' both.) Didactic in the best sense, with a wisdom born of experience and worn lightly, it speaks of the hidden understanding in any reciprocal love that endures. The line is one of my favourites. Perhaps it conveys more of a sense of a living relationship than any other in all the sequence. The immediacy of the first series, to the young man, is of a different nature.

The sequence is a passionate pilgrimage from the past to the present-day; from the ideal to the real; and, as it seems to me, from a Platonic to a sexual relationship. Love is the theme, the exploration like no other. In the first series the speaker is torn by the claims of the individual in a state of dependence, by a rebellion that cannot be. (It is noticeable that as the balance begins to shift in his favour, it comes to an end.) In the second the rebellion could scarcely be stronger but the chains of love stay stronger still. And yet, with the poet's ease in the reckoning-up of experience, they too can be worn lightly.

O call not me to justify the wrong
That thy unkindness lays upon my heart;
Wound me not with thine eye, but with thy tongue;   3
Use power with power, and slay me not by art.
Tell me thou lov'st elsewhere; but in my sight,
Dear heart, forbear to glance thine eye aside.   6
What need'st thou wound with cunning, when thy might
Is more than my o'erpressed defence can bide?
Let me excuse thee: ah, my love well knows   9
Her pretty looks have been mine enemies,
And therefore from my face she turns my foes,
That they elsewhere might dart their injuries.   12
    Yet do not so; but since I am near slain,
    Kill me outright with looks, and rid my pain.

One cannot take this as seriously as many of the sonnets. Shakespeare appears to have slipped into default mode, where the conventional courtly line provides the approach, and a pleasing jingle is added to the chain. And yet there would appear to be a "moment from life" at the back of it, a hurt at the way the woman looks at other men (or another man) while with him. He would rather be told she is intimate with others (another) than suffer its evidence in public – a very human reaction, and one in keeping with the long-suffering sensitive soul of the first series. The willingness to meet the truth head-on recalls sonnet 90, ' . . . so shall I taste / At first the very worst of fortune's might.' Now in contrast we are aware of the direct physicality of the attraction. Unequivocally pretty here, her looks, her eyes as they look at him, devastate him: he cannot bear their power, yet he must have their undivided attention.

    I am led to wonder if Shakespeare's emphasis on the young man and the ideal, and his stated preference for him over her, for the 'better angel' over the 'worser spirit' (144), may not reflect, at some level, a horror of the sexual act. A number of scenes from the plays come to mind that may stem in part from such a revulsion. At the same time nothing could be more "normal" than the contentedness of 138 or the explicit commentary of 151. It may be that his appetite for sexual punnery, which was possibly shared with the young man and certainly features in a number of the poems addressed to him, betrays a latent bisexuality. Much may be: one can only proceed along the path the sonnets take one, engaged with the diverse personality that gave them being, and forever coming to terms with their expressive power.

Even this one, a comparatively slight affair, has an urgency to it (mock or not) finely controlled by a series of imperatives, within which the softer language of the third quatrain lends a sympathetic air to the appeal. The pentameters are perfectly paced, perfectly spaced; there is no "traffic jam" of meaning or content; and the couplet allows a melodramatic climax. The plea in 13 ('Yet do not so'), the gasp of dire hurt ('since I am near slain'), the exposure to the full force of those looks and its result, fatal and liberating at once – it all puts the seal on a fine histrionic interlude, with as I surmise something real at the back of it. The musicality of the form seems to thrive on an idea of 'her pretty looks' (10), especially in that part of the poem; the contrary forces prevailing in the piece are welded effortlessly, as I think, by an inner openness on the part of the writer, despite the surface artifice; the whole is a pellucid piece of craftsmanship. And in that it is like about 140 of the others.

The art of composition in the great poets is a miracle. One can read Dante for his *terza rima* as well as for its panoramic content, his portrait of the mediaeval mind. In the Sonnets part of the pleasure, along the way, can simply be to note the constructional skill.

Be wise as thou art cruel: do not press
My tongue-tied patience with too much disdain,
Lest sorrow lend me words, and words express   3
The manner of my pity-wanting pain.
If I might teach thee wit, better it were,
Though not to love, yet, love, to tell me so;   6
As testy sick men, when their deaths be near,
No news but health from their physicians know.
For if I should despair I should grow mad,   9
And in my madness might speak ill of thee;
Now this ill-wresting world is grown so bad,
Mad slanderers by mad ears believèd be.   12
    That I may not be so, nor thou belied,
    Bear thine eyes straight, though thy proud heart go wide.

The situation is the same: but the speaker is angry now. The difference in tone from the last is perhaps the strongest evidence in the sequence for a deliberate and conscious dramatisation of a situation on the writer's part. The speaker has lost patience and quietly, but with an intensity to rival that of any stage villain, threatens the lady. He may 'speak ill of thee' (10), if she does not mend her ways with him in public. Of course the mood change may simply be the direct reflection of an altered mindset; but there is a strong argument for a staged element at least as a part of the whole. With a decisive sweep the last line states the request of 139.6 as an ultimatum. He does not plead now but demand. Through this poem too there is a steady increase in assertiveness. We hear of sorrow, pain, madness; but the voice of the couplet is ironic, in 'belied' (13), and the last line's almost scornful reference to taking poor aim in archery. As often in the collection the voice that plays at weakness ends a strong one; part of the hidden reason for the couplet, in the Shakespearian use.

As a dramatic moment it would act well. The tone is at once that of the lover fatally pierced by Cupid's dart, and of a no-holds-barred ultimatum. An exasperated finger-wagging, with a hint of menace; an overbearing, even bullying stance, as it were inching closer, begins to turn victor into victim. The electrons whirl in combat; yet the atom is perfectly composed. A glint of humour in the eye does not oust its opposite, the plea of the stricken heart not, for god's sake not to be humi-lated further. The sonnet follows directly on the last (otherwise line 2's 'disdain' would have to wait till line 14 for its expla-nation); the change is a swift one. Of a number of memorable moments in a dramatic reconstruction of the double series, a vignette involving the last poem and this might require the least planning.

Most of the poems to the woman lie more or less within the courtly tradition, if one includes the writer's own idiosyncratic twist to it, but some operate more or less outside it. These occur when the writer has something urgent to say of the here-and-now that can afford no more than a passing nod to the tradition, still so to speak the presiding genie of the sonnet form. So far I would class 129, 130 and 138 as independent creatures, with at least another three to come. In the whole of the far longer first series I find only three or four, 66, 94, 111 (perhaps) and 121. There is a reason for this. Somewhat as Polonius tells Reynaldo in *Hamlet*, 'By indirections find directions out,' in the context of spying on a son, so in the matter of an endeavour of the soul, the first series finds a roundabout way to its end. It is of a piece with the convention, which carries it along. The second series, in every way a more tangible and earthly affair, can the more easily switch to an immediate statement. Yet the convention, as here, is still the more instinctive choice.

In faith I do not love thee with mine eyes,
For they in thee a thousand errors note;
But 'tis my heart that loves what they despise,   3
Who in despite of view is pleased to dote;
Nor are mine ears with thy tongue's tune delighted,
Nor tender feeling to base touches prone,   6
Nor taste, nor smell, desire to be invited
To any sensual feast with thee alone.
But my five wits nor my five senses can   9
Dissuade one foolish heart from serving thee,
Who leaves unswayed the likeness of a man,
Thy proud heart's slave and vassal wretch to be.   12
    Only my plague thus far I count my gain,
    That she that makes me sin awards me pain.

The ingenuity that enables the writer to bear in anew on his topic, and deliver a fresh poetic package, complete with all the frills, can leave him remarkably exposed. When nothing more immediate presents itself the topic is the curse of his infatuation. We have posited something of the complex motive at the core of his stance, including a certain anger at himself; this anger itself may have more than one aspect to it. One appears to be a horror of sexual need and engagement. I have no idea if this can co-exist with a delighted happiness in the same, only that it appears to in our speaker. 'The heaven that leads men to this hell' (129) seems to underlie the second series: a necessary discussion for the writer at some part in the thesis of love. Its strength cannot be blinked; but it is not the whole story.

To make a lighter and more lasting point he denies what before he has claimed by implication, an enjoyment in intimacy, and at least once explicitly. 'I love to hear her speak' (130.9) hardly sits well with line 5 above. Yet they can both be true;

and perhaps the contradiction can spread and expand to fill the being. He wishes to say something about love, that it *is*, it is not to be explained, as memorably at 49.14. But here, with the physical side in the ascendant, the informing dye of the poem, its tone or mood, is of a different tinge.

Yet he makes the point beautifully. Lines 9–10 stay in the mind. A truth about love arises in the midst of what looks like a nonsense, but which may have its own, perhaps unknowing agenda. To let such an observation appear seems to me a root purpose of the series, though it may be almost hidden in an over-growth of minor issues, themselves inextricably bound up with the writer's or speaker's particular circumstance. But again and again it finds its way through. The accompanying complexity is a part of the real world, of things as they are.

'Dote' (4) is 'love distractedly', perhaps like a fool. The 'sensual feast with thee alone' (8), after the blanket rejection of lines 5–7, may indicate the sexual act. 'Who' (11) refers to the heart, as it does earlier (4). 'Unswayed' (11) means 'under no control', 'rudderless'. Line 12 is interestingly faithful to the language of the courtly convention. The twist in what follows is savage. His plague is his infatuation; at least, he says, she makes him pay for it. Some see a hint thereby of his having to pay or suffer less after death, in Purgatory; but I see it in a more modern way. Shakespeare was not much of a literalist in reli-gious matters. A grim humour, possibly encompassing the suggestion of a venereal disease he has contracted (see 144), or it may be a self-loathing after succumbing to her, acknowledges the power of sex. He may be saying that she does after all allow him to sleep with her, that he does after all want to. The sin may be that of adultery (see 152), or merely of being attracted to her, in spite of all. It is an unromantic ending. Yet an oasis of beauty nestles in the wilderness.

Love is my sin, and thy dear virtue hate,
Hate of my sin, grounded on sinful loving.
O, but with mine compare thou thine own state,   3
And thou shalt find it merits not reproving;
Or if it do, not from those lips of thine,
That have profaned their scarlet ornaments,   6
And sealed false bonds of love as oft as mine,
Robbed others' beds' revénues of their rents.
Be it lawful I love thee as thou lov'st those   9
Whom thine eyes woo as mine impórtune thee;
Root pity in thy heart, that when it grows,
Thy pity may deserve to pitied be.   12
    If thou dost seek to have what thou dost hide,
    By self-example mayst thou be denied.

The sin of 141.14 may simply be his love: at least it is so here,
where now her bed seems to be denied him. Lines 1–2 and to a
lesser extent 11–14 need more than one hearing, even if, as in
many of the couplets especially of the first series, the second
hearing does not disturb but retains a poetic propriety, so to
speak, both unobtrusive and enriching. That may be the case in
13–14, where what is hidden, withheld, would seem to be at
first sex and then pity and what it leads to. But the first two
lines seem deliberately to jolt the mind into an impasse. As I
take it: my sin is to love you – both according to you and
according to how I sometimes feel. If you hate my sin, that is
your virtue. My sinful loving – of an adulterous nature – makes
it absolutely right for you to reject me. And even as we read, and
the more so as we read on, it means the opposite. 'Dear' (1) is
sarcastic, the sinful loving applies to her as well, or her so-called
virtue; and we are looking in two directions at once. There is a
"ricochet" effect: the meaning never seems to find its shape, to

hold still. Then a stretch of calm waters, where we seem to know where we are going. A moment of epiphany hovers fleetingly; and the couplet wryly, and with a sense of acceptance, returns us to the speaker's own impasse.

I have come back and back to lines 11–12, unable to discover quite why they make my mind stop in its tracks, my being even, while still allowing the sonnet to reach its (somewhat perfunctory) ending. Katharine M. Wilson in *Shakespeare's Sugared Sonnets* has the clue: ' . . . the pity she has implanted grows into love . . . ' Pity is a key concept in Shakespeare. Here it is to flower into a love such as to reform the being and make it vulnerable.

And so again we have a couple of lines that belong to a larger world. The rest of the sonnet becomes their setting. It has its own reality as an account of a difficult, frustrating and self-contradictory situation; but Shakespeare uses that momentarily to snatch at the beyond. Yet it is compelling in itself. The dramatic situation of the second series – whose surface, like that of a Picasso portrait, is shot with counter-perspectives – is a riveting one.

Wilson sees all the sonnets as parodies of the traditional approach to the sonnet-sequence, as intentionally funny. There is a point of sorts, though she very much overdoes it. The poet defies conventionality in different ways in the two series, with an additional internal opposition (the 'fair, kind and true' man; the dark, unkind and dishonest woman). As a shock tactic, if it does nothing else, it rescues the form from its distemper, its 'goldengate' (83, 130). But of course there is much more going on. Overall this sonnet, too, argues for a more libertarian and less judgemental state of affairs, as does 121, more directly and powerfully.

The lips' 'scarlet ornaments' (6), indicating a vermilion cosmetic, segue to stamps of red sealing-wax on 'false bonds' (7), a nice conceit.

Lo, as a careful housewife runs to catch
One of her feathered creatures broke away,
Sets down her babe, and makes all swift dispatch   3
In pursuit of the thing she would have stay,
Whilst her neglected child holds her in chase,
Cries to catch her whose busy care is bent   6
To follow that which flies before her face,
Not prizing her poor infant's discontent;
So run'st thou after that which flies from thee,   9
Whilst I, thy babe, chase thee afar behind;
But if thou catch thy hope, turn back to me
And play the mother's part, kiss me, be kind.   12
    So will I pray that thou mayst have thy will
    If thou turn back, and my loud crying still.

An extended simile offers an unusual overview. Perhaps all heterosexual men have at one time or another, often in spite of themselves, behaved towards a woman they are sexually interested in more as a child towards its mother. As a young adult I remember in conversation with my father cursing a tendency in myself to turn a woman's sex drive into a maternal drive, and his reply which suggested it was a widespread phenomenon. This sonnet is beautifully honest in its laying bare of that aspect of a man's love. Shakespeare is of course subjective at all times; nothing in the way of a definitive theory of love is attempted; a sonnet-sequence is no treatise. But instinctively he will allow a significant aspect its presentation; and the "dark, unkind and untrue" stereotype of a mistress he has created, or assembled from certain less important facts of the situation, is forgotten.

In terms of sheer readability this is also very different from the last. The dodeka is absolutely of a piece, the narrative picture emerging with a semantic ease devoid of the "stop-go" nerviness noted in 142; and leading to a couplet that uses an alternative meaning to unexpected (and unrecognised) effect.

First, though, as to the farmyard scene. It may be that the creature making a break for it with a touch of comic pathos represents the speaker's friend, but we do not know this, only that the runaway is one of a number under the housewife's control. But the faint suspicion of a 'careful' woman not as 'attentive' but 'distracted', a stable of men at her beck and call, adds spice to the scene, its innocence preserved on the surface by the generic difference between child and bird. As the image is developed (9–12) the reader may wonder at the speaker's view of himself. There is no trace of self-mockery; rather, the statement of a need in unashamedly infantile terms. This though in the wider context we know he is asking to share her bed. The child in the man was never more exposed, nor ever more frankly recognised.

The direct way to take line 13 is as a fervent hope for the contentment of the housewife (pronounced "hussif", 1). Hints abound: the speaker is called Will, the young man may be too; there is probably an underlying promise of sexual satisfaction. (While the publisher italicises the final word with a capital W, it is no clear proof of the author's wish; and other words receive the same treatment.) Line 14 has an emphasis that seems to go unremarked. Surely the last word is the adverb. The final half-line then is far stronger than if 'still' is merely 'quieten'. (To make it clearer I insert a comma after 'back'.) As in 121 the more decisive – and far more effective – way to take the grammar of the final sentence is overlooked. What a telling conclusion, to see the infant in shock and still crying, even as it is picked up and cradled in the woman's arms, the man still at his complaining.

Two loves I have of comfort and despair,
Which like two spirits do suggest me still;
The better angel is a man right fair,   3
The worser spirit a woman coloured ill.
To win me soon to hell, my female evil
Tempteth my better angel from my side,   6
And would corrupt my saint to be a devil,
Wooing his purity with her foul pride.
And whether that my angel be turned fiend   9
Suspect I may, yet not directly tell;
But being both from me, both to each friend,
I guess one angel in another's hell.   12
    Yet this shall I ne'er know, but live in doubt,
    Till my bad angel fire my good one out.

Unlike 138, the other sonnet of this collection to feature in *The Passionate Pilgrim* of 1599 (see its note), this has altered little in its later edition. What changes there are bear out the sense of the first being a botched recall. The *Pilgrim* editor may have chosen these for the "human angle", the two poems in their way reflecting the author's love life as vividly as any. Yet they are opposites. 138 is engaged and this is not.

It is more like a scenario for a forthcoming series. The first line is sonething posited rather than felt. The octave sets up an infernal triangle and within it, a mystery: are the other two sleeping together? He allows himself to become cautiously involved in knowing the answer; but his anxiety on the account scarcely registers except as a lead-in to a dramatic last line. The sestet has the "I" of the speaker in a curiously undeveloped state. Who knows if this sonnet was not written in planning mode?

The poem usefully frames the 'two loves' (1), both as opposites and as differing presences within the speaker's mind. He is almost religiously attached to one; and, dare I say it, more interested in the other. Immediately, however, the piece takes its place in the narrative as a merciless description of a brutal state of affairs, as the speaker sees it; and indeed there is something brutish in the language used. 'Her foul pride' (8) carries a picture of an outrageous veneer of fine clothes and cosmetics perhaps; but in such a context 'pride' could also be the desire of a female animal in heat. When the writer snarls at the woman it is his own vicious quality (or that of the speaker) that knows no bounds. It is the dominant tone of the second series; but perhaps not the most significant, as we have seen and will see. Misogynistic without a doubt: but as within a mixed range of feeling, the series presents a bewildering tapestry, part at least of whose purpose was to take the fact of love by the scruff of the neck and depict it in its ugliness and beauty. The Platonic ideal of a chaste love between men, superior to the degrading physical attraction that fettered a man to a woman, is before us in as blind and blithe a display of male chauvinism as any second-rate writer may have given vent to. But this is no such writer and there is a great deal more to the picture. If we do not imagine the "dark lady" as having been given the sonnets that thus refer to her to read, let alone the writer/speaker reading them to her, the insult is not quite the same. And in the context of the overall opposition of the 'two loves', seen as types as well as characters, a negative force is recorded, and revealed to the light, as it needed to be.

'Suggest me' (2) is 'prompt me (to good or ill)'. 'Hell' (12) includes the meaning of a woman's sexual organ. The violent and abrupt expulsion of the final line ('fire . . . out') has an undertone to it of infecting with a venereal disease.

Those lips that Love's own hand did make
Breathed forth the sound that said 'I hate'
To me that languished for her sake;   3
But when she saw my woeful state,
Straight in her heart did mercy come,
Chiding that tongue that ever sweet   6
Was used in giving gentle doom,
And taught it thus anew to greet:
'I hate' she altered with an end   9
That followed it as gentle day
Doth follow night, who like a fiend
From heaven to hell is flown away.   12
    'I hate' from hate away she threw,
    And saved my life, saying, 'not you'.

To my mind this is a silly verse no poet would find space for in a collection that had any kind of serious point to it, let alone next to 146 (of all poems). Some have thought it may have been Shakespeare's first sonnet, written at the age of eighteen when courting Anne Hathaway. Her surname may have been pronounced "Hate-away" (see line 13). On the same lines, with 'and' sometimes pronounced 'an', it may end in a sheepish pun. If the author of the other sonnets did write it, which I tend to doubt, it might have been as a "blind" – to establish a false auto-biographical detail. The same argument can be made for the ludicrous over-use of "Will" in 135–6. It is a point for an anti-Stratfordian to make, to support the theory of the Stratford man's identity being used as a cover-up; but it carries little conviction. All three poems are too frivolous to be taken seriously in any way at all. Yet could it have been an early effort by the poet?

George Herbert wrote a double sonnet in 1610, at the age of

sixteen or seventeen, that may have been influenced by this collection (1609). He addresses God, ruing the lack of religious ardour in modern poets: ' . . . Doth poetry / Wear Venus' livery? only serve her turn? / Why are not sonnets made of thee?' The final six lines are worth quoting in full. 'Such poor invention burns in their low mind / Whose fire is wild, and doth not upward go / To praise, and on thee, Lord, some ink bestow. / Open the bones, and you shall nothing find / In the best face but filth; when Lord, in thee / The beauty lies in the discovery.' Callow or not, the stuff of great poetry is here. Shakespeare may well have had a less privileged education than Herbert; and the writing of 'Those lips . . . ' was not an occasion for moral earnestness. Yet it is hard to see him producing such a piece of trumpery nonsense as 145 at eighteen. Or if he did, wanting to keep it. Or if he did, having it printed. And nothing will persuade me that he would have wanted it printed where it is.

The tetrameters (rare in sonnets) make it an oddity; the sentiment makes it an irrelevance; the inclusion and especially the placing in this collection make it a sure bet Shakespeare did not oversee the printed edition. Yet such as it is, it is deft; and the language of lines 6–7 is charming in its way. Many born in Elizabethan times might have written it and one did. Perhaps it is our poet, the answer to a challenge, "Can you put your wife's name in a verse?" reeled off, and eventually appearing in the Sonnets by a kind of accident.

But it is an accident we have learned to live with, and even if its survival is no more than a quirk of history, it tells us something. Not what Shakespeare was like as a lad; but what *mere* verse is like in the presence of poetry. It is a quality of mind that makes the difference: the words follow on from that. Maybe the page it is on has a lasting value, after all.

Poor soul, the centre of my sinful earth,
Rich in these rebel powers that thee array,
Why dost thou pine within and suffer dearth,   3
Painting thy outward walls so costly gay?
Why so large cost, having so short a lease,
Dost thou upon thy fading mansion spend?   6
Shall worms, inheritors of this excess,
Eat up thy charge? Is this thy body's end?
Then, soul, live thou upon thy servant's loss,   9
And let that pine to aggravate thy store;
Buy terms divine in selling hours of dross;
Within be fed, without be rich no more.   12
    So shalt thou feed on death, that feeds on men,
    And death once dead, there's no more dying then.

First to the textual crux. The second line of the Q text is a manifest error: 'My sinful earth these rebel powers that thee array, . . . ' The last three words of line 1 have been repeated in place of what was presumably a two-syllable word or phrase linking soul or/and earth to rebel powers. There have been many suggestions. Mine is as above, a fairly simple solution that I believe offers an acceptable line of poetry in itself, and provides some of the threads needed for the poem's construction. Regardless of the line taken here, the tone of the piece is of especial interest. Aside from a melodramatic heightening at lines 7–8, it has a person-to-person softness to it, as of a final levelling with the self, or a private encounter at core. The poem is the plea of a spirit near tired to death.

    Rebel to servant to final surrender, the acceptance of the changing role of the outer self is all. The final phrase links the poem to the love-sequence, and particularly to this series: 'dying' in Elizabethan usage had a secondary meaning of sexual release. But sex, while it has or shares the last word, is by no means the whole story. It is his self-love, and all the pampering that goes with it, that the speaker is crying out at. In this sonnet he finally assumes the mantle, not merely of the protagonist of the poems, but of a great dramatic character in his own right. A fully acknowledged human being is speaking to us from the paper that for centuries was too hot to handle, the critical world unable deal with the gender issue; and that has always seemed to cloak itself in mystery. But here is no mystery. Whether it is Shakespeare himself we hear or his creation does not matter; art is more than an individual life. Whether song or play, the performance is almost at an end. It cannot end neatly but almost coughs its way out, with a number of poems on the "dark, unkind and untrue" theme, going back to the speaker's revulsion at what he sees that he loves, or what he sees inside himself. There is also a poem simply of man and woman together. The final two sonnets seem to be the work of an uninvolved hand, possibly hired, to draw things to a close.

Within the sequence this is one of a kind. One may fancy it carries the true voice of the author, a reflection *in propria persona* on the deepest human concern, the matter of the soul, its battle to continue to be. But what one hears is the true voice of the persona of the Sonnets. It is the interior address, and one as telling as any of his verse soliloquies, of a dramatic character. Finally, I think this is the best way to see the man behind the words: as the man in the words, an actor on the boards, forever wedded to his part.

'Aggravate' (10) has the literal sense of 'make heavier', 'increase', in balance with the then minor one of adding to a state of distress. The store's enrichment has its price. A word has the soul's burden.

My love is as a fever, longing still
For that which longer nurseth the disease,
Feeding on that which doth preserve the ill,   3
Th'uncertain sickly appetite to please.
My reason, the physician to my love,
Angry that his prescriptions are not kept,   6
Hath left me, and I desperate now approve
Desire is death, which physic did except.
Past cure I am, now reason is past care,   9
And frantic-mad with evermore unrest;
My thoughts and my discourse as madmen's are,
At random from the truth vainly expressed;   12
    For I have sworn thee fair, and thought thee bright,
     Who art as black as hell, as dark as night.

The conventional idea of love as a disease is seized upon and
wrenched round, to suit the speaker's adopted attitude, with a
kind of glee. Whether he hates the woman, or himself, or both,
scarcely matters; though I would note that if one reads 'self-love'
for 'love' the poem fits in with what is at times an open current
in the series, if at times a more veiled one. Its placing after 146
may have a hidden sense to it in this respect. As always it is a
complex matter: he has a loathing of the 'woman coloured ill'
(144.4), as well as of himself for loving her (her colour?); and all
the time we are reminded of an element of artificiality in the
pose, the twist on the convention for the sake of the twist, the
iconoclast sonneteer. But rising above all this is the surface
success of the poem merely as an expression of anger.

    It is extraordinary how the lines seem to race as the words go
slow. Here and there in the collection we see the same, a kind
of icy mounting rage, notably in 66, where the sheer strength
of what is listed, and of the listing itself, seems to topple over

into an exhaustion of despair. Here on the other hand the couplet is triumphant: anger finds its full focus in a stab of hatred . . . and yet one is unconvinced.

The writer has his own agenda. Four of the next five poems, as this, are concerned with the woman's visible 'defect' (149.11). It has come up unequivocally before (137, 141) but now it is used, at least as the sequence stands, to "wind down". I think one thing a close reading of the collection has done for me is to bring to the surface some of the different constituents in love's stew. It is a paradisal potion and a simmering hell-broth, in any individual case no doubt best left undisturbed. But we would be wrong to see the first series as positive and the second negative. The currents run deeper than that.

118 touches on the idea of infatuation, as well as of a weariness with it, as a feeding sickness. Now the conceit is more aggressively handled. And yet a humour lies behind it all; the gleam in the eyes is not of anger alone; and one wonders, yet again, if Shakespeare shared these poems with his 'fair friend', who was after all part of the situation. 'My reason . . . hath left me', a delightfully simple entrance to the gates of mayhem, is played out within an engaging personification, a doctor stumping off as his orders ('prescriptions', 6) are ignored. And the third quatrain is a brilliant example of the Baron Munchausen effect (68, 97), where the speaker is openly lying, as it were, in wonderfully convincing language. In a similar vein, the sudden glare in the absolute terms of the last line has a chuckle in its fury: trump that.

' . . . I desperate now approve / desire is death . . . ' (7–8) is oddly compressed. 'Approve' seems to be 'understand and accept', perhaps also 'am living proof of'. Certainly 'desire is death' fits with the gist of 146. A troubled conscience is forever in the background, quietly seething.

O me, what eyes hath love put in my head,
Which have no correspondence with true sight!
Or if they have, where is my judgement fled,   3
That censures falsely what they see aright?
If that be fair whereon my false eyes dote,
What means the world to say it is not so?   6
If it be not, then love doth well denote
Love's eye is not so true as all men's 'no'.
How can it? O how can love's eye be true,   9
That is so vexed with watching and with tears?
No marvel then though I mistake my view;
The sun itself sees not till heaven clears.   12
    O cunning love, with tears thou keep'st me blind,
    Lest eyes well-seeing thy foul faults should find.

This and the next, that centre on the idea of the speaker's blindness, are less robust in their questioning, less assertive in the overall statement, than is the general nature of their companions, in either part of the collection. Shakespeare may have reached a point where improvisation upon a theme was almost all he had left to offer. The repetition of the first half-line of 147.13 in 152.13, the 'blind, mind' final rhyme here and in 149, and more especially something merely querulous in these two, suggest someone "marking time", trying to get going again, and finally knowing when to stop. 151 finds new ground, after which nothing remains to be said. The enterprise has gone as far as it can go and is allowed to peter out.

    The discussion of the octave is consciously artificial, its note a little tinny, and the outcome is scarcely a surprise. But the writer manages it with a pretty turn in the sestet; and almost in spite of himself, as it would seem, stumbles upon a line that in a light and casual way, throws a magic chain of poetry round the unsuspecting mind. Line 10 stays with me when the rest of the poem has tidied itself away, and the image that it becomes part of is absorbed and dismissed and forgotten. Other readers find other phrases, other lines that leap from their context to strike home. Such can be the random appeal of poetry, in part something suddenly apt in itself, in part what T.S.Eliot called 'the inexplicable mystery of sound'.

The Q text punctuates lines 8–9 differently from the above: 'Loves eye is not so true as all mens: no, / How can it?' With some others I have adopted a version that gives the octave a strong ending ('eye' in line 8 also heard as 'ay'), and the sestet a start more in keeping with the natural demands of the form, not to speak of the writer's general approach. I imagine the manuscript left the question technically open. There is a good deal of evidence to suggest an erratic proof-reader's or editorial eye here and there in the collection. But the whimsical, plaintive tone of the piece may indeed justify the Q printing.

The 'foul faults' of the final line become more and more of a convenience to the writer, a hook to hang a poem on. This is not to say the speaker's revulsion is to be seen as a mere invention, but that it has perhaps been over-used. It is of course impossible to determine what precisely it is a reaction to, what has brought it on. I would hazard that the betrayal of his friendship with the youth, seen as the woman's doing, and his sporadic disgust at his own sex drive, are the chief factors; but there may well be others, as discussed. But there is something in this gallery of miniatures, so to speak, that is undeniable. The artist goes from shade to shade, tone to tone, from one end of the palette to the other. Each piece has its mood, often very different from the last; and it is the variation in the colouring, as much as the outline of the figures and what they are or are not up to, that makes up the whole.

Canst thou, O cruel, say I love thee not,
When I against myself with thee partake?
Do I not think on thee when I forgot   3
Am of myself, all tyrant for thy sake?
Who hateth thee that I do call my friend?
On whom frown'st thou that I do fawn upon?   6
Nay, if thou lour'st on me, do I not spend
Revenge upon myself with present moan?
What merit in myself do I respect,   9
That is so proud thy service to despise,
When all my best doth worship thy defect,
Commanded by the motion of thine eyes?   12
    But love, hate on, for now I know thy mind;
    Those that can see thou lov'st, and I am blind.

The tone is self-consciously that of the wounded lover, the courtly convention at first a retreat for the near-exhausted persona of the speaker, and finally providing a means of development of its individuality, if in a limited way. Much is a re-hash of a theme to be found in the first series (see 35); and yet the authentic voice of Shakespeare's to the woman does emerge by the end. With it, unexpectedly, an issue is touched on that is central to the collection.

First, another conundrum of the commas. The Q text punctuates lines 3–4 as above, and I have no difficulty with the speaker as tyrant (to himself); but some would like it to be the lady, 'all' acting retrospectively with 'forgot', or more widely, as a cordoned-off 'entirely'. Thus Duncan-Jones: ' . . . when I forgot / Am of myself, all, tyrant, for thy sake.' Booth has no comma in the line at all, leaving everything open under the sun. I suppose the question is, at what point does the convention begin to be set on its head?

It may not be till 'defect' of line 11; but the lines directly preceding that may have an almost violently physical second meaning. 'Do I not spend / Revenge upon myself with present moan?' (7–8) is awkward, a little odd. But Booth suggests 'lour'st' (7) was interchangeable with 'lower'st'; and suddenly we are the midst of an allusion to sexual intercourse, the woman dominant. Lines 9–10 may continue the theme: the speaker longs to be free of his physical compulsion but lacks the merit in himself to despise or dismiss it. The later frankness of 151 seems to allow such a reading, tucked away behind 'service' (10). Such a semantic progression offers a fascinating example of an individual comment cutting free of the conventional surround; just as Shakespeare does with the whole sonnet-series.

'Thy defect' (11) I take in wider context as her darkness, the dread hue. Line 12 is refreshingly direct, with 'motion' enjoying a further meaning of 'instruction'. The couplet has a curious force to it. On the surface it seems scarcely thought through: would not those who can see, see and recoil from her defect? While he may be implying that, perversely, she loves those who cannot love her, I think there is something else going on. The poet ignores the implication – let readers take it as they will – for an emphasis of sudden significance. The whole sonnet has been leading up to it, and yet it seems to announce itself. The final line stays in the head, surely, because it contains within itself a defining feature of the collection: the sacrifice of the self that is at the heart of love. In both series the speaker's desperate attachment to the other appears to set his being at risk. He lives in a night of error; his autonomy is under threat; the evolving statement of each and every poem can seem to be all that pulls him through, his one lifeline. And yet one of the joys of the collection is the sheer independence of the narrator, as he finds new ways to speak out, and new things to say.

O from what power hast thou this powerful might
With insufficiency my heart to sway?
To make me give the lie to my true sight,   3
And swear that brightness doth not grace the day?
Whence hast thou this becoming of things ill,
That in the very refuse of thy deeds   6
There is such strength and warrantise of skill,
That in my mind thy worst all best exceeds?
Who taught thee how to make me love thee more,   9
The more I hear and see just cause of hate?
O, though I love what others do abhor,
With others thou shouldst not abhor my state.   12
    If thy unworthiness raised love in me,
    More worthy I to be belov'd of thee.

Shakespeare has more of a grip on this poem's formation: while
the last two appeared somewhat tremulous in the handling, here
the pot is thrown with his old assurance. The questions hit
home, the rhetoric takes the reader along, the whole compels, if
it does not exactly persuade. That is, until the couplet, where in
148–9 the form found its feet; while here the ending loses breath
a little, a reverse sign of a certain general weakness at this stage
of the series. The represented situation is one of frustration: at
times the speaker is on intimate terms with the woman, at times
he is denied her bed, most of the time it seems he is castigated
by her for one reason or another; and all the time he is locked in
an attraction/repulsion syndrome, more infuriating to him than
all the rest of it. Then there is the question of liking, and of love;
which both appear naturally and openly in the series, a number
of times, without any sense of frustration at all. It is as if there
are two situations, as no doubt there often are; but generally the
more difficult one is kept in the background.

Shakespeare has it in the foreground in the form of a paradox. How can he find beautiful what is ugly? Paradox has a presence in the first series but in the second it runs the show. This piece embraces it with some force. It is interesting that in the 'becoming [making fine] of things ill' (5), the capacity to transform worst to more than best (8), physical appearance takes second place to deeds. What the woman has done, what she does is suddenly on the agenda as part of the wholesale reversal in his eyes; what he hears as well as what he sees is 'just cause of hate' (10). Perhaps the writer is committing himself to the essential trope, the all-consuming paradox, with more vigour, sensing it is near the end of its working life.

The opening wonderfully substantiates its sense with a mounting billow that seems noiselessly to crash into oblivion. 'Power . . . powerful might' gives way to the shuddering 'insufficency'. If one wished for an example of Shakespeare's genius, what sets him apart from other writers, one could do worse than adopt these two lines. The fourth line is a nice turn on the idea of the speaker's blindness. 'Refuse' (6) is as now the dregs, the least worthy or significant. Staccato monosyllables in 9–10 pinpoint the dilemma. Some see a sexual pun in the second syllable of 'abhor' (11, 12); also in 'raised' (13), the latter perhaps leading to the topic of the next poem. I have no view on the matter, except to say that where such a possible allusion does not add anything useful to what may be called the commanding tenor of the poem, but rather sets up a distraction (as here), it is perhaps better ignored.

'With others' (12) is the only indication in this series of what was so common in the first, the speaker's sense of being held in a general low regard. It is almost as if he is reminding himself, as well as the reader, of the figure he cuts in public, before it is all cast off.

Love is too young to know what conscience is,
Yet who knows not conscience is born of love?
Then, gentle cheater, urge not my amiss, 3
Lest guilty of my faults thy sweet self prove.
For thou betraying me, I do betray
My nobler part to my gross body's treason: 6
My soul doth tell my body that he may
Triumph in love; flesh stays no farther reason,
But rising at thy name doth point out thee 9
As his triumphant prize. Proud of this pride,
He is contented thy poor drudge to be,
To stand in thy affairs, fall by thy side. 12
    No want of conscience hold it that I call
    Her 'love' for whose dear love I rise and fall.

The lady is addressed from lines 3 to 12 but then the reader, perhaps a small clue as to this and others not actually having been written for her eyes. But one would like it to have been. It is tender, even merry; and as one reads one forgets the *angst*-bedevilled character that strides the stage over so much of the collection, at once colossus and Tom Thumb. She appears to have been berating him for an insincere profession of affection: what a reply.

That the moral sense is 'born of love' (2), of not wanting to hurt someone you care for, seems a truism – who knows [it] not? – and yet worth the saying. If there is a betrayal therein (of the 'nobler part', 6), he says she starts it, by leading him on or at the least attracting him, rousing his sexual interest: and suddenly everything is reversed. 'My soul' (7) is the lady herself (as I see it) and at the same time, and equally, all that is best in him. It is a beautiful expression of commitment, the sexual act sanctioned by love, the courtly compliment in tandem with a simple statement of metaphysical fact. 'My soul doth tell my body that he may / Triumph in love' on its own makes the Sonnets worth reading, for me. If 129 is an exposé of bad sex this is a tribute to good. The couplet finally dispels any lingering notion of betrayal, at least from his side. Somewhere, in some language, there must be a comparable poetic expression from a woman's point of view. I would dearly like to be introduced to it.

In the note to 140 I classed 129, 130 and 138 as sonnets of the second series with something to say too urgent to be confined within the courtly tradition, that furnishes the writer with his main base. To these I would add 143, 146 and 151; without this last, a detail would have been missing from the portrait of love that is too much part of life to be ignored.

It makes a fitting conclusion to the series, with an after-thought in 152 and the double *envoi* of 153–4. There really is no more to be said. In my comments I have made the assumption that the poems are all roughly in the right order, with some anomalies; that within either series the presentation is or has the general idea of a chronological one. I think that all in all they are semi-private poems; that Thorpe got hold of them and published without Shakespeare's final oversight; and that they cast an invaluable sidelight on the author of the plays. But they are not rounded, in their entirety, in the sense that an individual play is rounded. That being so, the collection is the more illustrative of the fragmentary things we in truth are.

I hear a very light emphasis on 'thou' and 'me' in line 5, the speaker urging the other's 'amiss' (3). In line 10 'proud' is perhaps also 'tumid'. Line 12 has clever double meanings, both parts suggesting a soldier's duties: to act on your behalf, to die for you. The final phrase is free of semantic distraction; a lurking military metaphor is no more; for a moment he is at peace with himself, with his mistress, with the world. But it could hardly end like that.

In loving thee thou know'st I am forsworn;
But thou art twice forsworn, to me love swearing,
In act thy bed-vow broke; and new faith torn,   3
In vowing new hate after new love bearing.
But why of two oaths' breach do I accuse thee
When I break twenty? I am perjured most,   6
For all my vows are oaths but to misuse thee,
And all my honest faith in thee is lost.
For I have sworn deep oaths of thy deep kindness,   9
Oaths of thy love, thy truth, thy constancy,
And to enlighten thee gave eyes to blindness,
Or made them swear against the thing they see.   12
    For I have sworn thee fair: more perjured eye,
    To swear against the truth so foul a lie.

The afterthought is needed. For the last poem of the live series
the dominant tone is restored; it would hardly have done to have
ended on a satisfied note. There is a suggestion that both parties
are married, though the state of being forsworn, and the broken
bed-vow, may merely refer to commitment elsewhere.
Otherwise there is no new material, but an effective twist on the
old. The writer seems to have taken the verb from 'I have sworn
thee fair' in 147.13 and shuttled it back and forth into a new
version of his customary dual-purpose outfit: damning rags for
her and a hair-shirt for himself. At the same time he has given
the current theme of blindness a more effective spin than in
148–150. One senses his relish as the argument takes a grip; and
line 9 in particular, while not convincing as a literal statement,
is a compelling one. But (as I hear it) the couplet stutters.

    Too much is going on with 'eye' (13) and its homophones 'I'
and 'ay'. Some editors have changed 'eye' to 'I', which I think
better, with 'eye' in the background, carried over from line 12

as it were. But still the carry-over is too prominent, unabsorbed; while the Q text as above, with the awkwardness of the heightened personification, makes for an even bumpier ride. 'Ay' ('indeed' or 'always') lurks there too; but while in 148.8–9 its unseen presence ('love's 'ay' ') does not obtrude, here it becomes too much of a good thing. The overlap is too manifold, too *felt*; and if this is indeed the final sonnet Shakespeare wrote of 1–152, it is my view that he may have decided such an entanglement, in the poetic territory that he made his own, was the clearest and final sign for him to quit.

As surely as Pope later did with sequential couplets, Shakespeare took the concluding sonnet-couplet option and put his stamp on it. Only he has allowed the muse of ambiguity to cast such a spell; again and again he negotiates with the reader a clear path through the thicket. It is an indulgence on my part but I like to see him at length slamming this sonnet down on the table, thinking with Hamlet, 'I am ill at these numbers;' and accepting that an epic poetic venture into new ground was over.

It is a further indulgence to complete the list of sonnets that I have taken to my heart (see notes to 63, 96 and 123). After 126, the last poem of the first series and one of the finest of the volume: 128, for an instant of sudden gaiety; 129, a tempest set in ice; 130, with its shock of beauty in the mundane; 138, an intimate *pas de deux*; 143, for its sketch of the child in the man; 144, a searing dispassionate epitome; 146, for its unparalleled depth of feeling; 151, for its acceptance of the physical, the metaphysical alongside. But a list of preferences leaves something unsaid. The whole is a poem, as close as a person is, with its own personality.

Cupid laid by his brand and fell asleep.
A maid of Dian's this advantage found,
And his love-kindling fire did quickly steep   3
In a cold valley-fountain of that ground;
Which borrowed from this holy fire of love
A dateless lively heat, still to endure,   6
And grew a seething bath, which yet men prove
Against strange maladies a sovereign cure.
But at my mistress' eye love's brand new-fired,   9
The boy for trial needs would touch my breast;
I, sick withal, the help of bath desired,
And thither hied, a sad distempered guest,   12
    But found no cure; the bath for my help lies
    Where Cupid got new fire, my mistress' eyes.

The last two poems are accomplished renditions of a Greek epigram by Marianus Scholasticus, a Byzantine poet of the 6th century AD. It appeared in the *Greek Anthology*, an old collection that had been translated into Latin. In both sonnets, in a departure from the original, the speaker enters the story. It seems they were written as a decorative close to the series, and to the sequence as a whole. The author uses the instrument of the sonnet merely to please; not to touch on some inner current, to tend towards a needed affirmation, on the part of his speaker. If Shakespeare was the author it was a different Shakespeare from the heady, half-possessed, driven instrumentalist we have come to know so well.

    The music of the sonnet is its guiding principle. It integrates the sense as it forms, one step away from the inchoate. Again and again our poet, playing the changes on the formal pattern, gives breath to the idea of a changing persona: one whose mind is never still, whose thoughts are unexpected, a questing spirit.

In any poem music and narrative conspire each to take the other's part, the former adding to the story, or continuing the argument, the latter supporting the harmonics; so the principle of interchange is always at work. A resultant energy is liberated in the reader's mind: it is on the alert, readier to meet the unknown. The words are there to make a discovery. The principle in Shakespeare's writing is at its most intent. Sonnets and plays, the reader or listener is on the *qui vive*. The sonnet-music, so much employed in the accentuation and continuation of points being made, and in their conclusion, is not self-conscious. Less apt than that of other sonneteers to produce a merely pretty effect, it is given to moments of beauty. The variant of the poetic style at use in the plays, overwhelmingly that of blank verse in the conversation of visible external characters, makes the same requirement of us as audience. This may be at core to recognise the dynamic impulse at the heart of all. The comparison of the two modes of the poet's craft is fertile ground for the researcher into the working of words at play. The material is different but the method is the same. In either case the recipient mind is itself active, explorative, creative: nothing is static.

It will be clear enough why I do not think 153 and 154 are by Shakespeare. The experience for the reader is a literary one only. Their need to be said lies wholly in the need of the series to find an ending; a far cry from 126, that so finely brings the first series to a close. I imagine Thorpe commissioned someone to provide an *envoi*; perhaps two versions were offered and he took both. But they are accomplished pieces. Perhaps the real difference is that it is not the writer, so much as the speaker, that we feel to be someone else. No *cri de coeur* is here; but only the neat tale of a raconteur. It is someone all too aware of his accomplishment.

The little love-god lying once asleep
Laid by his side his heart-inflaming brand,
Whilst many nymphs that vowed chaste life to keep   3
Came tripping by; but in her maiden hand
The fairest votary took up that fire,
Which many legions of true hearts had warmed;   6
And so the general of hot desire
Was sleeping by a virgin hand disarmed.
This brand she quenchèd in a cool well by,   9
Which from love's fire took heat perpetual,
Growing a bath and healthful remedy
For men diseased; but I, my mistress' thrall,   12
    Came there for cure, and this by that I prove:
    Love's fire heats water, water cools not love.

The little fable may have been chosen for its lesson, there is no cure for love; but its scope for bawdy will have played a part too. The male-chauvinistic mores of the literary world had a place for such hidden entertainment. One scarcely needs to visit a shadow-play of brands and wells; but it may be worth mentioning that the 'strange maladies' of 153.8 and 'men diseased' of 12 above could be taken as a reference to syphilis. The faint background chuckle, also to be overheard in earlier sonnets, may or may not relate to a (supposedly) real condition; in a mythic context it is the less likely. But I am bound to say there is one phrase that has me chuckling too. 'The general of hot desire' (7) is Cupid, but may also indicate another leading member of the male erotic cast. I am surprised that Booth, who can spot a galaxy of sexual allusions behind a clear sky, has nothing to say on it. Despite the undertones, however, that have something in common with what has gone before, I am as far as ever from seeing this and 153 as Shakespeare's work.

It is not only the type of narrative, descriptive rather than analytical; not only the language, the winsome 'hied' (153.12) and 'tripping' (4 above); not only the unconscionable distance between 'my mistress' eyes' of 153.14 and 130.1. All these seem to tell of another hand; and more so the disappearance of the adored one as any kind of tangible being. But what really sets these two poems apart is the lack of "bite" in the verse. For those who find my note to 153 over-analytical this has it in brief. It is the same in *A Lover's Complaint*, the long-winded poem in *rime royal* that acts as an end-piece to the Sonnets in Thorpe's edition. It was not unusual for such a contrasting section featuring a woman's voice to be added to a sequence; but if it is Shakespeare's (as Thorpe claims), it is the weakest poem he wrote by some way. (I except Sonnets 135, 136 and 145 from serious consideration.) *Venus and Adonis* and *Lucrece*, and a fair amount of his early verse for the stage, lack the inner compulsion of his mature work; but they are not sadly laboured and at the same time somehow self-admiring. These two final sonnets, while more finely crafted than the *Complaint*, carry something of the same narcissistic authorial echo, that to my mind simply is not Shakespeare.

We have come a long way since meeting Dali's golden Narcissus (sonnet 1, note). Yet the encounter with the Dark Lady, his counterpart, is part of the same journey. The sequence has a fragmentary surface, but an inner tensile strength: over the whole, as if finely welded within, it can seem a balance holds. It is one man's statement on the gift of love and the shock of loving; one man's voice, as if expressed from the marrow of his bones, on longing and belonging and exclusion. It is one poet's quest that has for a time been a part of us; and made of all these, in an air of fourteen lines, it is one craftsman's music.

Bibliographical Note

Stephen Booth's edition of the *Sonnets* (Yale University Press, 1977) is an invaluable companion to the studious reader. With a forensic eye for detail and alternative readings, his commentary takes infinite pains to enable one to choose one's own path through the forest. Katherine Duncan-Jones' edition for the Arden Shakespeare (Bloomsbury 1997) is finely selective in focus and always sharp. *Shakespeare's Sugared Sonnets* by Katharine M. Wilson (Allen and Unwin 1974) offers a useful background of themes and conceits from contemporary sequences. J.B. Leishman's *Themes and Variations in Shakespeare's Sonnets* (Hutchinson 1961) is to be recommended both for the literary-historical background it offers, and for its intuitive sympathies. I found John Kerrigan's small commentary-free edition for Penguin (1986) a sensitive guide to the text's punctuation. J.Dover Wilson's pamphlet, *Shakespeare's Sonnets: an Introduction for Historians and Others* (Cambridge University Press 1963), is far-reaching, balanced and discerning. Don Paterson's *Reading Shakespeare's Sonnets* (Faber and Faber 2010) has been entertaining to dip into. From each of these I have gained something, as at times from a variety of other published views. The text has inspired a number of different approaches, as I imagine it always will. Yet all will be for the same underlying reason. If there is one thing certain in the field of literary critical endeavour, it is that the *Sonnets* will not 'lack tongues to praise'.